THE ORIGIN OF
THE BIBLE

In memory of

Frederick F. Bruce

1910 – 1990

THE
ORIGIN
OF THE
BIBLE

EDITOR

Philip Wesley Comfort

Tyndale House Publishers, Inc.

WHEATON, ILLINOIS

Library of Congress Cataloging-in-Publication Data

The Origin of the Bible / editor, Philip Wesley Comfort.
    p.   cm.
    Includes bibliographical references.
    ISBN 0-8423-4735-6
    1. Bible—Introductions. 2. Bible—Canon. 3. Bible as
literature. 4. Bible—Manuscripts. 5. Bible—Versions.
I. Comfort, Philip Wesley.
BS480.077   1992
220—dc20   91-20339

Scripture quotations marked NIV are from the *Holy Bible,* New
International Version. Copyright © 1973, 1978, 1984 International Bible
Society. Used by permission of Zondervan Bible Publishers.

Scripture quotations marked KJV are taken from the *Holy Bible,*
King James Version.

Scripture quotations marked RV are from the *Holy Bible,* English Revised
Version, 1881.

Scripture quotations marked RSV are taken from the *Holy Bible,* Revised
Standard Version, copyright © 1946, 1952, 1971 by Division of Christian
Education of the National Council of Churches in the United States of
America.

Scripture quotations marked NRSV are taken from the *Holy Bible,* New
Revised Standard Version, copyright © 1989 by Division of Christian
Education of the National Council of Churches in the United States of
America.

Scripture quotations marked NASB are taken from the *New American
Standard Bible,* copyright © 1960, 1962, 1963, 1968, 1971, 1972, 1973,
1975, 1977 by The Lockman Foundation. Used by permission.

Scripture quotations marked TLB are taken from *The Living Bible,*
copyright © 1971 owned by assignment by KNT Charitable Trust.
All rights reserved.

Permission granted by Inter-Varsity Press, England, to reproduce three
articles from the *New Bible Dictionary* (editor, J. D. Douglas), revised
edition, 1982: "Bible" by F. F. Bruce, "Inspiration of the Bible" by
J. I. Packer, and "Canon of the Old Testament" by R. T. Beckwith.

Permission granted by Philip Comfort to reproduce and adapt portions
from *The Complete Guide to Bible Versions,* published by Tyndale House
Publishers Inc., 1991.

Permission granted by Baker Book House to reproduce and adapt
portions of *The Quest for the Original Text of the New Testament* by
Philip W. Comfort, 1992.

98   97   96   95   94   93   92
7   6   5   4   3   2   1

CONTRIBUTORS

Harold O. J. Brown, Ph.D.
Professor of Biblical and Systematic
  Theology
The Forman Professor of Ethics in
  Theology
Trinity Evangelical Divinity School

R. T. Beckwith, M.A.
Director, Latimer House, Oxford

F. F. Bruce, M.A.
formerly Rylands Professor of
  Biblical Criticism and Exegesis
University of Manchester, England

Philip W. Comfort, Ph.D.
Senior Editor, Bible Department,
  Tyndale House Publishers
Visiting Professor, New Testament,
  Wheaton College

Raymond Elliott, M.A. (Theology),
M.A. (Linguistics)
Member of Wycliffe Bible
  Translators/Summer Institute of
  Linguistics—translating the New
  Testament into Nebaj Ixil

Milton C. Fisher, Th.M., Ph.D., D.D.
Professor of Old Testament
Philadelphia Theological Seminary

R. K. Harrison, Ph.D., D.D.
Emeritus Professor, Wycliffe College
University of Toronto

Carl F. H. Henry, Th.D., Ph.D.
Visiting Professor
Trinity Evangelical Divinity School

Mark R. Norton, M.A.
Editor, Bible Department, Tyndale
  House Publishers

J. I. Packer, M.A., D.Phil., D.D.
Professor of Systematic Theology
Regent College

Leland Ryken, Ph.D.
Professor of English
Wheaton College

Larry Walker, Ph.D.
Professor of Old Testament and
  Semitic Languages
Mid-America Baptist Theological
  Seminary

Victor Walter, M.A., Th.M.
formerly Chairperson of Practical
  Theology
Trinity Evangelical Divinity School
Pastor, Cheyenne Evangelical Free
  Church

CONTENTS

SECTION FOUR
Bible Texts and Manuscripts

SECTION FIVE
Bible Translation

INTRODUCTION

THE BIBLE. No other book has had so many books written about it—so why yet another one? Though there are many books that help readers understand the content of the Bible, few explain its origins. This volume provides an overview of how the Bible was first inspired, canonized, read as sacred literature, copied in ancient Hebrew and Greek manuscripts, and translated into the languages of the world.

The first section, "The Authority and Inspiration of the Bible," focuses on the Bible's divine inspiration, lasting authority, and infallibility. The second section, "The Canon of the Bible," reveals the processes that went into selecting the thirty-nine books of the Old Testament and the twenty-seven books of the New Testament to be part of canonized Scripture. This section also has an essay on the Old Testament and New Testament apocrypha. The third section, "The Bible as a Literary Text," elucidates the literary background of the Bible and shows how the Bible is a literary masterpiece. The fourth section, "Bible Texts and Manuscripts," describes the ancient biblical manuscripts that have been discovered and used in forming editions of the Hebrew and Greek texts. The fifth section, "Bible Translation," provides information about the biblical languages (Hebrew, Aramaic, Greek) and Bible translation itself. Furthermore, this section gives a brief history of the English Bible and of other versions in many languages.

I hope this book will inspire fresh appreciation for our Bible and greater understanding of the processes that went into making the Bible the inspired text that it is.

Philip W. Comfort

SECTION

ONE

The Authority
and
Inspiration
of the Bible

The Bible
F. F. Bruce

The word "Bible" is derived through Latin from the Greek word *biblia* (books), specifically the books that are acknowledged as canonical by the Christian church. The earliest Christian use of *ta biblia* (the books) in this sense is said to be 2 Clement 14:2 (c. A.D. 150): "the books and the apostles declare that the church . . . has existed from the beginning." (Compare Dan. 9:2, "I, Daniel, understood from the Scriptures," where the reference is to the corpus of Old Testament prophetic writings.) Greek *biblion* (of which *biblia* is the plural) is a diminutive of *biblos*, which in practice denotes any kind of written document, but originally one written on papyrus.

A term synonymous with "the Bible" is "the writings" or "the Scriptures" (Greek *hai graphai, ta grammata*), frequently used in the New Testament to denote the Old Testament documents in whole or in part. For example, Matthew 21:42 says, "Have you never read in the Scriptures?" (*en tais graphais*). The parallel passage, Mark 12:10, has the singular, referring to the particular text quoted, "Haven't you read this Scripture?" (*ten graphen tauten*). 2 Timothy 3:15 (RSV) speaks of "the sacred writings" (*ta hiera grammata*), and the next verse says, "All Scripture is God-breathed" (*pasa graphe theopneustos*). In 2 Peter 3:16 "all" the letters of Paul are included along with "the other Scriptures" (*tas loipas graphas*), by which the Old Testament writings and probably also the Gospels are meant.

Content and Authority

Among Christians, for whom the Old Testament and New Testament together constitute the Bible, there is not complete agreement on their content. Some branches of the Syriac church do not include 2 Peter, 2 and 3 John, Jude, and Revelation in the New Testament. The Roman and Greek communions include a number of books in the Old Testament in addition to those that make up the Hebrew Bible; these additional books formed part of the Christian Septuagint.

While they are included, along with one or two others, in the complete Protestant English Bible, the Church of England (like the Lutheran Church) follows Jerome in holding that they may be read "for example of life and instruction of manners; but yet doth it not apply them to establish any doctrine" (Article VI). Other Reformed Churches give them no canonical status at all. The Ethiopic Bible includes 1 Enoch and the book of Jubilees.

In the Roman, Greek, and other ancient communions the Bible, together with the living tradition of the church in some sense, constitutes the ultimate authority. In the churches of the Reformation, on the other hand, the Bible alone is the final court of appeal in matters of doctrine and practice. Thus Article VI of the Church of England affirms: "Holy Scripture containeth all things necessary to salvation; so that whatsoever is not read therein, nor may be proved thereby, is not to be required of any man, that it should be believed as an article of the Faith, or be thought requisite or necessary to salvation." To the same effect the *Westminster Confession of Faith* (1.2) lists the 39 books of the Old Testament and the 27 of the New Testament as "all . . . given by inspiration of God, to be the rule of faith and life."

The Two Testaments

The word "testament" in the designations "Old Testament" and "New Testament," given to the two divisions of the Bible, goes back through Latin *testamentum* to Greek *diatheke,* which in most of its occurrences in the Greek Bible means "covenant" rather than "testament." In Jeremiah 31:31, a new covenant is foretold which will supersede that which God made with Israel in the wilderness (cf. Exod. 24:7ff). "By calling this covenant 'new,' he has made the first one obsolete" (Heb. 8:13). The New Testament writers see the fulfillment of the prophecy of the new covenant in the new order inaugurated by the work of Christ; his own words of institution (1 Cor. 11:25) give the authority for this interpretation. The Old Testament books, then, are so called because of their close association with the history of the "old covenant"; the New Testament books are so called because they are the foundation documents of the "new covenant." An approach to our common use of the term "Old Testament" appears in 2 Corinthians 3:14, "when the old covenant is read," although Paul probably means the law, the basis of the old covenant, rather than the whole volume of Hebrew Scripture. The terms "Old Testament" and "New Testament" for the two collections of books came into general Christian use in the later part of the second century; Tertullian rendered *diatheke* into Latin by *instrumentum* (a legal document) and also by *testamentum;* it was the latter word that survived, unfortunately, since the two parts of the Bible are not "testaments" in the ordinary sense of the term.

THE OLD TESTAMENT

In the Hebrew Bible the books are arranged in three divisions: the Law, the Prophets, and the Writings. The Law comprises the Pentateuch, the five "books of Moses." The Prophets fall into two subdivisions: the "Former Prophets," comprising Joshua, Judges,

Samuel, and Kings; and the "Latter Prophets," comprising Isaiah, Jeremiah, Ezekiel, and "The Book of the Twelve Prophets." The Writings contain the rest of the books: first Psalms, Proverbs, and Job; then the five "Scrolls," namely Song of Songs, Ruth, Lamentations, Ecclesiastes, and Esther; and finally Daniel, Ezra-Nehemiah, and Chronicles. The total is traditionally reckoned as twenty-four, but these twenty-four correspond exactly to our common reckoning of thirty-nine, since in the latter reckoning the Minor Prophets are counted as twelve books, and Samuel, Kings, Chronicles, and Ezra-Nehemiah as two each. There were other ways of counting the same twenty-four books in antiquity; in one (attested by Josephus) the total was brought down to twenty-two; in another (known to Jerome) it was raised to twenty-seven.

The origin of the arrangement of books in the Hebrew Bible cannot be traced; the threefold division is frequently believed to correspond to the three stages in which the books received canonical recognition, but there is no direct evidence for this.

In the Septuagint the books are arranged according to similarity of subject matter. The Pentateuch is followed by the historical books, these are followed by the books of poetry and wisdom, and these by the prophets. It is this order which, in its essential features, is perpetuated (via the Vulgate) in most Christian editions of the Bible. In some respects this order is truer to chronological sequence of the narrative contents than that of the Hebrew Bible; for example, Ruth appears immediately after Judges (since it records things that happened "in the days when the judges ruled"), and the work of the chronicler appears in the order Chronicles, Ezra, and Nehemiah.

The threefold division of the Hebrew Bible is reflected in the wording of Luke 24:44 ("the Law of Moses, the Prophets and the Psalms"); more commonly the New Testament refers to "the Law and the Prophets" (see Matt. 7:12) or "Moses and the Prophets" (see Luke 16:29).

The divine revelation that the Old Testament records was conveyed in two principal ways—by mighty works and prophetic words. These two modes of revelation are bound up indissolubly together. The acts of mercy and judgment by which the God of Israel made himself known to his covenant people would not have carried their proper message had they not been interpreted to them by the prophets—the "spokesmen" of God who received and communicated his word. For example, the events of the Exodus would not have acquired their abiding significance for the Israelites if Moses had not told them that in these events the God of their fathers was acting for their deliverance, in accordance with his ancient promises, so that they might be his people and he their God. On the other hand, Moses' words would have been fruitless apart from their vindication in the events of the Exodus. We may compare the similarly significant role of Samuel at the time of the Philistine menace, of the great eighth-century prophets when Assyria was sweeping all before her, of Jeremiah and Ezekiel when the kingdom of Judah came to an end, and so forth.

This interplay of mighty work and prophetic word in the Old Testament explains why history and prophecy are so intermingled throughout its pages; it was no doubt some realization of this that led the Jews to include the chief historical books among the Prophets. But not only do the Old Testament writings record this progressive twofold revelation of God; they record at the same time men's response to God's revelation—a response sometimes obedient, too often disobedient. In this Old Testament record of the response of those to whom the word of God came, the New Testament finds practical instruction for Christians; of the Israelites' rebellion in the wilderness and the disasters which ensued Paul writes: "These things happened to them as examples and were written down as warnings for us, on whom the fulfillment of the ages has come" (1 Cor. 10:11, NIV).

Regarding its place in the Christian Bible, the Old Testament is preparatory in character: what "God spoke to our forefathers through the prophets" waited for its completion in what was "spoken to us by his Son" (Heb. 1:1-2, NIV). Yet the Old Testament was the Bible that the apostles and other preachers of the gospel in the earliest days of Christianity took with them when they proclaimed Jesus as the divinely sent Messiah, Lord, and Savior: they found in it clear witness to Christ (John 5:39) and a plain setting forth of the way of salvation through faith in him (Rom. 3:21; 2 Tim. 3:15). For their use of the Old Testament they had the authority and example of Christ himself; and the church ever since has done well when it has followed the precedent set by him and his apostles and recognized the Old Testament as Christian Scripture. "What was indispensable to the Redeemer must always be indispensable to the redeemed" (G. A. Smith).

THE NEW TESTAMENT

The New Testament stands to the Old Testament in the relation of fulfillment to promise. If the Old Testament records what "God spoke of old to our fathers by the prophets," the New Testament records that final word which he spoke in his Son, in which all the earlier revelation was summed up, confirmed, and transcended. The mighty works of the Old Testament revelation culminate in the redemptive work of Christ; the words of the Old Testament prophets receive their fulfillment in him. But he is not only God's crowning revelation to man; he is also man's perfect response to God—the high priest as well as the apostle of our confession (Heb. 3:1). If the Old Testament records the witness of those who saw the day of Christ before it dawned, the New Testament records the witness of those who saw and heard him in the days of his flesh, and who came to know and proclaim the significance of his coming more fully, by the power of his Spirit, after his resurrection from the dead.

The New Testament has been accepted by the great majority of Christians, for the past 1,600 years, as comprising twenty-seven books. These twenty-seven fall naturally into four divisions: (1) the four Gospels, (2) the Acts of the Apostles, (3) twenty-one letters written by apostles and "apostolic men," and (4) Revelation. This order is not only logical, but roughly chronological so far as the subject matter of the documents is concerned; it does not correspond, however, to the order in which they were written.

The first New Testament documents to be written were the earlier epistles of Paul. These (together, possibly, with the Epistle of James) were written between A.D. 48 and 60, before even the earliest of the Gospels was written. The four Gospels belong to the decades between 60 and 100, and it is to these decades too that all (or nearly all) the other New Testament writings are to be assigned. Whereas the writing of the Old Testament books was spread over a period of a thousand years or more, the New Testament books were written within a century.

The New Testament writings were not gathered together in the form which we know immediately after they were penned. At first the individual Gospels had a local and independent existence in the constituencies for which they were originally composed. By the beginning of the second century, however, they were brought together and began to circulate as a fourfold record. When this happened, Acts was detached from Luke, with which it had formed one work in two volumes, and embarked on a separate but not unimportant career of its own.

Paul's letters were preserved at first by the communities or individuals to whom they were sent. But by the end of the first century there is evidence to suggest that his surviving correspondence began to be collected into a Pauline corpus, which quickly circulated among the churches—first a shorter corpus of ten letters and soon afterwards a longer one of thirteen, enlarged by the inclusion of the three Pastoral Epistles. Within the Pauline corpus the letters appear to have been arranged not in chronological order but in descending order of length. This principle may still be recognized in the order found in most editions of the New Testament today: the letters to churches come before the letters to individuals, and within these two subdivisions they are arranged so that the longest comes first and the shortest last. (The only departure from this scheme is that Galatians comes before Ephesians, although Ephesians is slightly the longer of the two.)

With the Gospel collection and the Pauline corpus, and Acts to serve as a link between the two, we have the beginning of the New Testament Canon as we know it. The early church, which inherited the Hebrew Bible (or the Greek version of the Septuagint) as its sacred Scriptures, was not long in setting the new evangelic and apostolic writings alongside the Law and the Prophets, and in using them for the propagation and defense of the gospel and in Christian worship. Thus Justin Martyr, about the middle of the second century, describes how Christians in their Sunday meetings read "the memoirs of the apostles or the writings of the prophets" (*Apology* 1.67). It was natural, then, that when Christianity spread among people who spoke other languages than Greek, the New Testament should be translated from Greek into those languages for the benefit of new converts. There were Latin and Syriac versions of the New Testament by A.D. 200, and a Coptic one within the following century.

The Message of the Bible

The Bible has played, and continues to play, a notable part in the history of civilization. Many languages have been reduced to writing for the first time in order that the Bible, in whole or in part, might be translated into them in written form. And this is but a minor sample of the civilizing mission of the Bible in the world.

This civilizing mission is the direct effect of the central message of the Bible. It may be thought surprising that one should speak of a central message in a collection of writings that reflects the history of civilization in the Near East over several millennia. But a central message there is, and it is the recognition of this that has led to the common treatment of the Bible as a book, and not simply a collection of books—just as the Greek plural *biblia* (books) became the Latin singular *biblia* (the book).

The Bible's central message is the story of salvation, and throughout both Testaments three strands in this unfolding story can be distinguished: the bringer of salvation, the way of salvation, and the heirs of salvation. This could be reworded in terms of the covenant idea by saying that the central message of the Bible is God's covenant with men, and that the strands are the mediator of the covenant, the basis of the covenant, and the covenant people. God himself is the Savior of his people; it is he who confirms his covenant-mercy with them. The bringer of salvation, the mediator of the covenant, is Jesus Christ, the Son of God. The way of salvation, the basis of the covenant, is God's grace, calling forth from his people a response of faith and obedience. The heirs of salvation, the covenant people, are the Israel of God, the church of God.

The continuity of the covenant people from the Old Testament to the New Testament is obscured for the reader of the common English Bible because "church" is an exclusively New Testament word, and he naturally thinks of it as something which began in the New Testament period. But the reader of the Greek Bible was confronted by no new word when he found *ekklesia* in the New Testament; he had already met it in the Septuagint as one of the words used to denote Israel as the "assembly" of the Lord's people. To be sure, it has a new and fuller meaning in the New Testament. The old covenant people had to die with him in order to rise with him to new life—a new life in which national restrictions had disappeared. Jesus provides in himself the vital continuity between the old Israel and the new, and his faithful followers were both the righteous remnant of the old and the nucleus of the new. The Servant Lord and his servant people bind the two Testaments together.

The message of the Bible is God's message to man, communicated "at many times and in various ways" (Heb. 1:1, NIV) and finally incarnated in Christ. Thus "the authority of the holy scripture, for which it ought to be believed and obeyed, dependeth not upon the testimony of any man or church, but wholly upon God (who is truth itself), the author thereof; and therefore it is to be received, because it is the word of God" (*Westminster Confession of Faith*, 1.4).

BIBLIOGRAPHY

Barr, J., gen. ed. *The Cambridge History of the Bible,* Volumes I–III, 1975.
Bruce, F. F. *The Books and the Parchments,* 1952.
Dodd, C. H. *According to the Scriptures,* 1952.
Reid, J. K. S. *The Authority of the Bible,* 1957.
Warfield, B. B. *The Inspiration and Authority of the Bible,* 1948.
Westcott, B. F. *The Bible in the Church,* 1896.

The Authority of the Bible
Carl F. H. Henry

Western civilization is in a severe "authority crisis," not confined solely to the realm of religious faith, nor specially or uniquely threatening to Bible believers. Parental authority, marital authority, political authority, academic authority, and ecclesiastical authority are all deeply questioned. Not only particular authorities—the authority of Scripture, of the pope, of political rulers, and so on—but the concept of authority itself is vigorously challenged. Today's crisis of biblical authority thus reflects a waning civilizational consensus on issues of sovereignty and submission.

In some respects the contemporary questioning of authority has a legitimate moral basis and is highly commendable. The twentieth century has witnessed the rise of ruthless and arbitrary tyrants imposing totalitarian dictates upon politically enslaved citizenries. In the United States political power was misused during the so-called Watergate era. Corporate power has been manipulated to institutional advantage both by huge business conglomerates and by massive labor unions.

Revolt against Biblical Authority
Judge of men and nations, the self-revealed God wields unlimited authority and power. All creaturely authority and power

is derived from that of God. As the sovereign Creator of all, the God of the Bible wills and has the right to be obeyed. The power God bestows is a divine trust, a stewardship. God's creatures are morally accountable for their use or misuse of it. In fallen human society God wills civil government for the promotion of justice and order. He approves an ordering of authoritative and creative relationships in the home by stipulating certain responsibilities of husbands, wives, and children. He wills a pattern of priorities for the church as well: Jesus Christ the head, prophets and apostles through whom redemptive revelation came, and so on. The inspired Scriptures, revealing God's transcendent will in objective written form, are the rule of faith and conduct through which Christ exercises his divine authority in the lives of Christians.

Revolt against particular authorities has in our time widened into a revolt against all transcendent and external authority. The widespread questioning of authority is condoned and promoted in many academic circles. Philosophers with a radically secular outlook have affirmed that God and the supernatural are mythical conceptions, that natural processes and events comprise the only ultimate reality. All existence is said to be temporal and changing; all beliefs and ideals are declared to be relative to the age and culture in which they appear. Biblical religion, therefore, like all other, is asserted to be merely a cultural phenomenon. The Bible's claim to divine authority is dismissed by such thinkers; transcendent revelation, fixed truths, and unchanging commandments are set aside as pious fictions.

In the name of man's supposed "coming of age," radical secularism champions human autonomy and creative individuality. Man is his own lord and the inventor of his own ideals and values, it is said. He lives in a supposedly purposeless universe that has itself presumably been engendered by a cosmic accident. Therefore, human beings are declared to be wholly free to impose upon nature and history whatever moral criteria they prefer. In such a view, to insist on divinely given truths and values, on transcendent principles, would be to repress self-fulfillment and retard creative personal development. Hence, the radically secular view goes beyond opposing particular external authorities whose claims are considered arbitrary or immoral; radical secularism is aggressively hostile to all external and objective authority, viewing it as intrinsically restrictive of the autonomous human spirit.

Any reader of the Bible recognizes rejection of divine authority and of a definitive revelation of what is right and good as an age-old phenomenon. It is not at all peculiar to contemporary man to "come of age"; it was found already in Eden. Adam and Eve revolted against the will of God in pursuit of individual preference and self-interest. But their revolt was recognized to be sin, not rationalized as philosophical "gnosis" at the frontiers of evolutionary advance.

If one takes a strictly developmental view, which considers all reality contingent and changing, what basis remains for humanity's decisively creative role in the universe? How could a purposeless cosmos cater to individual self-fulfillment? Only the biblical alternative of the Creator-Redeemer God, who fashioned human beings for moral obedience and a high spiritual destiny, truly preserves the permanent, universal dignity of the human species. The Bible does so, however, by a demanding call for personal spiritual decision. The Bible sets forth man's superiority to the animals, his high dignity ("little less than God," Ps. 8:5, NASB) because of the divine rational and moral image that he bears by creation. In the context of universal human involvement in Adamic sin, the Bible utters a merciful divine call to redemptive renewal through the mediatorial person and work of Christ. Fallen humanity is invited to experience the Holy Spirit's renewing work, to be conformed to the image of Jesus Christ, and to anticipate a final destiny in the eternal presence of the God of justice and justification.

Contemporary rejection of biblical tenets does not rest on any logical demonstration that the case for biblical theism is false; it turns rather on a subjective preference for alternative views of "the good life."

The Bible is not the only significant reminder that human beings stand daily in responsible relationship to the sovereign God. The Creator reveals his authority in the cosmos, in history, and in inner conscience, a disclosure of the living God that penetrates into the mind of every human being (Rom. 1:18-20; 2:12-15). Rebellious suppression of that "general divine revelation" does not succeed in wholly suspending a fearsome sense of final divine accountability (Rom. 1:32). Yet it is the Bible as "special revelation" that most clearly confronts our spiritually rebellious race with the reality and authority of God. In the Scriptures, the character and will of God, the meaning of human existence, the nature of the spiritual realm, and the purposes of God for human beings in all ages are stated in propositionally intelligible form that all can understand. The Bible publishes in objective form the criteria by which God judges individuals and nations, and the means of moral recovery and restoration to personal fellowship with him.

Regard for the Bible is therefore decisive for the course of Western culture and in the long run for human civilization generally. Intelligible divine revelation, the basis for belief in the sovereign authority of the Creator-Redeemer God over all human life, rests on the reliability of what Scripture says about God and his purposes. Modern naturalism impugns the authority of the Bible and assails the claim that the Bible is the Word of God written, that is, a transcendently given revelation of the mind and will of God in objective literary form. Scriptural authority is the storm center both in the controversy over revealed religion and in the modern conflict over civilizational values.

Higher Criticism

Discussion of biblical authority has been shadowed in the twentieth century both by sweeping claims for higher criticism from nonevangelical critics and by extravagant claims of what scriptural authority requires and implies from evangelical polemicists.

Skepticism toward the reliability of Scripture seems to survive in many academic circles despite the repeated collapse of critical theories. One still finds a disposition to trust secular writers whose credentials in providing historical testimony are often less adequate than those of the biblical writers. Not long ago many scholars rejected the historicity of the patriarchal accounts, denied that writing existed in Moses' day, and ascribed the Gospels and the Epistles to second-century writers. But higher criticism has sustained some spectacular and even stunning reverses, mainly through the findings of archaeology. No longer is it held that the glories of King Solomon's era are a literary fabrication, that "Yahweh," the redemptive God of the Hebrews, was unknown before the eighth-century prophets, or that Ezra's representations about the Babylonian captivity are fictional. Archaeologists have located the long-lost copper mines of Solomon's time. Tablets discovered at Ebla near Aleppo confirm that names similar to those of the patriarchs were common among people who lived in Ebla shortly before the events recorded in the later chapters of Genesis took place.

New Testament critic John T. Robinson conceded in *Redating the New Testament* (1906) that the late critical dating of New Testament books is wholly unpersuasive. Robinson argued that failure of the Gospels and Epistles to mention the destruction of the Temple in A.D. 70 is evidence that the writings were completed earlier, because otherwise that turn of events would have been used apologetically by the writers. It would be better, however, to arrive at dates of composition from what the writers teach and who they are rather than from what the writings do not contain; neither is it sound to be guided primarily by a supposed apologetic motivation that underlay their composition.

The "documentary" view of Scripture has long been considered by nonevangelical scholars the most firmly established achievement of literary and historical criticism. The theory (that the Old Testament narratives are a product of "redaction" by editors who blended separate reports into a single narrative) has had—until recently—the support of almost every prestigious Old Testament scholar outside evangelical circles. But the theory, also known is the "J-E-P-D hypothesis" (the letters standing for the supposed separate documents), has been under mounting attack. Umberto Cassuto (1883-1951), who held the chair of Bible at Hebrew University of Jerusalem, repudiated the prevalent critical notion that the biblical accounts gained their unity through literary redaction (editing), but retained relatively late datings for the completion of the Pentateuch and of Isaiah (*Biblical and Oriental Studies,* published posthumously, 1973). In a 1959 *Christianity Today* interview, Cyrus H. Gordon, a distinguished Jewish scholar, rejected the notion that the use of Elohim and Yahweh as divergent names for God implies different literary sources ("Higher Critics and Forbidden Fruit").

Recent linguistic research supports the argument that stylistic variations reflect the pace and mood of the narratives; it is less likely that they identify supposed redactors. Robert Longacre has argued that "the assumption of divergent documentary sources" in the Flood story, for example, is unnecessary and "obscures much of the truly elegant structure of the story." Thus, older critical views that refer the teaching of Scripture not to the originally named recipients of divine revelation but to late editorial redactors are *themselves coming under fresh criticism*. Furthermore, Bernard Childs has argued persuasively against the view that there exists behind the canonical writings earlier and more reliable sources that the biblical writers mythologized in the interest of the Hebrew cult.

The Bible's View of Itself

The intelligible nature of divine revelation—the presupposition that God's will is made known in the form of valid truths—is the central presupposition of the authority of the Bible. Much recent neo-Protestant theology demeaned the traditional evangelical emphasis as doctrinaire and static. It insisted instead that the authority of Scripture is to be experienced internally as a witness to divine grace engendering faith and obedience, thus disowning its objective character as universally valid truth. Somewhat inconsistently, almost all neo-Protestant theologians have appealed to the record to support cognitively whatever fragments of the whole seem to coincide with their divergent views, even though they disavow the Bible as specially revealed corpus of authoritative divine teaching. For evangelical orthodoxy, if God's revelational disclosure to chosen prophets and apostles is to be considered meaningful and true, it must be given not merely in isolated concepts capable of diverse meanings but in sentences or propositions. A proposition—that is, a subject, predicate, and connecting verb (or "copula")—constitutes the minimal logical unit of intelligible communication. The Old Testament prophetic formula "Thus saith the Lord" characteristically introduced propositionally disclosed truth. Jesus Christ employed the distinctive formula "But I say unto you" to introduce logically-formed sentences which he represented as the veritable word or doctrine of God.

The Bible is authoritative because it is divinely authorized; in its own terms, "All Scripture is God-breathed" (2 Tim. 3:16). According to this passage the whole Old Testament (or any element of it) is divinely inspired. Extension of the same claim to the New

Testament is not expressly stated, but it is not merely implied. The New Testament contains indications that its content was to be viewed, and was in fact viewed, as no less authoritative than the Old. The apostle Paul's writings are catalogued with "other Scriptures" (2 Pet. 3:15-16). Under the heading of "Scripture," 1 Timothy 5:18 cites Luke 10:7 alongside Deuteronomy 25:4 (compare 1 Cor. 9:9). The book of Revelation, moreover, claims divine origin (1:1-3) and employs the term "prophecy" in the Old Testament sense (22:9-10, 18). The apostles did not distinguish their spoken and written teaching but expressly declared their inspired proclamation to be the Word of God (1 Cor. 4:1; 2 Cor. 5:20; 1 Thess. 2:13). (See the chapter "The Inspiration of the Bible.")

The Inerrancy Question

The doctrine of biblical authority has been subverted by attacks on its historical and scientific reliability and by allegedly tracing its teaching to fallible human sources. Furthermore, the doctrine has sometimes been unnecessarily clouded by extreme conservative apologists who have overstated what biblical authority presupposes and implies. Some conservative scholars have repudiated all historical criticism as inimical to biblical authority and distinguished "true" from false Christians on the basis of subscription to "biblical inerrancy." If one accepts "plenary" divine inspiration of Scripture—that is, God's superintendence of the whole—the doctrine of biblical authority doubtless implies "inerrancy" of the content. But the Christian faith can hardly hope to advance its claims through a repudiation of historical criticism. To do so would imply that to support its position it must resort to uncritical views of history. To "higher criticism," which is so often pursued on arbitrary presuppositions that promote unjustifiable conclusions, the evangelical must reply with sound criticism that proceeds on legitimate assumptions and yields defensible verdicts.

Evangelical Christianity should champion the inerrancy of Scripture as a sound theological commitment, one that is consistent with what the Bible says about itself. But it need not repudiate the Christian integrity of all who do not share that commitment, nor regard them as hopelessly apostate. J. Gresham Machen, a brilliant evangelical apologist of the 1920s and 1930s and staunch champion of scriptural inerrancy, wrote that the doctrine of plenary inspiration "is denied not only by liberal opponents of Christianity, but also by many true Christian men . . . many men in the modern church . . . who accept the central message of the Bible and yet believe that the message has come to us merely on the authority of trustworthy witnesses unaided in their literary work by a supernatural guidance of the Spirit of God. There are many who believe that the Bible is right at the central point, in its account of the redeeming work of Christ, and yet believe that it contains many errors. Such men are not really liberals, but Christians, because they have accepted as true the message upon which Christianity depends" (*Christianity and Liberalism*, 75).

Yet Machen himself never wavered in his conviction that the whole Bible is to be considered "the seat of authority." He was convinced that the doctrine of inerrancy avoids instability in expounding authoritative doctrine and morals. He insisted that a "mediating" view of the Bible is not tenable. "Modernists" who claim to honor the authority of Jesus Christ rather than the authority of Scripture contradict Jesus' teaching since Jesus held a high view of Scripture. Moreover, the full explanation of Jesus' life and work depended on his crucifixion, resurrection, and heavenly ministry, and was derived from the Holy Spirit's inspiration of the apostles. It is illogical to pick and choose from the teaching of Jesus during his earthly ministry only those elements that serve one's own presuppositions. Rejection of the full trustworthiness of Scripture may finally lead one to ascribe to Jesus a life purpose different from the biblical one that Christ died and rose bodily to be the source of divine forgiveness of sinners.

The historic evangelical position is summed up in the words of Frank E. Gaebelein, general editor of *The Expositors' Bible Commentary*. In the preface to this commentary he spoke of a "scholarly evangelicalism [that was] committed to the divine inspiration, complete trustworthiness, and full authority of the Bible." Scripture is authoritative and fully trustworthy because it is divinely inspired. Lutheran theologian Francis Pieper directly connected the authority of the Bible with its inspiration: "The divine authority of Scripture rests solely on its nature, on its *theopneusty*"—that is, its character as "God breathed." J. I. Packer commented that every compromise of the truthfulness of the Bible must at the same time be regarded as a compromise of its authority: "To assert biblical inerrancy and infallibility is just to confess faith in (i) the divine origin of the Bible and (ii) the truthfulness and trustworthiness of God. The value of these terms is that they conserve the principles of biblical authority; for statements that are not absolutely true and reliable could not be absolutely authoritative." Packer reinforced that argument by demonstrating that Christ, the apostles, and the early church all agreed that the Old Testament was both absolutely trustworthy and authoritative. Being a fulfillment of the Old, the New Testament was no less authoritative. Christ entrusted his disciples with his own authority in their teaching so the early church accepted their teaching. As God's revelation, Scripture stands above the limitations of human assertion. (See the chapter "The Inerrancy and Infallibility of the Bible.")

Recent Challenges

In recent debate the authority of Scripture is compromised by some mediating scholars through their willingness to grant the infiltration of culturally dependent teaching. Some of the apostle

Paul's statements about women, or his views about a regathering of Israel in Palestine, are dismissed as reflective of the rabbinic teaching of the time and hence as evidence of Paul's culturally limited perspective. At some points biblical teaching obviously coincides with Jewish tradition. But where Hebrew tradition was elevated into a norm considered superior to or modifying and contravening Scripture, Jesus was critical of that tradition. That the apostle Paul may at some points have taught what was also taught by tradition historically rooted in the Old Testament proves nothing; at other points he was sharply critical of the rabbinical tradition.

The evangelical view has always been that what the inspired biblical writers teach they teach not as derived from mere tradition but as God-breathed; in their proclamation they had the mind of the Spirit to distinguish what was divinely approved and disapproved in current tradition. It is a sounder perspective therefore to speak of elements in which the Jewish tradition reflected prophetic revelation and of elements in which it departed from it. Once the principle of "culture dependency" is introduced into the content of scriptural teaching, it is difficult to establish objective criteria for distinguishing between what is supposedly authoritative and unathoritative in apostolic doctrine. Paul's views on homosexuality could then be considered as culturally prejudiced as his views of hierarchical authority or for that matter of the authority of Scripture.

In a further development some recent scholars have sought to ascribe to Scripture only a "functional" authority as an inner life-transforming stimulant, setting aside its conceptual-propositional authority. Recent neo-Protestant theologians—for example, Karl Barth, Rudolf Bultmann, Paul Tillich, and Fritz Buri—identify the supposed authoritative aspect of Scripture in radically divergent and even contradictory elements. All of them depart from the historic evangelical view (expounded, for example, by B. B. Warfield in *The Inspiration and Authority of the Bible,* 1948), that the authority of Scripture is concentrated in its disclosure of divinely revealed truths which constitute the rule of faith and morals. The "functional" view, which is reflected by David H. Kelsey in *The Uses of Scripture in Recent Theology* (1975), rejects the finality of any of the divergent views and accepts them equally (no matter how conflicting and contradictory they may be). Claims for external authority are subordinated into a supposed internal authority that dynamically alters the life of the community of faith. In spite of its profession of nondiscrimination toward divergent views, such a theory must of course explicitly exclude the traditional evangelical emphasis on the objective truth of the Bible. But once the validity of the biblical teaching in whole and part is forfeited, no persuasive reason remains why one's personal life ought to be transformed at all. One's life might be transformed in alternative and even expressly opposing patterns, or conformed sometimes in one way and sometimes in another, or transformed in correlation with ideas derived from non-Christian or anti-Christian sources as readily as in correlation with ideas derived from the Bible.

The issue of biblical authority can hardly be divorced from interest in the rational validity and historical factuality of the Scriptures. But evangelicals hold that the authority of the Bible is a divine authority; not all truths and historically accurate statements fall into that category. Scripture is authoritative because it is God's Word. The chosen prophets and apostles, some of them called by God in spite of their own indifference or even hostility—for example, the prophet Jeremiah and the apostle Paul—testify that the truth of God became theirs by divine inspiration. Judeo-Christian religion is based on historical revelation and redemption; instead of indifference to the concerns of history, the Bible asserts a distinctive view of linear history alien to that of ancient religions and philosophies.

Some Consequences of Rejection

The basic assumptions of modern secularism blunt in advance the personal force of many historic Christian claims. As a result young people are tempted, especially in a morally permissive age, to dismiss as superstition the special claims for Scripture. Even adult Christians sometimes show a certain discomfort concerning the Bible: they may bow to many of its penetrating ethical judgments but they are culturally conditioned to approach some of its authoritative claims with great reservation. Biblical language may ring strange in modern ears and the very notion of supernaturally revealed or inspired writings may seem like an echo from the historically conditioned past. Living almost two thousand years after the time of Jesus of Nazareth, some contemporary thinkers tend to dismiss as precritical, uncritical, or archaic the confident affirmations of Scripture's authority found in the historic Christian confessions. To them it may seem contrary to the contemporary mood or even repulsive to recognize Scripture as the divine rule of faith and conduct. No tenet of the inherited religious tradition suffers more abuse than assertion of the full authority of the Bible. Is it so incredible that a literature translatable into some 770,000 English words, printable on 1,000 small pages, and reducible photographically to a tiny negative should be regarded by Christians as the Word of God?

Yet it is clear from the history of theology and philosophy that efforts to preserve the reality of the living Creator-Redeemer God apart from the authority of the scriptural word always falter. Even the neoorthodox theology of "divine encounter," emphasizing as it did the distinctive interpersonal self-revelation of God, soon emptied into existentialist alternatives and finally into death-of-God speculation. The triune God is indeed the "ontological premise" on which the historic Christian faith is founded, but the case for biblical theism seems to require his definitive revelation in the inspired Word of Scripture.

Scriptural authority has often been needlessly blurred by appending to the Bible all kinds of secondary and tertiary authorities—apocryphal books, ecclesiastical tradition, and cultic interpretation. In earlier centuries, mediating scholars at times revised certain biblical doctrines and more radical critics completely rejected whatever articles of faith clashed with the temper of their age. In our own century such cumulative alterations, correlated with a naturalistic view of reality, have come to a climax. The historic Christian emphasis on biblical authority has in some places been totally repudiated. Officially atheistic regimes in communist countries, for example, may enlist all political and academic resources to undermine a theistic view. Even after signing the United Nations Declaration of Human Rights, they may repress Christian witness and evangelism, penalize those who do not uncritically support state absolutism, and at best allow only token distribution of the Bible. In other parts of the world, assaults on biblical authority by critical scholars have precipitated doubts in many influential academic communities.

The Power of God's Word

Yet the Bible remains the most extensively printed, most widely translated, and most frequently read book in the world. Its words have been treasured in the hearts of multitudes like none other. All who have received its gifts of wisdom and promises of new life and power were at first strangers to its redemptive message and many were hostile to its teaching and spiritual demands. In all generations its power to challenge persons of all races and lands has been demonstrated. Those who cherish the Book because it sustains future hope, brings meaning and power to the present, and correlates a misused past with the forgiving grace of God would not long experience such inner rewards if Scripture were not known to them as the authoritative, divinely revealed truth. To the evangelical Christian, Scripture is the Word of God given in the objective form of propositional truths through divinely inspired prophets and apostles, and the Holy Spirit is the giver of faith through that Word.

BIBLIOGRAPHY

Bruce, F. F. *The New Testament Documents: Are They Reliable?* 1960.
Childs, Brevard. *Introduction to the Old Testament as Scripture,* 1979.
Henry, Carl F. H. *God, Revelation, and Authority,* 1979.
Machen, J. Gresham. *Christianity and Liberalism,* 1923.
Robinson, John A. T. *Redating the New Testament,* 1976.
Warfield, B. B. *The Inspiration and Authority of the Bible,* 1948.

The Inspiration of the Bible
J. I. Packer

The word "inspiration" comes from Latin and English translations of *theopneustos* in 2 Tim. 3:16, which the KJV renders: "All Scripture is given by inspiration of God, and is profitable for doctrine, for reproof, for correction, for instruction in righteousness." "Inspired of God" in the RSV is no improvement on the KJV, for *theopneustos* means *out*-breathed rather than *in*-breathed by God—divinely *ex*-pired, rather than *in*-spired. In the last century Ewald and Cremer argued that the adjective bore an active sense, "breathing the Spirit," and Barth appears to agree. He glosses it as meaning not only "given and filled and ruled by the Spirit of God," but also "actively outbreaking and spreading abroad and making known the Spirit of God" (*Church Dogmatics,* 1.2); but B. B. Warfield showed decisively in 1900 that the sense of the word can only be passive. The thought is not of God as breathing out God, but of God as having breathed out Scripture. Paul's words mean, not that Scripture is inspiring (true though it is), but that Scripture is a divine product, and must be approached and estimated as such.

The "breath" or "spirit" of God in the Old Testament denotes the active outgoing of divine power, whether in creation (Ps. 33:6; Job 33:4; cf. Gen. 1:2; 2:7), preservation (Job 34:14), revelation to and through prophets (Isa. 48:16; 61:1; Mic. 3:8; Joel 2:28ff.), regeneration (Ezek. 36:27), or judgment (Isa. 30:28, 33). The New Testament reveals this divine "breath" (Greek *pneuma*) to be a Person of the Godhead. God's "breath" (the Holy Spirit) produced Scripture, as a means to the conveyance of spiritual understanding. Whether we render *pasa graphe* as "the whole Scripture" or "every text," and whether we follow the RSV or the RV in construing the sentence (the RV has "every scripture inspired of God is also profitable," which is a possible translation), Paul's meaning is clear beyond all doubt. He is affirming that all that comes in the category of Scripture, all that has a place among the "sacred writings" (*hiera grammata,* 2 Tim. 3:15, RV), just because it is God-breathed, is profitable for the guiding of both faith and life.

On the basis of this Pauline text, English theology regularly uses the word "inspiration" to express the thought of the divine origin and quality of Holy Scripture. Actively, the noun denotes God's out-breathing operation which produced Scripture: passively, the inspiredness of the Scriptures so produced. The word is also used more generally of the divine influence which enabled the human instruments of revelation—prophets, psalmists, wise men and apostles—to speak, as well as to write, the words of God.

The Idea of Biblical Inspiration

According to 2 Timothy 3:16, what is inspired is precisely the biblical writings. Inspiration is a work of God terminating, not in the men who were to write Scripture (as if, having given them an idea of what to say, God left them to themselves to find a way of saying it), but in the actual written product. It is Scripture—*graphe,* the written text—that is God-breathed. The essential idea here is that all Scripture has the same character as the prophets' sermons had, both when preached and when written (cf. 2 Pet. 1:19-21, on the divine origin of every "prophecy of Scripture"). That is to say,

Scripture is not only man's word—the fruit of human thought, premeditation, and art—but also and equally God's word, spoken through man's lips or written with man's pen. In other words, Scripture has a double authorship, and man is only the secondary author; the primary author, through whose initiative, prompting, and enlightenment, and under whose superintendence each human writer did his work, is God the Holy Spirit.

Revelation to the prophets was essentially verbal; often it had a visionary aspect, but even "revelation in visions is also verbal revelation" (L. Koehler, *Old Testament Theology,* E.T. 1957). Brunner has observed that in "the words of God which the Prophets proclaim as those which they have received directly from God, and have been commissioned to repeat, as they have received them . . . perhaps we may find the closest analogy to the meaning of the theory of verbal inspiration" (*Revelation and Reason*). Indeed we do; we find not merely an analogy to it, but the paradigm of it; and "theory" is the wrong word to use, for this is just the biblical doctrine itself. Biblical inspiration should be defined in the same theological terms as prophetic inspiration: namely, as the whole process (manifold, no doubt, in its psychological forms, as prophetic inspiration was) whereby God moved those men whom he had chosen and prepared (cf. Jer. 1:5; Gal. 1:15) to write exactly what he wanted written for the communication of saving knowledge to his people, and through them to the world. Biblical inspiration is thus verbal by its very nature, for it is of God-given words that the God-breathed Scriptures consist.

Thus, inspired Scripture is written revelation, just as the prophets' sermons were spoken revelation. The biblical record of God's self-disclosure in redemptive history is not merely human testimony to revelation, but is itself revelation. The inspiring of Scripture was an integral part in the revelatory process, for in Scripture God gave the church his saving work in history, and his own authoritative interpretation of its place in his eternal plan. "Thus says the Lord" could be prefixed to each book of Scripture with no less propriety than it is (359 times, according to Koehler) to individual prophetic utterances which Scripture contains. Inspiration, therefore, guarantees the truth of all that the Bible asserts, just as the inspiration of the prophets guaranteed the truth of their representation of the mind of God. ("Truth" here denotes correspondence between the words of man and the thoughts of God, whether in the realm of fact or of meaning.) As truth from God, man's Creator and rightful King, biblical instruction, like prophetic oracles, carries divine authority.

Biblical Presentation

The idea of canonical Scripture (i.e., of a document or corpus of documents containing a permanent authoritative record of divine revelation) goes back to Moses' writing of God's law in the wilderness (Exod. 34:27ff.; Deut. 31:9ff., 24ff.). The truth of all statements, historical or theological, that Scripture makes and their authority as words of God are assumed without question or discussion in both Testaments. The canon grew, but the concept of inspiration, which the idea of canonicity presupposes, was fully developed from the first and is unchanged throughout the Bible. As there presented, it comprises two convictions:

1. *The words of Scripture are God's own words.* Old Testament passages identify the Mosaic law and the words of the prophets, both spoken and written, with God's own speech (cf. 1 Kings 22:8-16; Neh. 8; Ps. 119; Jer. 25:1-13; 36, *etc.*). New Testament writers view the Old Testament as a whole as "the oracles of God" (Rom. 3:2, KJV), prophetic in character (Rom. 16:26; cf. 1:2; 3:21), written by men who were moved and taught by the Holy Spirit (2 Pet. 1:20; cf. 1 Pet. 1:10-12). Christ and his apostles quote Old Testament texts,

not merely as what men like Moses, David, or Isaiah said (see Mark 7:6, 10; 12:36; Rom. 10:5, 20; 11:9;), but also as what God said through these men (see Acts 4:25; 28:25), or sometimes simply as what "he" (God) says (1 Cor. 6:16; Heb. 8:5, 8), or what the Holy Spirit says (Heb. 3:7; 10:15). Furthermore, Old Testament statements, not made by God in their contexts, are quoted as utterances of God (Matt. 19:4ff.; Heb. 3:7; Acts 13:34, citing Gen. 2:24; Ps. 95:7; Isa. 55:2 respectively). Also, Paul refers to God's promise to Abraham and his threat to Pharaoh, both spoken long before the biblical record of them was written, as words which *Scripture* spoke to these two men (Gal. 3:8; Rom. 9:17), which shows how completely he equated the statements of Scripture with the utterance of God.

2. Man's part in the producing of Scripture was merely to transmit what he had received. Psychologically, from the standpoint of form, it is clear that the human writers contributed much to the making of Scripture— historical research, theological meditation, linguistic style, etc.

Each biblical book is in one sense the literary creation of its author. But theologically, from the standpoint of content, the Bible regards the human writers as having contributed nothing, and Scripture as being entirely the creation of God. This conviction is rooted in the self-consciousness of the founders of biblical religion, all of whom claimed to utter—and, in the case of the prophets and apostles, to write—what were, in the most literal sense, the words of another: God himself. The prophets (among whom Moses must be numbered: Deut. 18:15; 34:10) professed that they spoke the words of the Lord, setting before Israel what the Lord had shown them (Jer. 1:7; Ezek. 2:7; Amos 3:7). Jesus of Nazareth professed that he spoke words given him by his Father (John 7:16; 12:49). The apostles taught and issued commands in Christ's name (2 Thess. 3:6), so claiming his authority and sanction (1 Cor.

14:37), and they maintained that both their matter and their words had been taught them by God's Spirit (1 Cor. 2:9-13; cf. Christ's promises, John 14:26; 15:26ff.; 16:13ff.). These are claims to inspiration. In the light of these claims, the evaluation of prophetic and apostolic writings as wholly God's word, in just the same way in which the two tables of the law, "inscribed by the finger of God" (Exod. 31:18; cf.24:12; 32:16), were wholly God's word, naturally became part of the biblical faith.

Christ and the apostles bore striking witness to the fact of inspiration by their appeal to the authority of the Old Testament. In effect, they claimed the Jewish Scriptures as the Christian Bible: a body of literature bearing prophetic witness to Christ (Luke 24:25, 44; John 5:39; 2 Cor. 3:14ff.) and designed by God for the instruction of Christian believers (Rom. 15:4; 1 Cor. 10:11; 2 Tim. 3:14ff.; cf. the exposition of Ps. 95:7-11 in Heb. 3–4, and indeed the whole of Hebrews, in which every major point is made by appeal to Old Testament texts). Christ insisted that what was written in the Old Testament "cannot be broken" (John 10:35). He had not come, he told the Jews, to annul the law or the prophets (Matt. 5:17); if they thought he was doing that, they were mistaken. He had come to do the opposite—to bear witness to the divine authority of both by fulfilling them. The law stands forever because it is God's word (Matt. 5:18; Luke 16:17); the prophecies, particularly those concerning himself, must be fulfilled for the same reason (Matt. 26:54; Luke 22:37; cf. Mark 8:31; Luke 18:31). To Christ and his apostles, the appeal to Scripture was always decisive (cf. Matt. 4:4, 7, 10; Rom. 12:19; 1 Pet. 1:16).

The freedom with which New Testament writers quote the Old Testament (following the Septuagint, Targums, or an ad hoc rendering of the Hebrew, as best suits them) has been held to show that they did not believe in the inspiredness of the original words. But their interest was not in the words, as such, but in their meaning; and recent study has made it appear that these quotations are interpretative and expository—a mode of quotation well known among the Jews. The writers seek to indicate the true (i.e., Christian) meaning and application of their text by the form in which they cite it. In most cases this meaning has evidently been reached by a strict application of clear-cut theological principles about the relation of Christ and the church to the Old Testament.

Theological Statement

In formulating the biblical idea of inspiration, it is desirable that four negative points be made:

1. The idea is not of mechanical dictation, or automatic writing, or any process which involved the suspending of the action of the human writer's mind. Such concepts of inspiration are found in the Talmud, Philo, and the Fathers, but not in the Bible. The divine direction and control under which the biblical authors wrote was not a physical or psychological force, and it did not detract from but rather heightened the freedom, spontaneity, and creativeness of their writing.

2. The fact that in inspiration God did not obliterate the personality, style, outlook, and cultural conditioning of his penmen does not mean that his control of them was imperfect, or that they inevitably distorted the truth they had been given to convey in the process of writing it down. B. B. Warfield gently mocks the notion that, when God wanted Paul's letters written,

> He was reduced to the necessity of going down to earth and painfully scrutinizing the men He found there, seeking anxiously for the one who, on the whole, promised best for His purpose; and then violently forcing the material He wished expressed through him, against his natural bent, and with as

little loss from his recalcitrant characteristics as possible. Of course, nothing of the sort took place. If God wished to give His people a series of letters like Paul's, He prepared a Paul to write them, and the Paul He brought to the task was a Paul who spontaneously would write just such letters. (*The Inspiration and Authority of the Bible*)

3. Inspiredness is not a quality attaching to corruptions that intrude in the course of the transmission of the text, but only to the text as originally produced by the inspired writers. The acknowledgment of biblical inspiration thus makes more urgent the task of meticulous textual criticism, in order to eliminate such corruptions and ascertain what that original text was.

4. The inspiredness of biblical writing is not to be equated with the inspiredness of great literature, not even when (as is often true) the biblical writing is in fact great literature. The biblical idea of inspiration relates not to the literary quality of what is written but to its character as divine revelation in writing.

BIBLIOGRAPHY

Barth, Karl. *Church Dogmatics,* 1956.
Dodd, C. H. *According to the Scriptures,* 1952.
Ellis, Earl E. *Paul's Use of the Old Testament,* 1957.
Koehler, L. *Old Testament Theology,* 1957.
Stendahl, K. *The School of St. Matthew,* 1954.
Tasker, R. V. G. *The Old Testament in the New Testament,* 1954.
Warfield, B. B. *The Inspiration and Authority of the Bible,* 1951.

The Inerrancy and Infallibility of the Bible
Harold O. J. Brown

"Inerrancy" and "infallibility" are theological terms used by many Christians in defining the uniqueness of the Bible. Christians believe that God has communicated the Good News of salvation both "in person" through Jesus Christ and "in writing" through the Bible. The Bible, therefore, has always been regarded by Christians as unique and qualitatively different from other books.

Historical Background

God's people have always had an intense relationship to the written Scripture: the Jews to the Old Testament, the Christian church to the Old and New Testaments. Christians and Jews have both been characterized as "people of the Book." From the church's beginning, Christians acknowledged the Scriptures (first the Old Testament, then the New as well) to be inspired by God. The Greek word for "inspired" literally means "God outbreathed" (2 Tim. 3:16). The concepts of inerrancy and infallibility arose in theological discussions concerning the inspiration of the Scripture. Theologians asked themselves just how a book that was "God-breathed" would differ from other books.

At an early date, God's inspiration was understood to extend not merely to the writers of Scripture or to the concepts expressed in

Scripture, but to the very words written in the Scriptures. That understanding, known as the doctrine of "verbal" or "plenary" (complete) inspiration, was stated by Irenaeus, a second-century bishop of Lyons in Gaul (modern France), in his work *Against All Heresies*. Augustine (of the fourth century), bishop of Hippo in North Africa, expressed the same conviction—namely, that inspiration meant dictation by the Holy Spirit. To Irenaeus and Augustine, inspiration was not an ecstatic overpowering of a human writer's consciousness by the Holy Spirit, but was rather a high degree of illumination and calm awareness of God's revelation. Clement of Alexandria, his pupil Origen, and Jerome, the translator of the Bible into Latin, all spoke of inspiration as extending to every word of Scripture. The early Christian scholars, trusting in God as the God of truth and regarding him as incapable of deception or confusion, considered his verbally inspired Scripture to be equally trustworthy.

Meaning of the Terms

"Infallibility" may be called the subjective consequence of divine inspiration; that is, it defines the Scripture as reliable and trustworthy to those who turn to it in search of God's truth. As a source of truth, the Bible is "indefectable" (that is, it cannot fall away or defect from the standard of truth). Consequently, it will never fail or deceive anyone who trusts it.

"Inerrancy" is a closely related concept, but a later and less widely accepted term. It connotes that the Bible contains neither errors of act (material errors) nor internal contradictions (formal errors). The concept of infallibility addresses itself to one's personal knowledge of God and assurance of salvation. Inerrancy is concerned more specifically with the accurate transmission of the details of revelation.

Although in much theological writing the two terms are used interchangeably, infallibility is the broader term. Those who believe in an inerrant Bible also believe in an infallible Bible. The converse is not necessarily true. Although much depends on how "error" is defined, some scholars argue that the Bible can be infallible (in accomplishing God's purpose) without having to be free of error. They propose a more "dynamic" doctrine of infallibility that would continue to operate even if biblical errors were discovered.

A number of contemporary evangelical writers, such as the late Francis A. Schaeffer and John D. Woodbridge, have objected to any doctrine of "dynamic infallibility" as unbiblical, dualistic, or even nonsensical. Nevertheless, many respected evangelicals believe that one can regard the Bible as "the only perfect rule of faith and practice" without requiring or implying strict inerrancy.

Evangelicals acknowledge that the Bible is human as well as divine. The neoorthodox scholar Karl Barth (1886–1968) went further, maintaining that since "to err is human," a human book (even if also divine) must contain errors. Barth was cautious about attributing any specific errors to the Bible, yet he argued that error cannot be excluded on principle. Most nonevangelical scholars reject both infallibility and inerrancy and see no merit in attempting to separate them.

Recent Controversy

A publication of Harold Lindsell's, _The Battle for the Bible_ (1976), focused attention on the "inerrancy issue." The author charged that a number of prominent evangelical leaders, including some of his former colleagues, had begun to depart from an orthodox view of the Bible. Many who share Lindsell's concern regret any division among evangelicals, but see inerrancy as an important issue. Others regret the attention inerrancy has received and are concerned about inerrancy more as a threat to evangelical unity than as a significant theological issue.

One group, represented by the International Congress on Biblical Inerrancy (founded in 1977), considers the doctrine of inerrancy a watershed issue of Christian orthodoxy. A second group seems to claim that although inerrancy is true it should not be a "test of fellowship." A third group, represented by Jack Rogers of Fuller Theological Seminary, while not explicitly denying that inerrancy is true, contend that it is a late, historically conditioned formulation of the Christian position.

Rogers's position was set forth in his own contribution to a book he edited, *Biblical Authority* (1977). Rogers saw the doctrine of inerrancy as derived from Aristotelian-Thomistic roots. He argued that inerrancy conflicted with a more normative position based on Plato and Augustine and held by Luther and Calvin. Rogers pointed out that the doctrine of inerrancy did not receive explicit formulation until the seventeenth century.

According to his critics, Rogers tried unsuccessfully to demonstrate that since Luther and Calvin spoke of the human element of Scripture, they also accepted human errors in it. For such critics, a more plausible view is that Luther and Calvin neither assumed nor admitted errors in Scripture—that is, they took inerrancy for granted. Furthermore, they did not make inerrancy a test of orthodoxy because the question had not yet been formulated in those terms.

Those who affirm infallibility or inerrancy see their position as a theological conclusion from the bibical doctrines of God and of inspiration. Those who dispute the view, such as Karl Barth, almost always conclude that since the Bible is a human book it must necessarily contain error. In other words, the question is not primarily one of biblical interpretion but of theology and epistemology (the branch of philosophy concerned with the theory of knowledge). Of course, attempts to demonstrate that the Bible is totally without material error or internal contradiction require biblical interpretation.

Many biblical statements concern matters that cannot be either proved or disproved. However, many alleged contradictions have been resolved or diminished considerably by competent exegesis. For example, this would apply to the apparent discrepancies in the geneaolgies of Jesus (Matt. 1; Luke 3), the various accounts of the apostle Paul's conversion (Acts 9; 22; 26), and alleged errors of fact—such as the reference to the rabbit as a cud-chewing animal (Lev. 11:6) and the sun standing still over Gibeon (Josh. 10:12-14). Although logical and scientific difficulties remain, it is impossible to tell whether those difficulties are, strictly speaking, errors or only apparent contradictions, faults of a copyist or translator, or a problem of the cultural, historical, rhetorical gap between writer and reader.

Inerrancy and the Autographs

Properly speaking, inerrancy is attributed only to the original writings or "autographs" of Scripture, which no longer exist. Biblical scholars generally agree that the existing manuscripts of the Bible contain some copyists' errors, usually detectable by comparing later manuscripts with the earliest ones available and by applying textual criticism. Critics of inerrancy and infallibility sometimes argue that since the doctrine applies only to the autographs, it is essentially irrelevant today.

From a negative standpoint, if the original manuscripts contained errors, then of course the copies and translations available today would also. From a positive standpoint, defenders of inerrancy such as Francis Pieper, president of Concordia Theological Seminary (St. Louis) earlier in this century, have made a significant inference from the infallible and inerrant status of the autographs. They have insisted that for all practical purposes (that is, for questions of faith and life), present-day texts and good translations may also be regarded as inerrant. Supporters of inerrancy maintain that the confidence of Christian believers in modern translations of the Bible rests firmly on belief in the infallibility of the original writings.

If some copyists' errors have been detected in the existing biblical manuscripts, others more difficult to detect may also exist. Those asserting inerrancy in the autographs must share the concern of other biblical scholars to acknowledge and cope with textual problems in the existing copies.

Verbal Inspiration and Inerrancy

Jesus, like the Jews of the Old Testament era, believed that Scripture's trustworthiness extended not merely to its most important teachings but to the minutest details: "Until heaven and earth disappear, not the least stroke of a pen will by any means disappear from the Law until everything is accomplished" (Matt. 5:18, NIV). That view was reiterated by the apostle Paul (Acts 24:14; Tim 3:16). The authority of Jesus and Paul thus supports belief in all that Scripture affirms. Those who call Jesus Lord and accept his teaching should be expected to hold a high view of Scripture, as Jesus did.

The concepts of verbal inspiration and infallibility can be traced back to the early church fathers. They are not new ideas. Verbal inspiration seems to imply inerrancy, since otherwise the Holy Spirit would be the author of error. The medieval church, although giving tradition authority alongside Scripture, continued to assert verbal inspiration and infallibility, and even (in principle) the sufficiency of Scripture.

Martin Luther and other Protestant reformers had no need to exalt the authority and infallibility of Scripture, which the Roman Catholic church also accepted. Rather, they tried to combat Catholic exaltation of tradition to a status equal to or even superior to Scripture. Therefore, the Reformation did not produce explicit statements affirming the inerrancy or infallibility of Scripture. The successors of Martin Luther and John Calvin, however, did make such explicit statements.

After the Reformation, rationalism arose. In the eighteenth century, rationalism was characterized by an optimistic confidence in critical human reason and a disdain for supernatural influences in human affairs. Rationalists made the first serious claims that the Bible was like any other human book, and hence fallible. That presupposition led to repeated misunderstandings (and at times to falsifications) of the nature and content of Scripture.

Contemporary doubts about inerrancy or infallibility of Scripture by evangelical scholars often grow out of a desire to recognize or come to some sort of accommodation with the historical-critical method of studying the Bible. Yet many think that method begins with the supposition that the Bible cannot be what it claims to be. Among major American denominations, the Lutheran Church Missouri Synod, led by its president, Jacob A. O. Preus, took a definite stand on biblical inerrancy. It identified and repudiated the whole historical-critical method, with its assumptions, as the root from which contemporary inerrancy controversies spring. Missouri Synod Lutherans argued that rejection of the method does not imply rejection of scholarly research; what they rejected is any "research" in which the presuppositions preclude accepting the Bible as anything more than a human book. Supporters of inerrancy often assert that the case against it springs from an antisupernatural prejudice which, in principle, will repudiate not merely inerrancy but any divine superintendence or inspiration.

Two orthodox evangelical theologians arguing for inerrancy, Benjamin B. Warfield and Clark Pinnock, used the same graphic expression about inspiration, namely that an "avalanche of texts" from Scripture supports it. On examination, however, their "avalanche" seems to consist mainly of a few large boulders (Matt. 5:18; John 10:35; 2 Tim. 3:16; 2 Pet. 1:21). Scripture appears to presuppose its own inerrancy without explicitly stating it. For many Christians a compelling argument for inerrancy lies in Jesus' simple command to learn from him (Matt. 11:29; cf. John 13:13), coupled with the fact that Jesus accepted the Old Testament Scriptures as altogether trustworthy even in their details (Matt. 5:18; John 10:35).

Confessional Positions

Most mainline confessions of faith affirm the substance of inerrancy. It was the official position of the Roman Catholic church until that position, under liberal Protestant influence, loosened up somewhat at the Second Vatican Council (1962–1965). Among Reformed statements, the Belgic Confession (1561) and the Westminster Confession both affirm the perfection of Scripture. Similar stands are found in the Augsburg Confession (1530) of Lutheranism and in the Thirty-Nine Articles of the Church of England (1563). More recent confessions, such as the Baptist New Hampshire Confession of 1832, refer to the Bible as containing "truth without any mixture of error for its matter."

Problems or Errors?

Any alert reader of Scripture will become aware of problems in the text, although many apparent discrepancies or possible errors disappear under open-minded scrutiny. Even after careful study, however, some problems remain. The debate over inerrancy frequently comes down to choosing whether to tolerate such problems as "unanswered questions" or to transfer them to the category of "demonstrated errors." Often that decision reflects one's initial attitude toward Scripture and toward critical methods. If Scripture is accepted as the inspired Word of God, as "the standard that sets the standard," one will be reluctant to charge it with error—since to do so one must have some other, perhaps higher, norm by which to evaluate Scripture. Historically, doubt about inerrancy followed rather than produced the conviction that the Bible is merely a fallible human book. Hence, one should consider the possibility that recognition of an error in Scripture is the logical consequence of an earlier decision to judge the Bible rather than to let the Bible be the norm for all judgments.

Some have said that variations in chronological order constitute error—for example, in the sequence of Jesus' temptations (cf. Matt. 4:1-11 and Luke 4:1-13). But even as early as the second century, a Christian writer named Papias reported that the Gospel writers did not intend to record the events of Jesus' life in order, implying that their contemporaries found nothing strange or inaccurate in that practice.

Numbers in Scripture, which pose frequent problems are sometimes explicable on the basis of traditional practices of giving approximate or rounded values. For example, the value of the trigonometric constant (Π) calculated from the description of Solomon's basin (1 Kings 7:23) is accurate, but, as a scientist would say, only to "one significant figure." The duration of Israel's captivity in Egypt is predicted as roughly 400 years (Gen. 15.13) and reported more precisely as 430 years (Exod. 12:40-41). So-called scientific errors often stem from an improper understanding of the real meaning of obscure Hebrew or Greek texts. Certain difficulties remain, yet any that seemed formidable 50 years ago, or even 20 years ago, were resolved when new archaeological, textual, or scientific data came to light. No theory, either in theology or science, is ever completely devoid of difficulties. J. C. Ryle, an evangelical bishop of Liverpool (England), said, "The difficulties which beset any other theory of inspiration are tenfold greater than any which beset our own."

DIVERGENT EVANGELICAL POSITIONS
Among evangelicals a substantial group has always had little interest in the doctrine of inerrancy and some have actually rejected it.

Many British and German evangelicals, for example, maintain a uniformly high view of the Scripture's trustworthiness without adopting the terminology of inerrancy. They prefer terms like "infallibility," or "absolute trustworthiness," and so on. Some European evangelicals concede the presence of minor errors in the Bible; others who would not make that concession still do not wish to champion inerrancy.

In the United States, publication of Lindsell's book brought the inerrancy question to the attention of the evangelical public. Many evangelical theologians who would rather devote their energies to other issues have thus felt obliged to take a position on inerrancy. "Separatist" evangelical leaders have sometimes expressed suspicion that other evangelicals (such as Canadian theologian Clark S. Pinnock) took a "mediating" position on inerrancy in order to gain or maintain acceptance in liberal theological circles.

For many Christians of a liberal persuasion, as for non-Christians generally, a quarrel over inerrancy seems to be a quibble between two equally unacceptable views of Scripture. The concept of a book bearing supernatural authority is alien to the secular spirit of the age. Even Karl Barth, perhaps the most impressive theological mind of the twentieth century, had difficulty gaining a hearing for his basically conservative (but not "inerrantist") view of Scripture. Those evangelicals who propound a "dynamic" view of biblical authority are probably closer to Barth's "neoorthodoxy" than to the "Princeton orthodoxy" of B. B. Warfield. Like Barth, they may find it hard to keep their students and successors from moving toward a more relativistic and accomodating view of Scripture.

Conclusion

There can be no doubt that throughout its history the church of Jesus Christ has been committed to a view of inspiration that to most Christians implied inerrancy, even when the term itself was not used. Recent debate on the doctrine of inerrancy focuses attention both on questions of detail and on the fundamental question of the ultimate source of a Christian's authority. Christians affirm that Jesus Christ, not the doctrine of Scripture or of biblical infallibility, is the central reality of the Christian faith.

Although inerrancy, formulated to explain the doctrine of inspiration, has been described as a "late and derivative doctrine," many evangelical Christians accept it on the basis of the Bible's testimony to itself. Other Christians who also regard themselves as evangelicals do not accept the doctrine of inerrancy. A warning against compromise on scriptural infallibility and inerrancy was sounded in the nineteenth century by Bishop Pole: "Once allow the worm to gnaw the root, and we must not be surprised if the branches, the leaves, and the fruit, little by little decay."

BIBLIOGRAPHY

Cameron, Nigel M. de S. *Bibilical Higher Criticism and the Defense of Infallibilism in Nineteenth Century Britian*, 1987.
Carson, D. A. and John D. Woodbridge, eds. *Scripture and Truth*, 1986.
Conn, Harvie, ed. *Inerrancy and Hermeneutics: A Tradition, a Challenge, a Debate*, 1989
Rogers, Jack and Donald McKim. *The Authority and Interpretation of the Bible: An Historical Approach*, 1979.
Warfield, Benjamin B. *Limited Inspiration*, nd.

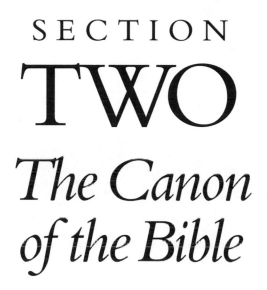

SECTION

TWO

The Canon of the Bible

The Canon of
the Old Testament
R. T. Beckwith

The Term "Canon"

The term "canon" is borrowed from Greek, in which *kanon* means a rule—a standard for measurement. With respect to the Bible, it speaks of those books that met the standard and therefore were worthy of inclusion. Since the fourth century *kanon* has been used by Christians to denote an authoritative list of the books belonging to the Old Testament or New Testament.

There has long been some difference of opinion about the books which should be included in the Old Testament. Indeed, even in pre-Christian times, the Samaritans rejected all its books except the Pentateuch; while, from about the second century B.C. onwards, pseudonymous works, usually of an apocalyptic character, claimed for themselves the status of inspired writings and found credence in certain circles. In the rabbinical literature it is related that in the first few centuries of the Christian era certain sages disputed, on internal evidence, the canonicity of five Old Testament books (Ezekiel, Proverbs, Song of Songs, Ecclesiastes, Esther). In the patristic period there was uncertainty among Christians whether the Apocrypha of the Greek and Latin Bible were to be regarded as inspired or not. Difference on the last point came to a head at the Reformation, when the church of Rome insisted that the

Apocrypha were part of the Old Testament, on an equal footing with the rest, while the Protestant churches denied this. Though some of the Protestant churches regarded the Apocrypha as edifying reading (the Church of England, for example, continued to include them in its lectionary "for example of life but not to establish any doctrine"), they were all agreed that, properly speaking, the Old Testament canon consists of the books of the Hebrew Bible—the books acknowledged by the Jews and endorsed in the teaching of the New Testament. The Eastern Orthodox Church was for a time divided on this issue, but has recently tended more and more to come down on the Protestant side.

What qualifies a book for a place in the canon of the Old Testament or New Testament is not just that it is ancient, informative and helpful, and has long been read and valued by God's people, but that it has God's authority for what it says. God spoke through its human author to teach his people what to believe and how to behave. It is not just a record of revelation, but the permanent written form of revelation. This is what we mean when we say that the Bible is "inspired," and it makes the books of the Bible in this respect different from all other books.

The First Emergence of the Canon

The doctrine of biblical inspiration is fully developed only in the pages of the New Testament. But far back in Israel's history we already find certain writings being recognized as having divine authority, and serving as a written rule of faith and practice for God's people. This is seen in the people's response when Moses reads to them the book of the covenant (Exod. 24:7), or when the Book of the Law found by Hilkiah is read, first to the king and then to the congregation (2 Kings 22–23; 2 Chron. 34), or when the Book of the Law is read to the people by Ezra (Neh. 8:9, 14-17; 10:28-39; 13:1-3). The writings in question are a part or the whole of the Pentateuch—in the first case quite a small part of Exodus, probably chapters 20-23. The Pentateuch is treated with the same reverence in Joshua 1:7ff.; 8:31; 23:6-8; 1 Kings 2:3; 2 Kings 14:6; 17:37; Hosea 8:12; Daniel 9:11, 13; Ezra 3:2, 4; 1 Chronicles 16:40; 2 Chronicles 17:9; 23:18; 30:5, 18; 31:3; 35:26.

The Pentateuch presents itself to us as basically the work of Moses, one of the earliest and certainly the greatest of the Old Testament prophets (Num. 12:6-8; Deut. 34:10-12). God often spoke through Moses orally, as he did through later prophets too, but Moses' activity as a writer is also frequently mentioned (Exod. 17:14; 24:4, 7; 34:27; Num. 33:2; Deut. 28:58, 61; 29:20-27; 30:10; 31:9-13, 19, 22, 24-26). There were other prophets in Moses' lifetime and more were expected to follow (Exod. 15:20; Num. 12:6; Deut. 18:15-22; 34:10), as they did (Judg. 4:4; 6:8), though the great outburst of prophetic activity began with Samuel. The literary work of these prophets started, as far as we know, with Samuel (1 Sam. 10:25; 1 Chron. 29:29), and the earliest kind of writing in which they seem to have engaged extensively was history, which afterwards became the basis of the books of Chronicles (1 Chron. 29:29; 2 Chron. 9:29; 12:15; 13:22; 20:34; 26:22; 32:32; 33:18ff.) and probably of Samuel and Kings too, which have so much material in common with Chronicles. Whether Joshua and Judges likewise were based on prophetic histories of this kind we do not know, but it is quite possible. That the prophets on occasion wrote down oracles also is clear from Isaiah 30:8; Jeremiah 25:13; 29:1; 30:2; 36:1-32; 51:60-64; Ezekiel 43:11; Habakkuk 2:2; Daniel 7:1; 2 Chronicles 21:12.

The reason why Moses and the prophets wrote down God's message and did not content themselves with delivering it orally was sometimes to send it to another place (Jer. 29:1; 36:1-8; 51:60ff.; 2 Chron. 21:12), but quite as often to preserve it for the future as a memorial (Exod. 17:14) or a witness (Deut. 31:24-26), that it might be there for the time to come (Isa. 30:8). The unreliability of oral tradition was well known to the Old Testament writers. An object-lesson here was the loss of the Book of the Law during the wicked reigns of Manasseh and Amon. When it was rediscovered by Hilkiah, its teaching came as a great shock, for it had been forgotten (2 Kings 22–23; 2 Chron. 34). The permanent and abiding form of God's message was therefore not its spoken but its written form, and this explains the rise of the Old Testament canon.

How long the Pentateuch took to reach its final shape we cannot be sure. However, we saw in the case of the book of the covenant, referred to in Exodus 24, that it was possible for a short document like Exodus 20-23 to become canonical before it had grown to anything like the length of the book which now embodies it. The book of Genesis also embodies earlier documents (Gen. 5:1), Numbers includes an item from an ancient collection of poems (Num. 21:14ff.), and the book of Deuteronomy was considered canonical even within Moses' lifetime (Deut. 31:24-26), for this writing was placed beside the ark. The ending of Deuteronomy, however, was written after Moses' death.

While there was a succession of prophets, it was of course possible for earlier sacred writings to be added to and edited in the manner indicated above, without committing the sacrilege about which warnings are given in Deuteronomy 4:2; 12:32; Proverbs 30:6. The same applies to other parts of the Old Testament. The book of Joshua embodies the covenant of its last chapter, 24:1-25, originally written by Joshua himself (24:26). Samuel embodies the document on the manner of the kingdom (1 Sam. 8:11-18), originally written by Samuel (1 Sam. 10:25). Both these documents were canonical from the outset, the former having been written in the very Book of the Law at the sanctuary of Shechem, and the latter having been laid up before the Lord at Mizpeh. There are signs of the growth of the books of Psalms and Proverbs in Psalms 72:20 and Proverbs

25:1. Items from an ancient collection of poems are included in Joshua (10:12ff.), Samuel (2 Sam. 1:17-27) and Kings (1 Kings 8:53, LXX). Kings names as its sources the *Book of the Acts of Solomon*, the *Book of the Chronicles of the Kings of Israel* and the *Book of the Chronicles of the Kings of Judah* (1 Kings 11:41; 14:29ff.; 2 Kings 1:18; 8:23). The latter two works, combined together, are probably the same as the *Book of the Kings of Israel and Judah*, often named as a source by the canonical books of Chronicles (2 Chron. 16:11; 25:26; 27:7; 28:26; 35:27; 36:8; and, in abbreviated form, 1 Chron. 9:1; 2 Chron. 24:27). This source book seems to have incorporated many of the prophetic histories which are also named as sources in Chronicles (2 Chron. 20:34; 32:32).

Not all the writers of the Old Testament books were prophets, in the narrow sense of the word; some of them were kings and wise men. But their experience of inspiration led to their writings also finding a place in the canon. The inspiration of psalmists is spoken of in 2 Samuel 23:1-3; 1 Chronicles 25:1, and of wise men in Ecclesiastes 12:11ff. Note also the revelations made by God in Job (38:1; 40:6), and the implication of Proverbs 8:1–9:6 that the book of Proverbs is the work of the divine Wisdom.

The Closing of the First Section of the Canon—the Law

The references to the Pentateuch (in whole or part) as canonical, which we saw in the other books of the Old Testament, and which continue in the intertestamental literature, are remarkably numerous. This is doubtless due in part to its fundamental importance. References to other books as inspired or canonical are, within the Old Testament, largely confined to their authors: the chief exceptions are probably Isaiah 34:16; Psalms 149:9; Daniel 9:2. Another reason for this frequency of reference to the Pentateuch may, however, be that it was the first section of the Old Testament to be written and recognized as canonical. The likelihood that this was so arises from the fact that it was basically the work of a single prophet of very early date, which was edited after his death but was not open to continual addition, whereas the other sections of the Old Testament were produced by authors of later date, whose number was not complete until after the return from the Babylonian exile. No one doubts that the Pentateuch was both complete and canonical by the time of Ezra and Nehemiah, in the fifth century B.C., and it may have been so considerably earlier. In the third century B.C. it was translated into Greek, thus becoming the first part of the Septuagint. In the mid-second century B.C. we have evidence of all five books, including Genesis, being attributed to Moses (see Aristobulus, as cited by Eusebius, *Preparation for the Gospel* 13.12). Later in the same century the breach between Jews and Samaritans seems to have become complete, and the preservation of the Hebrew Pentateuch by both parties proves that it was already their common property. All this is evidence that the first section of the canon was now closed, consisting of the five familiar books, neither more nor less, with only minor textual variations persisting.

The Development of the Second and Third Sections of the Canon—the Prophets and Hagiographa

The rest of the Hebrew Bible has a different structure from the English Bible. It is divided into two sections: the Prophets, and the Hagiographa (sacred writings). The Prophets comprise eight books: the historical books Joshua, Judges, Samuel, and Kings, and the oracular books Jeremiah, Ezekiel, Isaiah, and the Twelve (the Minor Prophets). The Hagiographa comprise eleven books: the lyrical and wisdom books Psalms, Job, Proverbs, Ecclesiastes, Song of Songs, and Lamentations, and the historical books Daniel (see below), Esther, Ezra-Nehemiah, and Chronicles. This is the traditional order, according to which the remaining book of the Hagiographa, Ruth, is prefaced to Psalms, as ending with the genealogy of the psalmist David, though in the Middle Ages it was moved to a later position, alongside the other four books of similar brevity (Song of Songs, Ecclesiastes, Lamentations and Esther). It is noteworthy that in Jewish tradition Samuel, Kings, the Minor Prophets, Ezra-Nehemiah, and Chronicles are each reckoned as a single book. This may indicate the capacity of an average Hebrew leather scroll at the period when the canonical books were first listed and counted.

Doubt has sometimes been cast, for inadequate reasons, on the antiquity of this way of grouping the Old Testament books. More commonly, but with equally little real reason, it has been assumed that it reflects the gradual development of the Old Testament canon, the grouping having been a historical accident and the canon of the Prophets having been closed about the third century B.C., before a history like Chronicles and a prophecy like Daniel (which, it is alleged, naturally belong there) had been recognized as inspired or perhaps even written. The canon of the Hagiographa, according to this popular hypothesis, was not closed until the Jewish synod of Jamnia or Jabneh about A.D. 90, after an open Old Testament canon had already been taken over by the Christian church. Moreover, a broader canon, containing much of the Apocrypha, had been accepted by the Greek-speaking Jews of Alexandria, and was embodied in the Septuagint; and the Septuagint was the Old Testament of the early Christian church. These two facts, perhaps together with the Essene fondness for the pseudonymous apocalypses, are responsible for the fluidity of the Old Testament canon in patristic Christianity. Such is the theory.

The reality is rather different. The grouping of the books is not arbitrary, but according to literary character. Daniel is half narrative, and in the Hagiographa (according to the traditional order), it seems to be placed with the histories. There are histories in the Law (covering the period from the creation to Moses) and in the

Prophets (covering the period from Joshua to the end of the monarchy), so why should there not be histories in the Hagiographa also, dealing with the third period, that of the Babylonian exile and return? Chronicles is put last among the histories, as a summary of the whole biblical narrative, from Adam to the return. It is clear that the canon of the Prophets was *not* completely closed when Chronicles was written, for the sources it quotes are not Samuel and Kings but the fuller prophetic histories which seem to have served as sources for Samuel and Kings as well. The earliest elements in the Prophets, incorporated in books such as Joshua and Samuel, are certainly very old, but so are the earliest elements in the Hagiographa, incorporated in books such as Psalms, Proverbs, and Chronicles. These elements may have been recognized as canonical before the final completion of even the first section of the canon. The latest elements in the Hagiographa, such as Daniel, Esther, and Ezra-Nehemiah, belong to the end of Old Testament history. But the same is true of the latest elements in the Prophets, such as Ezekiel, Haggai, Zechariah, and Malachi. Even though the books of the Hagiographa do tend to be later than the Prophets, it is only a tendency, and the overlap is considerable. Indeed, the very assumption that the Hagiographa are a late collection may have led to their individual books being dated later than they otherwise would have been.

Since the books in both these sections are by a variety of authors and are usually independent of one another, it may well be that they were recognized as canonical individually, at different dates, and at first formed a single miscellaneous collection. Then, when the prophetic gift had been for some while withdrawn, and their number was seen to be complete, they were more carefully classified, and were divided into two distinct sections. "The books," spoken of in Daniel 9:2 (NRSV), may have been one growing body of literature, loosely organized and containing not only works by prophets like Jeremiah but also works by psalmists like David. The tradition in 2 Maccabees 2:13 about Nehemiah's library reflects such a mixed collection: "He, founding a library, gathered together the books about the kings and prophets, and the books of David, and letters of kings about sacred gifts." The antiquity of this tradition is shown not only by the likelihood that some such action would be necessary after the calamity of the exile, but also by the fact that the "letters of kings about sacred gifts" are simply being preserved because of their importance and have not yet been embodied in the book of Ezra (6:3-12; 7:12-26). Time had to be given after this for books like Ezra to be completed, for the recognition of the latest books as canonical, and for the realization that the prophetic gift had ceased, and only when these things had happened could the firm division between Prophets and Hagiographa and the careful arrangement of their contents be made. The division had already been made towards the end of the second century B.C., when the prologue to the Greek translation of Ecclesiasticus was composed, for this prologue repeatedly refers to the three sections of the canon. But it seems likely that the division had not long been made, for the third section of the canon had not yet been given a name; the writer calls the first section "the Law," and the second section (because of its contents) "the Prophets" or "the Prophecies," but the third section he simply describes. It is "the others that have followed in their steps," "the other ancestral books," "the rest of the books." This language implies a fixed and complete group of books, but one less old and well-established than the books it contains. The three sections are also referred to in the first century A.D. by Philo (*De Vita Contemplativa* 25) and by Christ (Luke 24:44), both of whom give the third section its earliest name of "the Psalms."

The Closing of the Second and Third Sections of the Canon

The date when the Prophets and Hagiographa were organized in their separate sections was probably about 165 B.C. The

2 Maccabees tradition just quoted speaks of the second great crisis in the history of the canon: "And in the same way Judas [Maccabaeus] collected all the books that had been lost on account of the war which had come upon us, and they are still in our possession" (2 Macc. 2:14). The "war" mentioned here is the Maccabaean war of liberation from the Syrian persecutor Antiochus Epiphanes. The hostility of Antiochus against the Scripture is on record (1 Macc. 1:56ff.), and it is indeed probable that Judas would have needed to gather copies of them together when the persecution was over. Judas knew that the prophetic gift had ceased a long time before (1 Macc. 9:27), so it seems likely that when he gathered together the scattered Scriptures he arranged and listed the complete collection in the traditional order. Since the books were as yet in separate scrolls, which had to be "collected," what he would have produced would not have been a volume but a collection, and a list of the books in the collection, divided into three.

In drawing up his list, Judas probably established not only the firm division into Prophets and Hagiographa but also the traditional order and number of the books within them. A list of books has to have an order and number, and the traditional order has Chronicles as the last of the Hagiographa. This position for Chronicles can be traced back to the first century A.D., since it is reflected in a saying of Christ's in Matthew 23:35 and Luke 11:51, where the phrase "from the blood of Abel to the blood of Zechariah" probably means all the martyred prophets from one end of the canon to the other, from Genesis 4:3-15 to 2 Chronicles 24:19-22. The traditional number of the canonical books is twenty-four (the five books of the Law, together with eight books of the Prophets and the eleven books of the Hagiographa listed above), or twenty-two (Ruth being in that case appended to Judges, and Lamentations to Jeremiah, in order to conform the count to the number of letters in the Hebrew alphabet). The number twenty-four is first recorded in 2 Esdras 14:44-48, about A.D. 100. The number twenty-two is first recorded in Josephus (*Contra Apion* 1.8), just before A.D. 100, but also, probably, in the fragments of the Greek translation of the book of *Jubilees* (first century B.C.?). If the number twenty-two goes back to the first century B.C., so does the number twenty-four, for the former is an adaptation of the latter to the number of letters in the alphabet. And since the number twenty-four, which combines some of the smaller books into single units but not others, seems to have been influenced in this by the traditional order, the order too must be equally old. There is no doubt about the identity of the twenty-four or twenty-two books—they are the books of the Hebrew Bible. Josephus says that they have all been accepted as canonical from time immemorial. Individual attestation can be provided for the canonicity of nearly all of them from writings of the first century A.D. or earlier. This is true even of four out of five disputed by certain of the rabbis: only the Song of Songs, perhaps because of its shortness, remains without individual attestation.

Such evidence implies that by the beginning of the Christian era the identity of all the canonical books was well known and generally accepted. How, then, has it come to be thought that the third section of the canon was not closed until the synod of Jamnia, some decades after the birth of the Christian church? The main reasons are that the rabbinical literature records disputes about five of the books, some of which were settled at the Jamnia discussion; that many of the Septuagint manuscripts mix apocryphal books among the canonical, thus prompting the theory of a wider Alexandrian canon; and that the Qumran discoveries show the apocalyptic pseudepigrapha to have been cherished, and perhaps reckoned canonical, by the Essenes. But the rabbinical literature records similar, though more readily answered, academic objections to many other canonical books, so it must have been a question of removing books from the list (had this been possible), not adding them. Moreover, one of the five disputed books (Ezekiel) belongs to the second section of the canon, which is admitted to have been closed long before the Christian era. As to the Alexandrian canon, Philo of Alexandria's writings show it to have been the same as the Palestinian. He refers to the three familiar sections, and he ascribes inspiration to many books in all three, but never to any of the Apocrypha. In the Septuagint manuscripts, the Prophets and Hagiographa have been rearranged by Christian hands in a non-Jewish manner, and the intermingling of Apocrypha there is a Christian phenomenon, not a Jewish. At Qumran the pseudonymous apocalypses were more likely viewed as an Essene appendix to the standard Jewish canon than as an integral part of it. There are allusions to this appendix in Philo's account of the Therapeutae (*De Vita Contemplativa* 25) and in 2 Esdras 14:44-48. An equally significant fact discovered at Qumran is that the Essenes, though at rivalry with mainstream Judaism since the second century B.C., reckoned as canonical some of the Hagiographa and had presumably done so since before the rivalry began.

From Jewish Canon to Christian

The Septuagint manuscripts are paralleled by the writings of the early Christian Fathers, who (at any rate outside Palestine and Syria) normally used the Septuagint or the derived Old Latin version. In their writings, there is both a wide and a narrow canon. The former comprises those books from before the time of Christ which were generally read and esteemed in the church (including the Apocrypha), but the latter is confined to the books of the Jewish Bible, which scholars like Melito, Origen, Epiphanius, and Jerome take the trouble to distinguish from the rest as alone inspired. The Apocrypha were known in the church from the start, but the further back one goes, the more rarely are they treated as inspired. In the New Testament itself, one finds Christ acknowledging the Jewish Scriptures, by various of their current titles, and accepting the three sections of the Jewish canon and the traditional order of its books; one finds most of the books being referred to individually as having divine authority—but not so for any of the Apocrypha. The only apparent exceptions are found in Jude: Jude 9 (citing the apocryphal work, *The Assumption of Moses*) and Jude 14, citing *Enoch*. Jude's citations of these works does not mean he believed they were divinely inspired, just as Paul's citation of various Greek poets (see Acts 17:28; 1 Cor. 15:33; Tit. 1:12) does not attribute divine inspiration to their poetry.

What evidently happened in the early centuries of Christianity was this: Christ passed on to his followers, as Holy Scriptures, the Bible which he had received, containing the same books as the Hebrew Bible today. The first Christians shared with their Jewish contemporaries a full knowledge of the identity of the canonical books. However, the Bible was not yet between two covers: it was a memorized list of scrolls. The breach with Jewish oral tradition (in some matters a very necessary breach), the alienation between Jew and Christian, and the general ignorance of Semitic languages in the church outside Palestine and Syria, led to increasing doubt concerning the canon among Christians, which was accentuated by the drawing up of new lists of the biblical books, arranged on other principles, and the introduction of new lectionaries. Such doubt about the canon could only be resolved, and can only be resolved today, in the way it was resolved at the Reformation—by returning to the teaching of the New Testament and the Jewish background against which it is to be understood.

BIBLIOGRAPHY

Green, W. H. *General Introduction to the Old Testament: the Canon*, 1899.
Harris, R. L. *Inspiration and Canonicity of the Bible*, 1957.
Kline, M. G. *The Structure of Biblical Authority*, 1972.

Leiman, S. Z. *The Canonization of Hebrew Scripture,* 1976.

Lewis, J. P. *Journal of Bible and Religion* 32, 1964, pp. 125–132.

Margolis, M. L. *The Hebrew Scriptures in the Making,* 1922.

Purvis, J. D. *The Samaritan Pentateuch and the Origin of the Samaritan Sect,* 1968.

Ryle, H. E. *The Canon of the Old Testament,* 1895.

Sundberg, A. C. *The Old Testament of the Early Church,* 1964.

Westcott, B. F. *The Bible in the Church,* 1864.

Zeitlin, S. *A Historical Study of the Canonization of the Hebrew Scriptures,* 1933.

The Canon of
the New Testament
Milton Fisher

The New Testament was written within the period of half a century, several hundred years after the completion of the Old Testament. Both halves of that statement would be questioned by modern critics, who would extend the time span for completion of both testaments. The writer of this survey is confident of its truthfulness to historic fact, however, and the approach taken to canonization of both Old Testament and New Testament is based solidly upon that twofold premise.

The Old Testament is so far removed from us in time that its formation as a body of Scripture might be considered too remote for certification of its contents. Such is not the case. In a sense, we possess far higher certification of the Old Testament canon than of the New Testament canon (see the chapter "The Canon of the Old Testament" for definition). We refer to the fact of our Lord's own imprimatur by way of his use of the Hebrew Scriptures as the authoritative Word of God.

Yet there is a sense in which Jesus Christ did establish the New Testament content or canon as well, by way of anticipation. It was he who promised, "the Counselor, the Holy Spirit, whom the

Father will send in my name, will teach you all things and will remind you of everything I have said to you" and "he will guide you into all truth" (John 14:26; 16:13, NIV).

From this we can derive, in turn, the basic principle of canonicity for the New Testament. It is identical to that of the Old Testament, since it narrows down to a matter of divine inspiration. Whether we think of the prophets of Old Testament times or the apostles and their God-given associates of the New, the recognition at the very time of their writing that they were authentic spokesmen for God is what determines the intrinsic canonicity of their writing. It is altogether God's Word only if it is God-breathed. We can be assured that the books under question were received by the church of the apostolic age precisely when they had been certified by an apostle as being thus inspired. The apparent variation, relative to geographic area, in acknowledgment of some of the New Testament epistles may well reflect the simple fact that this attestation was by its very nature localized at the first. Conversely, that all twenty-seven books of the now universally received New Testament were ultimately agreed upon is evidence that proper attestation was indeed confirmed after rigorous investigation.

Tertullian, an outstanding Christian writer in the first two decades of the third century, was one of the first to call the Christian Scriptures the "New Testament." That title had appeared earlier (c. 190) in a composition against Montanism, the author of which is unknown. This is significant. Its use placed the New Testament Scripture on a level of inspiration and authority with the Old Testament.

From available information, the gradual process which led to full and formal public recognition of a fixed canon of the twenty-seven books comprising the New Testament takes us down into the fourth century of our era. This does not necessarily mean that these Scriptures were lacking recognition in their entirety before that time, but that a need for officially defining the canon was not pressing until then. Analogous to this would be the way certain theological doctrines have been enunciated at particular periods of church history, as—for example—the Christological formulations of early centuries of the church and the doctrine of justification by faith at the time of the Reformation. The fact that Tertullian is credited by some to be the first to define the Trinity clearly is not taken to mean that the doctrine of the triune God came into existence at that point in history or that the Bible did not contain that truth. Just so, the New Testament was actually completed with the writing of its final portion (which was not necessarily the Book of Revelation), not *constituted* Scripture by statements about it by men, speaking either as individuals or corporately.

While the New Testament is very much the counterpart and completion of the revelation given in the Old Testament, its formal structure is somewhat dissimilar. The organizing principle of the Old Testament canon was its nature as a covenant document. The Pentateuch, in particular, partakes of the pattern set by other treaties and written agreements of the ancient Near East. The principle of authoritative sacred writings established by the Old Testament for God's people obviously carried over to the New.

Though a much shorter period of time was involved in the writing of the New Testament, the geographic range of its origin is far wider. This circumstance alone is sufficient to account for a lack of spontaneous or simultaneous recognition of the precise extent of the New Testament canon. Because of the geographic isolation of the various recipients of portions of the New Testament, there was bound to be some lag and uncertainty from one region to another in the acknowledgment of some of the books.

In order to appreciate just what did transpire in the process of canonization of the New Testament books, we must review the facts available to us. This will enable us to analyze *how* and *why* our early Christian forebears settled upon the twenty-seven books in our New Testament.

The historic process was a gradual and continuous one, but it will help us understand it if we subdivide the nearly three and one-half centuries involved into shorter periods of time. Some speak of three major stages toward canonization. This implies, without justification, that there are readily discernible steps along the way. Others simply present a long list of the names of persons and documents involved. Such a list makes it difficult to sense any motion at all. A somewhat arbitrary breakdown into five periods will be made here, with the reminder that the spreading of the knowledge of sacred literature and the deepening consensus as to its authenticity as inspired Scripture continued uninterruptedly. The periods are:

1. First Century
2. First Half of Second Century
3. Second Half of Second Century
4. Third Century
5. Fourth Century

Again, without meaning to imply that these are clear-cut stages, it will be helpful to notice the major trends observable in each of the periods just identified. In the first period, of course, the various books were written, but they also began to be copied and disseminated among the church. In the second, as they became more widely known and cherished for their contents, they began to be cited as authoritative. By the end of the third period they held a recognized place alongside the Old Testament as "Scripture," and they began to be both translated into regional languages and made the subject of commentaries. During the third century A.D., our fourth period, the collecting of books into a whole "New Testament" was underway, together with a sifting process which was separating them from other Christian literature. The final, or fifth, period finds the church fathers of the fourth century stating that conclusions regarding the canon have been reached which indicate acceptance by the whole church. Thus, in the most strict and formal sense of the word, the canon had become fixed. It remains to list in greater detail the forces and individuals which produced the written sources witnessing to this remarkable process through which, by God's providence, we have inherited our New Testament.

Period One: First Century

The principle determining recognition of the authority of the canonical New Testament writings was established within the content of those writings themselves. There are repeated exhortations for public reading of the apostolic communications. At the close of his first letter to the Thessalonians, possibly the first book of the New Testament to be written, Paul says, "I command you in the name of the Lord to read this letter to all the Christians" (1 Thess. 5:27, TLB). Earlier in the same letter Paul commends their ready acceptance of his spoken word as "the word of God" (2:13), and in 1 Corinthians 14:37 he speaks similarly of his "writings," insisting that his message be recognized as a commandment from the Lord himself. (See also Col. 4:16; Rev. 1:3.) In 2 Peter 3:15-16 Paul's letters are included with "the other Scriptures." Since Peter's is a general letter, widespread knowledge of Paul's letters is thereby implied. Highly indicative also is Paul's usage in 1 Timothy 5:18. He follows up the formula "the Scriptures say" by a combined quotation about not muzzling an ox (Deut. 25:4) and "the worker deserves his wages" (cf. Luke 10:7). Thus, an equivalence is implied between Old Testament Scripture and a New Testament Gospel.

In A.D. 95 Clement of Rome wrote to the Christians in Corinth using a free rendering of material from Matthew and Luke. He seems to be strongly influenced by Hebrews and is obviously familiar with Romans and Corinthians. There are also reflections of 1 Timothy, Titus, 1 Peter, and Ephesians.

Period Two: First Half of Second Century

One of the earliest New Testament manuscripts yet discovered, a fragment of John from Egypt known as the John Rylands papyrus, demonstrates how the writings of the apostle John were revered and copied by about A.D. 125, within thirty to thirty-five years of his death. There is evidence that within thirty years of the apostle's death all the Gospels and Pauline letters were known and used in all those centers from which any evidence has come down to us. It is true that some of the smaller letters were being questioned as to their authority in some quarters for perhaps another fifty years, but this was due only to uncertainty about their authorship in those particular locales. This demonstrates that acceptance was not being imposed by the actions of councils but was rather happening spontaneously through a normal response on the part of those who had learned the facts about authorship. In those places where the churches were uncertain about the authorship or apostolic approval of certain books, acceptance was slower.

The first three outstanding church fathers, Clement, Polycarp, and Ignatius, used the bulk of the material of the New Testament in a revealingly casual manner—authenticated Scriptures were being accepted as authoritative without argument. In the writings of these men only Mark (which closely parallels the material of Matthew), 2 and 3 John, Jude, and 2 Peter are not clearly attested.

The *Epistles of Ignatius* (c. A.D. 115) have correspondences in several places with the Gospels and seem to incorporate language from a number of the Pauline letters. The *Didache* (or *Teaching of the Twelve*), perhaps even earlier, makes references to a written Gospel. Most important is the fact that Clement, Barnabas, and

Ignatius all draw a clear distinction between their own and the inspired, authoritative apostolic writings.

It is in the *Epistle of Barnabas*, c. A.D. 130, that we first find the formula "it is written" (4:14) used in reference to a New Testament book (Matt. 22:14). But even before this, Polycarp, who had personal acquaintance with eyewitnesses of our Lord's ministry, used a combined Old Testament and New Testament quotation. Citing Paul's admonition in Ephesians 4:26, where the apostle quotes Psalm 4:4 and makes an addition, Polycarp in his *Epistle to the Philippians* introduces the reference by, "as it is said in *these Scriptures*" (12:4). Then Papias, Bishop of Hierapolis (c. 130-140), in a work preserved for us by Eusebius, mentions by name the Gospels of Matthew and Mark, and his use of them as the basis of exposition indicates his acceptance of them as canonical. Also around A.D. 140, the recently discovered *Gospel of Truth* (a Gnostic-oriented work probably authored by Valentinius) makes an important contribution. Its use of canonical New Testament sources, treating them as authoritative, is comprehensive enough to warrant the conclusion that in Rome (at this period) there was a New Testament compilation in existence corresponding very closely to our own. Citations are made from the Gospels, Acts, letters of Paul, Hebrews, and the book of Revelation.

The heretic Marcion, by defining a limited canon of his own (c. 140), in effect hastened the day when the orthodox believers needed to declare themselves on this issue. Rejecting the entire Old Testament, Marcion settled for Luke's Gospel (eliminating chapters 1 and 2 as too Jewish) and Paul's letters (except for the pastoral ones). Interestingly, especially in the light of Colossians 4:16, he substitutes the name "Laodiceans" for Ephesians.

Near the end of this period Justin Martyr, in describing the worship services of the early church, puts the apostolic writings on a par with those of the Old Testament prophets. He states that the voice which spoke through the apostles of Christ in the New Testament was the same as that which spoke through the prophets—the voice of God—and the same voice that Abraham heard, responding in faith and obedience. Justin was also free in his use of "it is written" with quotations from New Testament Scriptures.

Period Three: Second Half of Second Century

Irenaeus had been privileged to begin his Christian training under Polycarp, a disciple of apostles. Then, as a presbyter in Lyons, he had association with Bishop Pothinus, whose own background also included contact with first generation Christians. Irenaeus quotes from almost all the New Testament on the basis of its authority and asserts that the apostles were endowed with power from on high. They were, he says, "fully informed concerning all things, and had a perfect knowledge . . . having indeed all in equal measure and each one singly the Gospel of God" (*Against Heretics,* 3.3). Irenaeus gives reasons why there should be four Gospels. "The Word," he says, ". . . gave us the Gospel in a fourfold shape, but held together by one Spirit." In addition to the Gospels, he makes reference also to Acts, 1 Peter, 1 John, all the letters of Paul except Philemon, and the book of Revelation.

Tatian, pupil of Justin Martyr, made a harmony of the four Gospels, the *Diatessaron,* attesting to the equal status they had in the church by A.D. 170. Other "gospels" had come into existence by then, but he recognized only the four. Also dating from about 170 was the *Muratorian Canon.* An eighth-century copy of this document was discovered and published in 1740 by librarian L. A. Muratori. The manuscript is mutilated at both ends, but the remaining text makes it evident that Matthew and Mark were included in the now missing part. The fragment begins with Luke and John, cites Acts, thirteen Pauline letters, Jude, 1 and 2 John, and Revelation. There follows a statement, "We accept only the Apocalypse of

John and Peter, although some of us do not want it [Apocalypse of Peter is 2 Peter?] to be read in the Church." The list goes on to reject by name various heretical leaders and their writings.

Translated versions existed by this period. In the form of Syriac and Old Latin translations we secure, by A.D. 170, adequate witness from the extreme eastern and western branches of the church, as we might well expect from the other evidence in hand. The New Testament canon is represented with no additions and the omission of only one book, 2 Peter.

Period Four: Third Century

The outstanding Christian name of the third century is that of Origen (A.D. 185–254). A prodigious scholar and exegete, he made critical studies of the New Testament text (alongside his work on the *Hexapla*) and wrote commentaries and homilies on most of the books of the New Testament, emphasizing their inspiration by God.

Dionysius of Alexandria, pupil of Origen, indicates that while the Western church accepted the book of Revelation from the first, its position in the East was variable. In the case of the letter to the Hebrews, the situation was reversed. It proved to be more insecure in the West than in the East. When it comes to other contested books (note, incidently, that all in that category have the hindmost position in our present Bibles—Hebrews to Revelation), among the so-called "Catholic Epistles" Dionysius supports James and 2 and 3 John, but not 2 Peter or Jude. In other words, even at the end of the third century there was the same lack of finality about the canon as at its beginning.

Period Five: Fourth Century

Early in this period the picture begins to clarify. Eusebius (A.D. 270–340, bishop of Caesarea before 315), the great church historian, sets forth his estimate of the canon in his *Church History* (3, chpts. iii–xxv). Herein he makes a straightforward statement on the status of the canon in the early part of the fourth century. (1) Universally agreed upon as canonical were the four Gospels, Acts, Letters of Paul (including Hebrews, with question about his authorship), 1 Peter, 1 John, and Revelation. (2) Admitted by a majority, including Eusebius himself, but disputed by some were James, 2 Peter (the most strongly contested), 2 and 3 John, and Jude. (3) The *Acts of Paul,* the *Didache,* and *Shepherd of Hermas* were classified "spurious," and still other writings were listed as "heretical and absurd."

It is in the latter half of the fourth century, however, that the New Testament canon finds full and final declaration. In his *Festal Letter* for Easter, 367, Bishop Athanasius of Alexandria included information designed to eliminate once and for all the use of certain apocryphal books. This letter, with its admonition, "Let no one add to these; let nothing be taken away," gives us the earliest extant document which specifies our twenty-seven books without qualification. At the close of the century the Council of Carthage (A.D. 397) decreed that "aside from the canonical Scriptures nothing is to be read in church under the Name of Divine Scriptures." This too lists the twenty-seven books of the New Testament.

The sudden advance of Christianity under Emperor Constantine (Edict of Milan, 313) had a great deal to do with the reception of all the New Testament books in the East. When he assigned Eusebius the task of preparing "fifty copies of the Divine Scriptures," the historian, fully aware of which were the sacred books for which many believers had been willing to lay down their very lives, in effect established the standard which gave recognition to all of the once-doubtful books. In the West, of course, Jerome and Augustine were the leaders who exercised a determinitive influence. Publication of the twenty-seven books in the Vulgate version virtually settled the matter.

Principles and Factors Determining the Canon

By its very nature, Holy Scripture, whether Old or New Testament, is a production given of God, not the work of human creation. The key to canonicity is divine inspiration. Therefore, the method of determination is not one of selection from a number of possible candidates (there *are no* other candidates, in actuality) but one of reception of authentic material and its consequent recognition by an ever-widening circle as the facts of its origin become known.

In a sense the movement of Montanus, which was declared heretical by the church of his day (mid-second century), was an impetus toward the recognition of a closed canon of the written Word of God. He taught that the prophetic gift was permanently granted to the church and that he himself was a prophet. The pressure to deal with Montanism, therefore, intensified the search for a basic authority, and apostolic authorship or approval became recognized as the only sure standard for identifying God's revelation. Even within the Scripture record, first-century prophets were subordinate and subject to apostolic authority. (See, for example, 1 Cor. 14:29-30; Eph. 4:11.)

When in the Protestant Reformation all things were being reexamined, some of the reformers sought means of reassuring themselves and their followers about the canon of Scripture. This was in some ways an unfortunate aspect of reformation thinking, because once God in his providence had determined for his people the fixed content of Scripture, that became a fact of history and was not a repeatable process. Nevertheless, Luther established a theological test for the books of the Bible (and questioned some of them)—"Do they teach Christ?" Equally subjective, it would seem, was Calvin's insistence that the Spirit of God bears witness to each individual Christian in any age of church history as to what is his Word and what is not.

Actually, even for the initial acceptance of the written Word, it is neither safe nor sound (as far as Scripture or history teaches us) to say that recognition and reception was an intuitive matter. It was rather a matter of simple obedience to the known commands of Christ and his apostles. As we saw at the outset, our Lord promised (John 14:26; 16:13) to communicate all things necessary through his agents. The apostles were conscious of this responsibility and agency as they wrote. Paul's explanation in 1 Corinthians 2:13 is apropos: "In telling you about these gifts we have even used the very words given to us by the Holy Spirit, not words that we as men might choose. So we use the Holy Spirit's words to explain the Holy Spirit's facts" (TLB).

Hence the early church, with closer ties and greater information than is available to us today, examined the testimony of the ancients. They were able to discern which were the authentic and authoritative books by their apostolic origin. Mark's association with Peter and Luke's with Paul gave them such apostolic approval, and epistles like Hebrews and Jude were also tied in with the apostolic message and ministry. Incontrovertible consistency of doctrine in all the books, including the sometime contested ones, was perhaps a subordinate test. But historically the procedure was essentially one of acceptance and approval of those books which were vouched for by knowledgeable church leaders. Full acceptance by the original recipients followed by a continued acknowledgment and use is an essential factor in the development of the canon.

The church's concept of canon, derived first of all from the reverence given the Old Testament Scriptures, rested in the conviction that the apostles were uniquely authorized to speak in the name of the One who possessed all authority—the Lord Jesus Christ. The development from there is logical and straightforward. Those who heard Jesus in person were immediately subject to his authority. He personally authenticated his words to the believers. These same believers knew that Jesus authorized his apostles to speak in his name, both during and (more significantly) after his earthly ministry. Apostolic speaking on behalf of Christ was recognized in the church, whether in personal utterance or in written form. Both the spoken word of an apostle and the letter of an apostle constituted the word of Christ.

The generation that followed that of the apostles themselves received the witness of those who knew that the apostles had the right to speak and write in the name of Christ. Consequently, the second and third generation of Christians looked back to apostolic words (writings) as the very words of Christ. This is what is really meant by canonization—recognition of the divinely authenticated word. Hence, the believers (the church) did not establish the canon but simply bore witness to its extent by recognizing the authority of the word of Christ.

Canon Criticism

By way of a footnote to the case for confidence in the New Testament canon of twenty-seven books with which we are familiar, it must be observed that there are still some who feel the issue is not yet settled, or perhaps *should not* have been settled as it was. Two objections are raised. One has to do with the inadequacy of the solutions the Reformers proposed to their own questions. We would submit that the questions were already answered historically and that the tests of canonicity proposed by both Luther and Calvin are improper. The other objection is based on an assumption that the church Fathers operated on wrong information. Several of the New Testament books, they suggest, were not written until after the apostolic age, or at least have questionable authorship. These suspicions have been dealt with and dispelled, I believe, in the above presentation. No Christian, confident in the providential working of his God and informed about the true nature of canon-icity of his Word, should be disturbed about the dependability of the Bible we now possess.

BIBLIOGRAPHY

Bruce, F. F. *The Canon of Scripture,* 1988.

Gamble, Harry Y. "The Canon of the New Testament" in *The New Testament and Its Modern Interpreters.* eds. E. J. Epp and G. W. McRae, 1989.

Harrison, Everett. *Introduction to the New Testament,* 1971.

McRay, John R. "New Testament Canon" in the *Baker Encyclopedia of the Bible,* ed. Walter Elwell, 1988.

Old Testament and
New Testament Apocrypha
R. K. Harrison

The writings of the Old and New Testaments tended to attract certain additional compositions in the form of books, parts of books, letters, "gospels," apocalypses, and so on. Most of the authors wrote anonymously but some presented their writings to the public under the name of a familiar Old Testament figure or member of the Christian church. Such compositions formed a small but important part of the great body of Jewish literature which emerged during the period between the Old and New Testaments. Much of it was the result of religious and political ferment, for the Jews felt their faith and their very existence threatened first by the pagan influences of Hellenistic Greek culture, then by the oppression of invading Roman forces.

Historical Background

A brief review of the history of that intertestamental period will establish the background against which the majority of the Old Testament apocryphal books were composed. When Alexander the Great died in 323 B.C., his empire was split up among his four generals. Judea was included in the territory governed by Seleucus I, but in 320 B.C. it was annexed by Ptolemy of Egypt to his own territory. That kind of activity characterized much of the intertestamental period, placing the Palestinian people under severe political and social pressure. In general their conquerors sought to conciliate the Jews, and in the case of the Ptolemies even encouraged them to migrate to Egypt. However, the threat of military oppression was never far from Judea, and became a reality once more in 205 B.C. when Ptolemy V died suddenly and Antiochus III of Syria decided to annex Judea. An Egyptian army moved to check his advance but was defeated near Sidon in 198 B.C., after which Judea became part of the Seleucid kingdom. Although Antiochus was tolerant toward the Jews, he maintained firm political control over the country, just as the Egyptians had done. Eventually the civil strife which had been breaking out in various parts of the Near East toward the end of the Greek period attracted the attention of the Romans, who were coming to the forefront as a military and political power. Roman legions entered Asia Minor in 197 B.C. and were attacked by the Syrians. After a long campaign Scipio Africanus crushed Syrian forces at Magnesia in 190 B.C., thus paving the way for further Roman inroads into Palestine.

In the meantime the Seleucid kings clung precariously to their power and began to behave with increasing severity toward the Jews. Part of the difficulty lay in the fact that the Seleucids had become propagandists for pagan Hellenic culture and were bent upon introducing Greek traditions into orthodox Judaism. "Hellenizing" occurred with particular severity under Antiochus IV (175–164 B.C.), causing the Hasmonean family to rise up in revolt. The resistance under Judas Maccabeus was so successful that the Syrian regent Lysias guaranteed the return of Jewish liberties, an obvious setback for the hellenizing party in Judea. In 142 B.C. Judea became independent from Syria, and under John Hyrcanus (135–105 B.C.) achieved some political and territorial solidarity. But the whole situation was unstable at best and was complicated by the

conflicts between the Hellenizers and the more traditional Saddu-
cees, Pharisees, and scribes. In the meantime, purist religious
groups such as the members of the Dead Sea community broke
away from the orthodox Jews and founded their own settlements
in the inhospitable wilderness of Judea.

In 64 B.C. Pompey attacked Syria and made it into a Roman
province. While endeavoring to quell unrest in Judea, the Romans
were attacked by fanatical Jews who were ultimately slaughtered
on the Temple mount. The Romans kept a garrison in Jerusalem
thereafter and incorporated Judea into the newly fashioned province of Syria. The subsequent Herodian dynasty governed under
the supervision of Rome, which maintained legions in Judea until
after the second Jewish Revolt (A.D.132–135).

The period that saw the writing of the Apocryphal material was
thus one of unprecedented political, military, social, and religious
turbulence. It has been estimated that at the birth of Christ, one
person out of every two in the Roman Empire was a slave. Jewish
resistance to hellenizing influences produced times of repression
and persecution that made the Jews long for deliverance and
stimulated the interest of at least some in the possiblity of a messiah
coming from God to remedy the situation. The apocalyptic writings dealt at length with the problem of the struggle between good
and evil and with the expectation of a new age in which God
would reward the faithful with spiritual blessings. Messianic figures
who appeared in apocalyptic writings, especially in New Testament
Apocrypha, were not infrequently balanced by an antichrist, both
of them being attended by many angelic personages. It was a
literary and spiritual world of partial fact and partial fantasy, the
fantasy being an important ingredient for maintaining the expectations of the less emotionally stable.

While the Dead Sea scrolls cannot be regarded as apocryphal,
some passages are apocalyptic—e.g., the Manual of Discipline

3:13–4:26, the War Scroll (1QM) 1:15-19, and the New Jerusalem (5Q15). Some scholars have interpreted parts of the Copper Scroll (3Q15) apocalyptically, but most writers simply regard the material as a list of concealed treasure.

Apocryphal and Canonical Writings

Although the earliest Old Testament apocryphal works may have been written as early as the end of the fourth century B.C., the majority appeared from the second century B.C. onward. Some of them quite closely approximated counterparts in the canonical Scriptures, and there is no doubt that in some circles their authority and inspiration were regarded as similar to that of the scriptural compositions venerated by the Jews and later by Christians.

Other religious writings from that period made no claim to be scriptural. Such compositions preserved the familiar traditions of both Judaism and primitive Christianity, although on occasion they enriched or embellished them by means of legends and unhistorical narratives. Because very few books of any kind were in circulation at that time, the Palestinians tended to read whatever literary material came into their possession. Although the Torah or Law of Moses had always been recognized as the standard of theological orthodoxy for the Jews, narratives of endurance under persecution or accounts of the way that the enemies of God's people received their just reward had an obvious attraction for those under the pressures of a pagan society.

In the same way, although the Gospels and Epistles—along with the Old Testament—comprised the basic canon or approved list of Scriptures for Christians, many additional narratives claimed the attention of Christ's early followers. Those compositions often dealt with the supposed activities of Jesus and his followers, as well as with martyrdoms, revelations, and spiritual teachings. Some works contained material that was not only unhistorical but downright bizarre, but others reflected the spirit of Christ and the apostolic teachings to a certain extent. For the early Christians, as also for the Jews, the establishment of a formal canon of scriptural writings must have been prompted in part by a necessity to separate the record of revealed truth from other written forms of religious tradition as well as from actual heresy.

Writings that failed to gain acceptance into the Old and New Testament canons were described in the writings of some early Christian scholars by the term "apocrypha." The Greek word means "hidden things," and when applied to books it described those works which religious authorities wished to be concealed from the reading public. The reason was that such books were thought to contain mysterious or secret lore, meaningful only to the initiate and therefore unsuitable for the ordinary reader. But the word "apocrypha" was also applied in a less complimentary sense to works that deserved to be concealed. Such works contained harmful doctrines or false teachings calculated to unsettle or pervert rather than edify those who read them. The suppression of unde- sirable writings was comparatively easy at a time when only a few copies of any book were in circulation at a given time. Offensive writings would more likely have been burned by the authorities than "hidden" (compare Acts 19:19).

Hidden or esoteric teachings were not part of the Hebrew tradition, which based its spirituality on the first five books of the Hebrew canon. Insofar as mysterious doctrines came into Hebrew life, they did so from pagan sources and generally involved magical practices which were forbidden to Israel. Only when the concept of wisdom emerged in such writings as Proverbs, Ecclesiastes, Job, and certain psalms did Jewish teachers such as Jesus Ben Sirach advise their hearers to search out the "hidden things" of divine wisdom (Ecclus. 14:20-21; 39:1-3, 7). Even so, the emphasis was upon knowing the mind and revealed will of God, not on the study of esoteric treatises of a kind popular among Hellenistic authors and readers.

By the end of the first century A.D., a clear distinction was being made in Jewish circles between writings which were suitable for use by the general public and esoteric works which were to be restricted to the knowledgeable and the initiated. Thus in 2 Esdras 4:1-6, the writer tells how Ezra was supposedly instructed by God to publish openly certain writings (that is, the Torah of Moses), and keep others secret (that is, apocalyptic traditions dealing with the coming end of the age). In 2 Esdras 14:42-46 reference is made to seventy books, evidently noncanonical material, written after the twenty-four books of the Hebrew canon.

Use of the term "apocrypha" to mean "noncanonical" goes back to the fifth century A.D., when Jerome urged that the books found in the Septuagint and in the Latin Bibles that did not occur in the canon of the Hebrew Old Testament writings should be treated as apocryphal. They were not to be disregarded entirely, since they were part of the great contemporary outpouring of Jewish national literature. At the same time they should not be used as sources for Christian doctrine, but at best for supplementary reading of an uplifting or inspirational nature.

Protestant theologians generally have followed the tradition established by Jerome, regarding the Old Testament Apocrypha as the excess of the Septuagint canon over the Hebrew Scriptures. When the Hebrew Bible began to be translated into Greek in Egypt during the reign of Ptolemy II (285–246 B.C.), the scholars concerned included a number of books that, while remaining outside the generally accepted list of Hebrew canonical writings, still had a bearing upon Jewish history and society. That procedure reflected contemporary attitudes in Palestine, where, as the Dead Sea scrolls show, many people made little serious attempt to separate canonical writings from other forms of religious literature.

The decision made by Jewish authorities about what to regard as canonical Scripture naturally had a bearing on what would constitute Old Testament Apocrypha.

Textual evidence represented by certain manuscripts and fragments from the Dead Sea caves makes it reasonably certain that the last of the canonical Hebrew writings had been completed several decades before the time Alexander the Great (356–323 B.C.) began his conquests in the Near East. The process by which those compositions came to be accepted as canonical was more protracted, however. Only when they had been circulated, read, and assessed favorably by comparison with the spirituality of the Torah were they accorded general canonicity. Hence the distinction between the canonical and apocryphal writings came as much through usage and general consent on the part of orthodox Judaism as in any other manner. Earlier scholars suggested that the so-called "Council of Jamnia," held in Palestine about A.D. 100, was responsible for drawing up a list of Old Testament books suitable for use by the faithful. However, subsequent studies have thrown considerable doubt upon the historicity of such a council, at the same time showing that the Jewish authorities of that period considered their noncanonical writings to be more of an obstacle than a help to devotion.

Old Testament Apocrypha

The books the Jews regarded as being specifically "outside the canon," and therefore apocryphal, are as follows: 1 Esdras; 2 Esdras; Tobit; Judith; the additions to Esther; the Wisdom of Solomon; Ecclesiasticus; Baruch; the Letter of Jeremiah; the additions to the Book of Daniel (the Prayer of Asariah and the Song of the Three Young Men; Susanna; and Bel and the Dragon); the Prayer of Manasseh; 1 Maccabees; and 2 Maccabees. Several Septuagint manuscripts included some pseudohistorical material under the titles of 3 and 4 Maccabees; thus even the Apocrypha varied somewhat in content, depending upon the manuscript tradition being followed. Among early Christian scholars there was also some difference of opinion about the precise limits of canonical Hebrew Scripture, and hence of apocryphal material. A serious break with Hebrew and rabbinic tradition came with the writings of Augustine, who advanced the view that the books of the Apocrypha were of equal authority with the other writings of the canonical Hebrew and Christian Scriptures. A few dissenting voices were raised in support of Jerome's position, but the views of Augustine were embraced by the Council of Trent (1546) and became official Roman Catholic teaching.

The book called 1 Esdras seems to be a compilation of historical material drawn from various parts of the Old Testament, notably Chronicles, Ezra, and Nehemiah. It includes one interesting interpolation, the Debate of the Three Soldiers (1 Esdras 3:1–5:6), in which the supremacy of truth is demonstrated by some unfortunate historical errors and inconsistencies that are found in the book, in sharp contrast to the accuracy of the canonical sources upon which the compiler of 1 Esdras drew. The book called 2 Esdras consists mostly of a Jewish apocalypse in which Ezra, in a series of visions, bewails the predicament of exiled Israel and looks for a Messianic figure to restore the nation to its former glory.

The book of Tobit is a mixture of folklore and romance, written perhaps about 200 B.C. and apparently intended to instruct the Jews in proper attitudes of piety toward God. Tobit himself appears as resolute in suffering and an example to his fellows in matters of charity, justice, morality, and religious obligations. As with 1 Esdras, the book contains historical as well as geographical mistakes.

The book of Judith narrates the way in which an enterprising Jewish woman kills an enemy leader and saves her people. The narrative, however, seems to have no basis in historical fact and is also marked by chronological and other errors.

The additions to the Book of Esther comprise the following sections: the dream of Mordecai; the edict of Artaxerxes; prayers of Mordecai and Esther; Esther before the king; the counter-edict; an epilogue. These sections were meant to be interpolated into the text of the canonical book, and were probably written originally in Greek.

The Wisdom of Solomon, compiled perhaps about 100 B.C., represents an elaboration of the teaching about wisdom found in Proverbs and Ecclesiastes: but in its doctrines is considerably closer to Greek than to Hebrew thought. The book was read widely in the early Christian era.

The Book of Ecclesiasticus, also called the Wisdom of Jesus the Son of Sirach, was valued highly by both Jews and Christians. The author was a scribe who wished to give his teachings a more permanent form, for which he utilized the canonical Proverbs as a model. His instruction adheres closely to Jewish orthodoxy, though the author shows Sadducean tendencies. The book was probably written about 180 B.C.

Baruch draws heavily for its content upon certain Old Testament prophets and sages and is in the form of an address purportedly sent to the exiled Judeans in Babylonia. Its principal themes are the sin, punishment, and forgiveness of Israel. The Letter of Jeremiah, a document supposedly sent to the Judeans about to be taken captive in Babylonia, is actually a religious tract condemning idolatry.

The additions to the book of Daniel consist of three supplementary sections foreign to the Hebrew and Aramaic of the canonical work. The Prayer of Azariah, which recognizes the divine justice of the Babylonian exile, is followed by the Song of the Three Young Men when they were delivered from death in the fiery furnace. The story of Susanna tells how Daniel saves an innocent woman from death and seems to have been based upon a popular Babylonian tale. Bel and the Dragon contains two stories that ridicule idolatry and show the powerlessness of the Babylonian gods.

The Prayer of Manasseh consists of a short penitential psalm representing the king's supposed petition for divine mercy during a period of imprisonment in Babylonia (compare 2 Chron. 33:10-13).

Evidently 1 Maccabees was written, much as Chronicles was, to record a "spiritual" history of the nation, except that it deals exclusively with the Maccabean period. It drew upon some genuine literary sources, although the authenticity of parts of the work has been questioned. Whereas 1 Maccabees endeavors to present a reasonably objective account of the Hasmoneans, 2 Maccabees comprises a rhetorical summary of a considerably larger work on the subject of the Maccabean era. It is even more theologically oriented than 1 Maccabees, and contains several chronological errors along with other actual contradictions.

The Old Testament Apocrypha depicts graphically the conditions of the desperate days before Christ's birth. Unfortunately, military, political, and ideological conflicts were to be part of Jewish life until resistance to Roman rule ended in the second century A.D. There were times, as in the Maccabean period, when a brief respite was obtained from military and pagan religious pressures, but for the most part the orthodox Jew was a beleaguered figure in his own land. A people hardened by successive atrocities and by the omnipresent forces first of Egypt, then of Syria, and finally of Rome, could look for true freedom only in the messianic assurances of their national literature. In any event, the deliverance of the nation could be only in the somewhat distant future. For the time being the Jews in their struggles with alien political and religious influences had to be content with stories of heroism and self-sacrifice in time of war, bravery in the face of persecution, resolution in defeat, and the prospect of a coming golden age that was described in some of the apocalyptic writings.

New Testament Apocrypha

Christians of the New Testament period were already familiar with Jewish apocryphal works, including the apocalyptic speculations found in 2 Esdras. Therefore it was hardly surprising that a similar body of literature should grow up around their own Scriptures when they began to be composed and circulated.

New Testament Apocrypha, however, like its Old Testament counterpart, could be considered only in relationship to an established canon of scriptural writings. Since the earliest catalog of New Testament writings, the Muratorian Canon, was not compiled until about A.D. 200, a considerable period of time elapsed before an official church statement could appear on what was to be considered New Testament Apocrypha. In the meantime a large assortment of materials of a predominantly religious nature appeared, purporting to be orthodox in nature and dealing with various aspects of historic Christianity. As events turned out, this apocryphal literature defeated the purposes it was intended to serve. Because of the scarcity of information about such matters as the childhood, adolescence, and early manhood of Jesus, the "infancy" gospels undertook to supply the reader with what was meant to pass for historical fact. Much of the material, however, was entirely within the realm of fantasy and could never have been accepted as fact by any intelligent reader. For example, in the Gospel of Thomas the five-year-old Jesus is accused of breaking the Sabbath by making sparrows of clay beside a stream. When his father Joseph investigates the situation, Jesus claps his hands and the clay birds come to life and fly away chirping.

"Passion" gospels were written to embellish the canonical accounts of Christ's crucifixion and resurrection. As supplements to Christian teaching, many of the apocryphal writings seemed to be proclaiming ideas that were actually outside the scope of New Testament doctrine. Attempts to fill in the "hidden years" of Christ's life had no foundation whatever in the traditions of the Gospels. Works dealing with the last state of unbelievers were embellished in a manner that went far beyond anything stated in the New Testament. In some notable instances, as in the writings of various Gnostic sects, the authors set out deliberately to propagate heretical teachings they had accepted under the authority of some apostolic figure. The Gospel of Thomas, recovered around 1945 from Nag Hammadi (Chenoboskion) near the Nile River, is an example of an attempt to perpetuate curious sayings and dogmas by attributing them to Jesus, so that they would receive wide currency and acceptance.

Because the writings under discussion bear some resemblance to the principal literary types and divisions of the New Testament, scholars have often grouped them together in a similar manner for the convenience of students. The principal Apocrypha Gospels are:

Arabic Gospel of the Infancy
Armenian Gospel of the Infancy
Bartholomew's Book of the Resurrection of Christ
Bartholomew, Gospel of
Basilides, Gospel of
Birth of Mary, Gospel of the
Ebionites, Gospel of the
Hebrews, Gospel According to the
James, Protevangelium of
Joseph the Carpenter, History of
Marcion, Gospel of

Matthias, Gospel of

Nazarenes, Gospel of the

Peter, Gospel of

Philip, Gospel of

Pseudo-Matthew, Gospel of

Thomas, Gospel of

There are also some apocryphal Acts, which are purported to be accounts of apostolic achievements not recorded in Scripture. Such "Acts" are the source of much tradition such as Peter's being crucified upside down and Thomas's mission to India. The reliability of the traditions is questionable because the writings contain clearly unorthodox material. Yet small fragments of accurate information may be embedded in this mass of largely fictitious literature.

Because of their often heretical character, the church consistently reacted against such books, sometimes even demanding that they be burned (for example, at the Nicene Council of 787). The Acts of John pictured Jesus talking to John on the Mount of Olives during the crucifixion, explaining that it was only a spectacle. In the Acts of Thomas, Jesus appeared in the form of Thomas, exhorting a newly married couple to dedicate themselves to virginity. Sexual abstinence was a dominant theme, reflecting Platonic ideas, which disparaged the physical body.

Many scholars date the earliest work, the Acts of John, before A.D. 150. The major Acts (of John, Paul, Peter, Andrew, and Thomas) were probably written during the second and third centuries. These gave rise to other Acts that were primarily miracle stories, written more to entertain than to teach. Works classified in one way or another under the heading of Acts include:

Abdias, Apostolic History of

Andrew, Acts of

Andrew, Story of
Andrew and Matthias, Acts of
Andrew and Paul, Acts of
Barnabas, Acts of
Bartholomew, Acts of
James, Ascents of
John, Acts of
John, Acts of, by Prochorus
Martyrs, Acts of
Matthew, Acts and Martyrdom of
Paul, Passion of
Paul and Thecla, Acts of
Peter, Acts of
Peter, Passion of
Peter, Preaching of
Peter, Slavonic Acts of
Peter and Andrew, Acts of
Peter and Paul, Acts of
Peter and Paul, Passion of
Peter and the Twelve Disciples, Acts of
Philip, Acts of
Pilate, Acts of
Simon and Judas, Acts of
Thaddaeus, Acts of
Thomas, Acts of

A host of apocryphal works are classified as epistles. These generally pseudonymous works originated from many widely separated periods of time. For example, one group of epistles is primarily Jewish and relates to the Old Testament, such as the Letter of Jeremiah (mentioned earlier in this article). The larger group focuses around persons and places mentioned in the New Testament. Such epistolary writings include:

Abgarus and the Letters of Christ
Apostles, Epistle of the
Barnabas, Epistle of
Corinthians, Third
Laodiceans, Epistle to the
Lentulus, Epistle of
Paul and Seneca, Epistles of
Titus, Epistle of

Many liberal scholars have considered 2 Peter and Jude to be apocryphal also.

Many other apocryphal works are apocalyptic in nature. These works are supplemented by material such as the Apostolic Constitutions and Canons. Added to these are the Gnostic compositions found at Nag Hammadi, which include works purporting to represent the teachings of Christ as well as "secret" instructions compiled by the Gnostic writers and a few apocryphal compositions.

Comparative studies have shown without doubt that the New Testament apocryphal writings preserve at best a series of debased traditions about the Founder and teachings of early Christianity. At worst, the narratives are entirely devoid of historical value and in some respects are totally alien to New Testament spirituality. Even where they seem to support a tradition current in some part of the early church, the evidence they present is inferior to what can often be had from other sources. Sometimes the compositions are so trivial and inconsequential that it is difficult to account for their survival. Certain apocryphal writings did in fact become lost, and are now known only in the form of quotations in larger works.

Nevertheless, the New Testament apocryphal compositions are important in indicating what was attractive to the ordinary people of the day. For them an element of the romantic seemed necessary to supplement the body of received spiritual truth. Certain of the stories recounted were vivid and imaginative, and others such as the apocalypses provided a form of escapism from harsh temporal realities. No matter what their nature, the New Testament apocryphal writings exerted an influence out of all proportion to their fundamental worth.

BIBLIOGRAPHY

Allegro, J. M. *The Treasure of the Copper Scroll,* 1960.
Charles, R. H. *The Apocrypha and Pseudepigrapha of the Old Testament,* 1913.
Charlesworth, J. H. *The Old Testament Pseudepigrapha,* 2 vols., 1983, 1985.
James, M. R. *The Apocryphal New Testament,* 1924.
Kirkpatrick, P. G. *The Old Testament and Folklore Study,* 1988.
Robinson, J. M., ed. *The Nag Hammadi Library,* 1988 (third, revised edition).
Schneemelcher, W., ed.; R. M. Wilson, trans. *New Testament Apocrypha,* 1963.
Sparks, H. F. D. *The Apocryphal Old Testament,* 1984.

SECTION
THREE
The Bible as a Literary Text

Literature in Bible Times
Milton Fisher

The Bible can be better understood and more fully appreciated if we view it in its historical setting. This includes a knowledge of other writings that existed both before and during the composition of the Holy Scriptures.

Some Bible readers assume this matchless Book to be so vastly different from all other writings that no comparison whatsoever ought to be attempted. On the other extreme, some put the Bible on the same level as other writings of that period—writings that have come to light primarily within the past century or so. It is in part a reaction to this mistake coupled with a conscious rejection of the Apocrypha that has caused many evangelical Christians to ignore the great wealth of literary works from Bible times now known to us. The best way to acquaint ourselves with the relationship of the Scriptures to the literature of the surrounding cultural environment and to become convinced of the importance of such information is to cite some specific examples. This will also serve to introduce the background information necessary for an understanding of the nature of the connection between the Bible and these extrabiblical writings. We can then go on to answer questions about the origins of writing among various peoples of the biblical world and to examine the types of literature dating centuries and even millennia before Christ.

Extrabiblical Literature and the Earliest Books of the Bible

Apart from an inner circle of pioneer scholars and those with professional or academic reasons for reading their publications, the religious literature of the ancient Near East is not widely known. Much that has been unearthed by the archaeologist's spade has been deciphered and published, but few have read it at any length. Without motivation and guidance for doing so, few Bible students will investigate an extremely significant corpus of literature which has remarkable bearing upon the Bible, especially upon the earliest books of the Bible.

To begin with, let us take a look at the Pentateuch, the five Books of Moses—first, at the Book of Genesis in particular. The reader of Genesis ought to be struck immediately by the contrast between the pace and style of the first eleven chapters and those remaining. Genesis 1-11 is formal, tightly structured, highly selective and concentrated in content. Beginning at chapter 12, on the contrary, we find the lives of Abraham and the patriarchs of the three succeeding generations treated in the greatest of detail.

One might argue that some facts from the earlier period were simply lost and, therefore, were not accessible to Moses in his day. But to those who recognize the divine inspiration of the Holy Scriptures it is more acceptable to believe that it was God's purpose to place the emphasis on his redemptive plan for his elect people and for the world at large, inasmuch as that plan was to be effected through the seed of Abraham. Therefore, information expands as we get into the heart of the Abrahamic story.

With respect to comparative literature, however, there is another significant thing about the contrast observed between Genesis 1–11 and chapters 12–50. The earlier section has much of the heavy, somber tone and the almost symmetrical structure of the literature of the Mesopotamian culture out of which Abraham came. The succeeding narrative partakes of the more sensitive and at times bright flavor of Egyptian creativity. Recall how Moses, the human author, was well trained in "all the wisdom of the Egyptians and was powerful in speech and action" (Acts 7:22, NIV). This man was best suited of anyone known to us in that age to have authored the first five books in the biblical canon.

Even more basic and significant, however, is the matter of the literary form of the Pentateuch as a whole. Much new light has been shed on this over the past few decades. The historical setting for the writing of the Pentateuch is the amazing Exodus of the Israelites from Egypt and their constitution as a nation under God at Sinai. There the Redeemer made a covenant with his people. The opening books of the Hebrew Scriptures are by nature a *covenant document,* recording the origin, intent, and requirements of this covenant relationship between Israel and God, her King.

Recent studies of ancient Near Eastern covenants, especially treaty documents of the second millennium B.C., have revealed striking parallels to the Mosaic corpus. In particular, the suzerainty treaties drawn up by kings of the Hittite empire have several characteristics that are remarkably similar to the book of Deuteronomy and also to the Pentateuch as a whole. While Israel's experience and her special relationship to the Lord God is unique, the format in which the Lord confirmed that relationship fits beautifully into this familiar pattern of their contemporary society.

A word of explanation about these suzerainty agreements is necessary. Unlike the absolute rule of a sovereign over his local nation or of an emperor over the divisions of his empire, a suzerain exercised control over a smaller or weaker nation in international affairs, while allowing a large measure of independence on the domestic level. In fact, the contract or treaty he offered his subjugated neighbor was usually quite advantageous, both economically and in regard to military security. Just as in the Sinai covenant, which the sovereign God presented to the chosen people, it was the *great king* himself who drew up the terms of the covenant—on a take-it-or-leave-it basis (the latter under threat of abandonment to a worse fate). The Lord's offer to Israel was in terms of "if you obey . . . then I will bless you."

Several specific elements in these treaties are clearly reflected in the Mosaic law. Following a short preamble, a prologue details the occasion of the agreement, often some military victory over the region. Then the stipulations are spelled out—the basic terms (like the biblical decalogue), followed by the ancillary laws or statutes. So far, these four elements are found in that order in the book of Deuteronomy, a covenant renewal document (for the second generation out of Egypt), as are a document clause and sanctions. These latter items include provision for ceremonies of acceptance and instructions for placing a copy in the shrine (for Israel, the ark of the covenant) and public reading of the laws. The threat of curses for breaking of terms and the blessings for faithfulness are also seen in the biblical counterpart. Applied to the Pentateuch as a whole, we can compare the opening chapters of Genesis to the preamble, the rest of Genesis and part of Exodus to the historical prologue, and Exodus 19 through Leviticus to the stipulations of a treaty.

These comparisons have been treated at some length because they serve so well to illustrate the general relationship of Bible content to extrabiblical writings. That is, while the Bible is truly distinct from all human writings in one sense, it was providentially designed to be readily understood and adapted to the thought life of the people who received it. Today, we can better understand what it is saying and how to apply its teaching to our own day by learning something of the context in which it had its origin.

The oft-debated "dual account" of creation, Genesis 1–2, can perhaps also best be explained by this covenant orientation of the material. The first covenant sign God designed for his creatures, to express their recognition of him as Creator, was the Sabbath—to which the six creative days of the first chapter point. Chapter 2, in turn, leads up to that most essential covenant relationship on earth, the marriage bond.

Long before Bible scholars became aware of the above comparison with suzerainty treaties, the Mosaic laws themselves were viewed in the light of even older legal codes. Hammurabi's code, for example, antedates Moses by at least two centuries, and those of Eshnunna (Babylonian), Ur-Nammu, and Lipit-Ishtar (both Sumerian) are older still. More will be said, below, about this and about some mythological materials as they relate to the creation and flood narratives of Genesis.

The actual history of literary activity in ancient times has been pieced together by analysis of often fragmentary remains unearthed over a wide area by a number of archaeological expeditions. Clay tablets with Sumerian cuneiform (incised wedge writing) dating to about 1750 B.C. were recovered by the University of Pennsylvania excavation at Nippur (Iraq, ancient Mesopotamia), some seventy-five years ago. Among them was a catalogue of literature dating to at least 2000 B.C., indicating that writing had been invented and literature produced back into the third millennium B.C. It is the opinion of most scholars that the Egyptian hieroglyphic picture-writing was an independent development, perhaps under the stimulus of earlier Sumerian writing. Not long after king Menes, founder of Egypt's first dynasty around 3000 B.C., a phonetic system of hieroglyphics seems to have been developed. The Babylonian and Assyrian scribes simply borrowed Sumerian ideograms and adapted them into a phonetic syllabary for recording their own Semitic speech, known collectively as Akkadian. By the middle of the second millennium B.C., the Canaanites at Ugarit had simplified cuneiform script into a true alphabet of just thirty single letters, while to the south of them a linear alphabet was produced. The latter was used by the Hebrews and was later carried into Europe and elsewhere by the Phoenicians.

Thousands of clay tablets, dating to the reign of the Assyrian king Ashurbanipal (about 650 B.C.), were found in the royal library at Nineveh during twenty-five years of excavation in the second half of the nineteenth century. These were but copies of far older compositions, handed down from Sumerian times. Among them were the creation epic, *Enuma Elish,* and the Babylonian-Assyrian version of the great flood, part of the Epic of Gilgamesh. An even greater number of tablets (over 20,000) were discovered in the 1950s at Mari, on the Euphrates River northwest of Babylon. The majority of these were secular documents, business and political records and exchanges.

Religious, epic, and commercial documents and letters came to light about the same time at Ugarit, on the Mediterranean coast of Syria. These are dated by their contents to the period from 1400 to 1200 B.C. In recent years an equally valuable discovery has been made of numerous tablets from ancient Ebla, northeast of Ugarit, the contents of which deal with a period antedating Abraham by about four hundred years.

From these sporadic finds, viewed in comparison with the complete canon of the Hebrew Scriptures, we can get a surprisingly full picture of the types of literary interests found among the ancients. The Sumerian-Akkadian tradition stands as one major block, over against more creatively entertaining productions of the Egyptians. The Egyptians also had their very complex myths and a *Book of the Dead,* a guide to life after death. Between those two cultures and influenced by both were the Canaanites, whose literature, in language closely akin to biblical Hebrew, affords some of the closest parallels to the Bible itself—theologically far off, but similar in poetic expression and religious terminology. What little we possess of Moabite, Aramaic, and Phoenician texts also shows how close their literary forms were to those of the Hebrews.

It was long taught that ancient Greek and Roman (Latin) culture and literature must be seen as worlds apart from that of eastern life. Studies by Professor Cyrus H. Gordon and others, however, have indicated far more contact and exchange of ideas between peoples of the Mediterranean basin than had been allowed for by traditional scholars. The cultural differences were indeed more pronounced by intertestamental and New Testament times. But the farther back one travels in time—back to the period idealized by Homeric epic and epitomized in Israelite history by the exploits of Hebrew judges and kings of the united monarchy—the closer the cultural roots are entwined. Even Virgil's Latin epic, the *Aeneid,* contains elements reflective of biblical times.

It is the New Testament writings, of course, that lie within the Graeco-Roman context in which Koine Greek prevailed as the *lingua franca.* Letters on papyrus, preserved in dry Egyptian sands, are similar in style to the New Testament Epistles. Herodotus, a historian of the fifth century B.C., set a high standard of observation and reporting, helping prepare the way for the factual accounts of the ministry of Christ and the apostles in the four Gospels and Acts.

Ancient Literary Types and Genres

Before summing up the actual influence of these religious and secular literatures on the production of the Bible, it is necessary to review the several genres or types of literary material found among these various nations, languages, and cultures. The literary types number between eight and fifteen, according to whether one combines or distinguishes among certain subgenres.

Let us settle for nine major types of literature, bearing in mind that similar types (purged of theological and factual aberrations) show up in greater or lesser degree in our Bible.

1. Commercial documents constitute a majority of the finds at some sites. Business operations made practical use of writing for record keeping and confirmation of agreements from very early times.

2. Not far removed as to purpose would be epistolary usage, personal communications between officials or friends.

3. Legal codes and court records were also essential to settled community life. Only such written documents could assure uniformity of practice.

4. Political documents, such as the treaties described above, were considered sacrosanct and inviolable among the ancients. Copies were made for all parties concerned, for sacred deposit and for public notice. Fresh clues to the surprisingly wide extent of literacy in ancient times are still being discovered.

5. Historiographic materials are not far removed from the previous category, since records of current events such as royal annals were often of a politically propagandistic nature. Epic writings were a combination of fact and fable. The ancient prophetic omen texts could be placed under either of two categories yet to be itemized, but they are mentioned here for good reason. The "scientific" system of prediction they pretend to afford would be patently unworkable if the events these texts record were not historically accurate. Omen texts often prove to be demonstrably more trustworthy than the royal annals.

6. Poetic compositions occur in all the cultures already enumerated, often with religious content, sometimes epic, occasionally

entertaining, and even found in the prologue and epilogue of the famous Hammurabi law code.

7. Religious literature of the neighboring peoples is what the nonspecialist would think of first, surely, when asked to consider comparative materials. The Bible itself is above all a "religious" book. Hopefully, what has been said thus far has informed the reader sufficiently to make him aware that in reality many different categories of human writing have bearing on various portions and aspects of our Scriptures. In truth, religious texts or inscriptions of funerary, votive (vow-making), and ritualistic nature all have bearing on some details within the Bible. But the subgenre we generally refer to as mythological has always attracted the major interest and analysis, whether or not this deserves to be the case.

8 and 9. Closely allied with religious expression per se would be (8) wisdom literature and (9) prophetic writings. The former is found in variant forms among the Babylonians (cosmological writings focusing on Ishtar, Queen of Heaven), Egyptians, Canaanites, and Aramacans. Each of these has been claimed to have had direct influence on Hebrew thought and writing, especially the Egyptian and Canaanite sources. Soothsayers, seers, and ecstatic prophets were prevalent throughout the biblical world, and much has been written to identify the Hebrew prophets with them. The fact is, however, both the type of message and the writings of Israel's prophets are without parallel.

Apocalyptic ("uncovered, revealed") writings are a specialized type of (pseudo-) prophetic material. They constitute a unique class of intertestamental Jewish and early Christian writings which both imitate passages found in Ezekiel, Daniel, and the New Testament book of Revelation and pretend authorship by some famous Old Testament saint. This was done to lend authority to the writing at a time when authentic prophetic utterance had ceased.

The Influence of Ancient Literature on the Bible

As to the influence of ancient literature on the Bible itself, it has already been shown that whereas the Bible has elements that do parallel all these literary categories, it is itself a distinct production. The effects upon it by extrabiblical writings are decidedly limited and controlled by virtue of its divine origin. Though the Bible in a few instances cites other literature (for example, see Num. 21:14; Josh. 10:13; 2 Sam. 1:18; 2 Kings 1:18; 1 Chron. 29:29; Acts 17:28; 1 Cor. 15:33; Tit. 1:12; Jude 9, 14), the relationship is one of shared media and mode of expression, rather than of source or direct determination.

As mentioned above, most people would think the ancient mythological writings, both cosmological and epic in theme, would be the closest to biblical subject matter. But the theological and historical presentations are so utterly contrastive they are not worthy to be compared. Closer comparison may legitimately be drawn between the poetic structure and repertoire, as well as the ritualistic (cultic) terminology of Ugaritic (Canaanite) and the Old Testament, but here again the theological presuppositions of the two are poles apart.

We have already drawn sharp distinction between prophetism in Israel and the outwardly similar phenomenon in surrounding cultures. The source or causation factor makes the crucial difference here also. Perhaps the closest tie or sharing of style and content appears in the wisdom literature. This deserves explanation.

Throughout the ancient Near East there developed a class of wise men—scribes who both created and collected sagacious sayings. They were usually under patronage of royalty (see Prov. 25:1) or the priesthood. Egyptian lads were urged by their instructors to aspire to a scribal profession as the most noble and influential station. The scribes were trained by wisdom literature and also wrote wisdom literature. This particular form of writing was shared so much in common by the various cultures that a running debate continues, for example, over who borrowed from whom in the case of close parallels between Proverbs 22:17 to 23:14 and "The Wisdom of Amenemope" from Egypt. In addition to the apocalyptic genre mentioned above, wisdom literature was popular with the intertestamental writers of such apocryphal books as Ecclesiasticus (or Wisdom of Sirach) and Wisdom of Solomon, along with the rabbinical tractate *Pirqe Aboth* (Sayings of the Fathers).

Nineteenth-century critics of the Bible proposed that both the ancient narratives and the complex legal codes of the Pentateuch were of multiple authorship, composed and reworked over centuries of time. Theirs was a developmental or evolutionary theory. By the twentieth century archaeologists had unearthed and translated myths relating to creation and the flood and royal law codes dated long before Moses. Critics then modified their theories, insisting that the Hebrews *borrowed* from Babylonian sources. Further discovery and careful comparative analysis has adequately substantiated the independence of the Bible as to the origin of content. It is in areas of language and style, various formalities, that the extrabiblical literature helps us place the Holy Scriptures in their proper historic and literary context.

The world of the New Testament was largely shaped by Greek culture ("Hellenism") and Roman administration. The combined Graeco-Roman society contributed to the *form* of New Testament Scripture, yet without real loss of its Judaic roots. This has been demonstrated by extensive study and comparison of the Gospels, Acts (actually Luke-Acts as a "general history" genre of Hellenistic literature), and the several types of New Testament letters with ancient documents and fragments from the Mediterranean world.

It is interesting to observe how scholars in the combined field of classics (Greek and Latin studies) and New Testament strain and struggle—and differ from one another—to pinpoint exact parallels between scriptural and secular writings. Literary experts speak of the generic features: "form" (linguistic style and idiom), "content" (subject matter), and "function" (author's purpose). Not surprisingly, in the first category there are close and useful (for understanding and appreciation) parallels. The third feature has general but not precise bearing. It is when we come to "content" that the Bible largely stands alone. For here we have inspired revelation, God-given as to message and in its origin.

One aspect of such analysis should serve to illustrate the similar-yet-different nature of the biblical-secular comparison. The Gospels may be seen as falling into the pattern of Graeco-Roman biographical writings, as long as the biography is understood to record "history." But for the Greeks, biographies tended to display an antihistorical idealism due to the author's determination to present personalities as types or paradigms for readers to emulate, rather than as truly historic individuals. The Bible text does indeed present historical fact. But in stark contrast to the Greek compositions, with the exception of the God-man Jesus Christ, none of the participants in the narrative are presented as ideal persons.

In all, then, the sacred Scriptures, both Old and New Testaments, are not at all isolated from the normal types and expression of their day. Yet they stand out as exceptional and truly incomparable in their authority and instructional value.

BIBLIOGRAPHY

Aune, David E. *The New Testament in Its Literary Environment,* 1989.
Deissmann, Adolf. *Light from the Ancient East,* 1927.
Gordon, Cyrus H. *The Ancient Near East,* 1965.
————. *The Common Background of Greek and Hebrew Civilizations,* 1965.
Livingston, G. Herbert. *The Pentateuch in Its Cultural Environment,* 1974.
McNamara, Martin. *Palestinian Judaism and the New Testament,* 1983.
Ramsay, William M. *The Bearing of Recent Discovery on the Trustworthiness of the New Testament,* 1915.

The Bible as Literature
Leland Ryken

Christianity is the most literary religion in the world. This should not surprise us, for the sacred book of Christianity is a thoroughly literary book.

This is a truth that the world of biblical scholarship has rediscovered in the last quarter of the twentieth century, as a quiet revolution has occurred in approaches to the Bible. Conventional preoccupations with historical background, theological content, and the process of composition have given way to a focus on the biblical text itself, a preoccupation with the forms and style of biblical writing, and a concern to see the unity and wholeness of texts.

A genuinely literary approach to the Bible can take two directions. One is to relate the Bible to the literary milieu in which it was produced. This is the domain of biblical scholars and experts in comparative literature of the ancient world, and it is the subject of a companion essay to this one in the present volume. Scholars in this camp tend to be preoccupied with identifying sources for what we find in the Bible.

What is known as the literary approach to the Bible more customarily involves placing the Bible into the familiar literary context that people pick up during the course of their literary education in high school and college. This means applying to the Bible the familiar tools of literary analysis that literary critics and teachers of literature use, and it involves comparing the Bible to familiar literary texts from Homer to modern drama and movies.

Such a literary approach is the subject of the present essay. It is relatively uninterested in accounting for sources of biblical literature. It is concerned simply to show what is in the Bible, not to speculate how it got there. It is not surprising that literary criticism of this type should see a great deal of correspondence between the Bible and other literature, for the simple reason that the Bible has been the single biggest influence on Western literature.

A Brief History of "the Bible as Literature"

The current fashionableness of the Bible-as-literature movement may convey the misconception that literary critics have discovered something new. But a look at the history of the topic shows that viewing the Bible as literature is as old as the Bible itself.

LITERARY AWARENESS OF BIBLICAL WRITERS

The biblical data consists of both explicit and implicit evidence. One writer within the canon comes right out and states his philosophy of writing, and it turns out to be a thoroughly literary view of composition. The passage occurs near the end of the Old Testament book of Ecclesiastes:

> Besides being wise, the Preacher also taught the people knowledge, weighing and studying and arranging proverbs with great care. The Preacher sought to find pleasing words, and uprightly he wrote words of truth. (Eccl. 12:9-10, RSV)

Several things are important here. One is the picture of the writer as self-conscious composer, carefully choosing from among available options as he selects and arranges his material. A second theme is the preoccupation with artistry and beauty of expression, as suggested by the phrase "pleasing words" or "words of delight." A third literary aspect of this writer's theory of writing is his awareness that he is writing in a definite literary genre ("type" or "kind"), in this case by using proverbs.

A second piece of explicit evidence that the writers of the Bible were self-conscious literary craftsmen is the way in which they apply technical generic labels to works in the Bible. They talk about such genres as chronicle, saying or proverb, song, hymn, complaint, parable, gospel, apocalypse, epistle, and prophecy. What this shows is a relatively sophisticated knowledge of literary genres.

The implicit evidence of literary awareness among biblical writers is even more compelling. For one thing, biblical writings display literary qualities. Biblical storytellers evidently knew that stories are structured on a principle of beginning-middle-end. Their stories exhibit the same techniques of dramatic irony, foreshadowing, and climax that we find everywhere in the stories of the world.

Biblical poets knew that praise psalms have three main parts (introduction, development, resolution) and that lament psalms have five ingredients (invocation, complaint or definition of the crisis, petition, statement of confidence in God, and vow to praise God). They were adept at discovering metaphors and similes and at employing such figurative devices as personification, apostrophe, and hyperbole.

The literary sophistication of biblical writers is evident simply in the excellence with which they exploited the resources of literary art, but the case is strengthened if we place their writings in their ancient context. When we do so, we find that biblical writers wrote in apparent awareness of the literature being produced in surrounding nations. The Ten Commandments and book of Deuteronomy, for example, bear all the marks of the suzerainty treaty of ancient Hittite kings. Psalm 29 is a parody of Canaanite poems written about the exploits of Baal. The Song of Solomon contains poems resembling Egyptian love poetry. And the book of Acts contains elements of similarity to travelogues and trial defenses in Greek literature.

THE DEBATE IN THE EARLY CHURCH

The question of whether the Bible is literary became a point of debate among the church fathers. Steeped in classical rhetoric as well as the Bible, these men struggled to know how to relate the Bible to the rules and practice of classical writing. Their general tendency was to set up an opposition between the Bible and classical literature, and to celebrate the superiority of Christianity to paganism by arguing that the simplicity of the Bible triumphed over the ornateness of classical art.

But a few people took issue with this dismissal of the literary nature of the Bible. Some of them, for example, claimed that certain Old Testament poetic passages were written in identifiable classical meters. Jerome defended his own habit of alluding to classical authors by observing that Paul did the same in the New Testament.

But the towering medieval figure is Augustine (see especially *On Christian Doctrine,* IV, 6-7). Augustine's approach is admittedly narrow (an analysis of rhetoric or style), but he established four crucial principles that are still valid in literary approaches to the Bible. First, he asserted that the writers of the Bible followed the ordinary rules of classical rhetoric. He explicated passages from Amos and the Epistles to prove that the Bible can be compared to familiar literature. Secondly, Augustine admired the eloquence and beauty of the Bible as having inherent value. Thirdly, he foreshadowed a cornerstone of modern literary theory when he claimed that the style of the Bible is inseparable from the message that it expresses. Finally, for all his enthusiasm over the literary eloquence of the Bible, Augustine showed an uneasiness about viewing the Bible as being totally similar to other literature, claiming, for example, that the eloquence of the Bible was not "composed by man's art and care" but instead flowed "from the Divine mind."

THE RENAISSANCE AND REFORMATION SYNTHESIS

The sixteenth and seventeenth centuries represented a great flowering of the literary understanding of the Bible. Whereas Augustine had voiced a minority opinion, viewing the Bible as literary became the majority opinion during the Renaissance. While Augustine's approach was a narrowly focused rhetorical one, the Renaissance and Reformation championed a manysided literary inquiry into both the content and form of the Bible. Further synthesis emerges when we observe that the attempt to view the Bible as literature was conducted by both exegetes (Luther, Calvin, and the Puritans) and writers of imaginative literature.

Among literary figures, much of the impetus for seeing the Bible as literature originally came from the attempt to provide a Christian defense of imaginative literature. Sir Philip Sidney's *Apology for Poetry* is a typical example. In defending literature, Sidney appealed to the concreteness or "figuring forth" of human experience in the Bible, as well as emphasizing the importance of literary genres and figurative language in the Bible.

Barbara Lewalski's book *Protestant Poetics and the Seventeenth-Century Religious Lyric* documents the extent to which Reformation exegetes and Renaissance poets agreed on a set of postulates about the literary nature of the Bible. The chief principles were that the Bible is made up of literary genres, that the texture of the Bible is frequently figurative and poetic, and that the Bible relies heavily on a system of symbolism. The noteworthy point is that the literary interpretation of the Bible went hand in hand with a religious belief in the Bible as a sacred book.

THE ROMANTIC SECULARIZING OF THE BIBLE

Such a synthesis was lost during the next great era of literary interest in the Bible—the Romantic movement of the early nineteenth century. I have labelled the Romantic approach to the Bible as "secular" because it represented a literary interest devoid of the religious faith that centuries of Christianity had attributed to the Bible. In many ways the Romantic veneration of the Bible as literature was a poet's movement.

The Romantics valued two literary aspects of the Bible. They loved the primitive simplicity of the biblical world and the passionate sublimity of much of its poetry. C. S. Lewis speaks of the era's "taste for the primitive and the passionate," adding the following:

> The primitive simplicity of a world in which kings could be shepherds, the abrupt and mysterious manner of the prophets, the violent passions of bronze-age fighting men, the background of tents and flocks and desert and mountain, the village homeliness of our Lord's parables and metaphors, now first . . . became a positive literary asset. (*The Literary Impact of the Authorized Version*, 27)

As Western society itself became increasingly secular, poets strove to put spiritual reality back into life. Hungry for mythology, they came to look upon the Bible as containing (in the words of the English poet William Blake) "the great code of art." Romantic poets were interested in the Bible as a literary source and model, but not as a source of religious belief. The truth that Romanticists saw in the Bible was the truth that they found in other works of imaginative literature—truthfulness to human experience, especially human feelings. The secular valuing of the Bible as literature has persisted into the twentieth century, a phenomenon that has produced its own reaction in Christian circles that value the Bible chiefly for its religious content.

THE TRIUMPH OF LITERARY CRITICISM OF THE BIBLE

The current interest in literary approaches to the Bible is largely the result of efforts by literary critics. During the first half of the twentieth century the movement was little noticed. A handful of college literature teachers taught successful courses in the English Bible at universities, and occasionally they published books of literary appreciation of the Bible and anthologies intended for use in literature courses.

By 1960 the movement had come to the surface. The most influential literary critic of the century, Northrop Frye, claimed that "the Bible forms the lowest stratum in the teaching of literature. It should be taught so early and so thoroughly that it sinks straight to the bottom of the mind, where everything that comes along later can settle on it" (*The Educated Imagination*, 110). By 1990 the Bible had become the latest fad in secular literary circles.

Biblical scholarship shares the current interest in literary approaches. A paradigm shift has occurred in which the theological and historical preoccupations of traditional biblical scholarship have given way to literary methods of analysis. Attempts to find the roots of this paradigm shift in earlier schools of biblical scholarship are misleading. The current literary interest in the Bible among biblical scholars became possible only as scholars repudiated the methods and preoccupations that had dominated their discipline for more than a century, in deference to the methods of literary critics in the humanities.

SUMMARY

The willingness to approach the Bible with literary expectations and to analyze it with the tools of literary criticism is more than the latest fashion. It is rooted in the nature of the Bible itself. Beyond that, throughout the centuries the best interpretation of the Bible has accepted the premise that the Bible is in significant ways a work of literature whose meaning and enjoyment depend partly on an ability to approach it with literary methods.

Premises of a Literary Approach to the Bible

Any exploration of what it means to approach the Bible as literature is based on presuppositions. Failure to acknowledge these presuppositions has often obscured the issues.

OBSTACLES TO ACCEPTANCE OF A LITERARY APPROACH

A literary approach to the Bible has always faced a challenge from people who have religious scruples over viewing the Bible as literature. Upon analysis, these scruples turn out to be groundless.

One objection centers on the equation of literature with fiction. Although literary critics with secular or liberal leanings make it clear that they regard much of the Bible as fictional, these claims are not a necessary part of a literary approach. We should not overlook that historians and biblical scholars with secular and liberal leanings have been making the claim of fictionality for decades. The question of whether the Bible is historically factual and accurate belongs not to literary criticism (which has nothing new to add to the discussion) but to the debate over historicity that has long raged among biblical scholars.

The fear that a literary approach to the Bible requires an acceptance of the fictionality of biblical narrative is based on a misconception about literature. Fictionality, though common in literature, is not an essential feature of it. The properties that make a text literary are unaffected by the historicity or fictionality of the material. A literary approach depends on a writer's selectivity and molding of the material, regardless of whether the details actually happened or are made up.

Nor does the presence of artifice and convention in a biblical text imply fictionality. By way of analogy, the genre of the live television sports report is replete with conventions and artifice that do not not detract from its factuality. The reporter is filmed with a sports arena in the background. During the course of the report the reporter either interviews an athlete or is momentarily replaced by a film clip of sports action. The artifice of such conventions is obvious. Yet they do not undermine the factuality of the report itself.

Yet another obstacle to a literary approach to the Bible is a fear that such an approach means only a literary approach, without the special religious belief and authority that Christians associate with the Bible. Because the Bible is a special book, some people have argued that it cannot be like ordinary literature. By such logic, the Bible cannot be studied with the ordinary tools of linguistics, grammar, or history, a position that no one would argue.

The fact that the Bible is in some ways unlike other books does not mean that it is unlike them in every way. Even a cursory look at the Bible shows that it uses ordinary language and grammar, and that it contains history. It is equally evident that the Bible employs the techniques of literature that we find in literature generally.

To approach the Bible as literature does not mean that we read it *only* as literature. A literary approach itself can be trusted to reveal the points at which the Bible is like and unlike the familiar literature that we find in an anthology of English or American literature.

THE UNIQUENESS OF THE BIBLE

A literary approach to the Bible by definition emphasizes how the Bible resembles other works of literature. Since this will be the focus of my own discussion, it is well to note first the most obvious ways in which the Bible is unlike such literature.

The God-centeredness and supernatural orientation of the Bible make it stand out. God is the leading character or actor in the Bible in a way that is without parallel in other literature. Furthermore, although ancient literature presupposes the existence of a supernatural world with otherworldly scenes and characters, the Bible is more consistent in portraying the interpenetration of a divine world into the ordinary realm of earthly life.

Secondly, the Bible makes stronger claims to inspiration and authority than ordinary literature does. Erich Auerbach, in his classic essay, "Odysseus' Scar," comparing storytelling technique in Homer's *Odyssey* and Genesis, emphasized this difference. He wrote that "the religious intent" of stories in the Bible "involves an absolute claim to historical truth. . . . The Bible's claim to truth is not only far more urgent than Homer's, it is tyrannical—it excludes all other claims" (14). Another literary scholar, C. S. Lewis, made a similar observation:

> In most parts of the Bible everything is implicitly or explicitly introduced with "Thus saith the Lord." It is . . . not merely a sacred book but a book so remorselessly and continuously sacred that it does not invite, it excludes or repels, the merely aesthetic approach. (*The Literary Import of the Authorized Version,* 32-33)

Thirdly, the Bible is a unique mingling of three types of writing. They are the historical, the theological, and the literary. Usually one of these dominates a passage, though not to the exclusion of the others. The more literary the treatment of an event is, the more a literary approach will yield. But even in these cases, biblical passages invite historical and theological approaches as well as a literary approach in a way that literature in general does not. Obviously, then, the plea for literary criticism of the Bible does not imply the sufficiency of such an approach by itself.

THE LITERARY UNITY OF THE TWO TESTAMENTS
The tendency of literary and biblical scholars has been to drive a wedge between the literature of the Old and New Testaments. The

fashion has been to treat the literary forms of the two testaments as distinct from each other, and the overwhelming result has been to value Old Testament literature to the disparagement of the New Testament.

The rigid distinction between the literary forms of the two testaments is a fallacy. It is partly the generic labels that mislead us. Because the Old Testament advertises such genres as chronicles, psalms, and prophets, it is easy to assume that the New Testament labels of gospels, acts, epistles, and apocalypse belong to a different world.

But underlying the books of the Old and New Testaments are literary forms that cut across the external labels. These literary forms are the deep structure of biblical literature, and they are what make the Bible literary in nature. They also provide a literary unity to the Bible as a whole that is obscured by conventional classifications. These foundational literary forms are story or narrative, poetry, proverb, satire, oration, and visionary writing. Narrative and poetry, of course, have numerous subtypes. Most basic of all is the concept that literature itself has identifiable characteristics.

In the discussion that follows, I have used the deep structure as my organizing framework. Whether we find a story or poem in the Old Testament or the New does not make much difference so far as its literary form and meaning are concerned. A story is a story, and a poem is a poem. What changes from the Old Testament to the New is not the literary forms (except for the addition of the epistle) but the theological content that those forms carry.

SUMMARY

A literary approach to the Bible is compatible with virtually any theological or religious stance. It does not require acceptance of premises that are hostile to an evangelical understanding of the Bible. Although a literary approach by definition involves seeing the Bible as similar to literature in general, such comparison can be trusted to show ways in which the Bible is also unique.

To approach the Bible as literature requires two activities. One is to know what it means to approach the Bible as literature. The other is to define the "canon" of biblical literature—to know where literature appears in the Bible. These two topics—the methods of literary analysis and the places in the Bible where those methods are required—will provide the focus for the discussion that follows.

Literature as a Genre

Before we consider the specific genres of biblical literature, it is necessary to define literature itself. When we do, we find that literature as a whole is a genre—a type of writing that has its own identifiying traits. Before a piece of writing is a story or poem or any other specific genre, it belongs to the larger category of "literature."

HUMAN EXPERIENCE AS THE SUBJECT

The simplest of all touchstones for literature is that the subject of literature is human experience, in contrast to abstract facts or information. Literature aims to get the reader to share an experience, not primarily to grasp ideas.

Literature is "incarnational." It embodies its ideas or meanings in concrete form. It enacts rather than states. Instead of expressing abstract propositions about virtue and vice, for example, literature presents stories of good and evil characters in action. The commandment "you shall not murder" gives us a precept; literature incarnates the same truth in the story of Cain and Abel. Instead of defining "neighbor," Jesus told a story about neighborly behavior (the parable of the Good Samaritan). The truthfulness of literature is not simply a matter of true ideas but also takes the form of truthfulness to human experience—to the way things are in the world.

Literature thus appeals to the imagination—our image-making and image-perceiving capacity. In terms popularized by recent brain research, it is "right-brain" discourse. The corresponding skill that it requires from a reader or interpreter of the Bible is the ability to picture scenes, characters, and events. Literature appeals to our intelligence through the imagination.

Because literature is incarnational, the first thing it requires of a reader is a willingness to relive the text as vividly and concretely as possible—sharing scenes and events with characters in a story or the images in a poet's meditation. Furthermore, a piece of literature cannot be reduced to an idea or proposition. The whole story or whole poem is the meaning because it is an experience, not an abstraction.

Because the truthfulness of literature is partly truthfulness to human experience, literature is universal. Whereas history tells us what happened, literature tells us what happens—what is true for all people at all times. Of course, in the Bible these two impulses are typically combined. Still, the degree to which we can see universal human experience in a text remains a useful touchstone of whether it is literary in nature.

LITERARY GENRES

The most common way by which literature has been defined through the centuries is by its genres (literary types). The human race has generally agreed that some genres (such as story, poetry, and drama) are literary in nature. Other genres, such as historical chronicles, theological treatises, and genealogies, are expository ("informational") writing. Still others fall into one category or the other, depending on how a writer handles them. Letters, sermons, and orations, for example, can move in the direction of literature if they display the ordinary elements of literature.

Every literary genre has its distinctive features and conventions. These are a set of expectations that should govern our encounter with a text, enabling us to ask the right questions of a passage. An awareness of genre can program our reading of a passage, giving it a familiar shape and allowing the details to fall into an identifiable pattern. Knowing how a given genre operates can also prevent misinterpretation of a text.

Even if we did not have other evidence, we would know that the Bible is literary simply by its abundance of literary genres. The list of genres is approximately what we find in an anthology of world literature: epic, story of origins, hero story, tragedy, drama, satire, lyric poetry, epithalamion (wedding poem), elegy (funeral poem), encomium (a poem or essay in praise of an abstract quality or character type), proverb, parable, visionary writing, epistle, and oratory.

SPECIAL RESOURCES OF LANGUAGE

Regardless of the specific genre in which a literary text is written, literature uses a higher proportion of certain resources of language than ordinary discourse does. The most obvious of these resources is figurative language, including metaphor, simile, symbolism, connotative language, allusion, pun, paradox, irony, and word play. Such language is of course the very essence of poetry, but it appears throughout the Bible, even in parts that might be considered predominantly expository rather than literary, such as the New Testament Epistles.

In addition to possessing such features of vocabulary, a text can become literary by its arrangement of sentences or rhetorical patterning. An example is the parallel clauses that is the verse form of biblical poetry but that is also evident in much biblical prose. Any arrangement of clauses that strikes us as unusually patterned might qualify as an example of literary rhetoric—series of questions or statements that follow a common pattern, rhetorical questions, question-and-answer constructions, imaginary dialogues, and (very important in the Bible) the conciseness of a proverb.

All of this is a way of saying that style is one of the things that makes the Bible literary. Whenever writers do things with language that call attention to the expression itself and that get more mileage out of language than ordinary discourse does, the resulting style lends a literary quality to a passage. Biblical writers consistently manipulate the literary resources of language, syntax, and rhetoric.

ARTISTRY

Literature is an art form, characterized by beauty, craftsmanship, and technique. The "how" of literature is as important as the "what."

The elements of artistic form that all types of literature share include pattern or design, theme or central focus, organic unity (also called unity in variety, or theme and variation), coherence, balance, contrast, symmetry, repetition or recurrence, variation, and unified progression. These elements of artistry take one form in narrative, another in poetry, another in proverb, and so forth. But whatever the genre, the sheer abundance of literary technique and artistry that we find in many parts of the Bible make it a literary masterpiece.

Artistic form serves the purpose of intensifying the impact of what is said, but it also provides pleasure, delight, and enjoyment. One of the things that a literary approach to the Bible offers over conventional approaches is that it opens the way for readers to enjoy the aesthetic beauty of the Bible. Literary analysis is capable of showing that the Bible is an interesting book rather than a dull book. The artistic excellence of the Bible is not extraneous to its total effect. It is one of the glories of the Bible.

MEANING THROUGH FORM

A literary approach is preoccupied with literary form. In any discourse, meaning is communicated through form. The concept of form should be construed very broadly in this context. It includes anything that touches on *how* a writer has expressed the content of an utterance.

While the principle of meaning through form is true for all types of writing, it is especially crucial for literature. Literature has its own forms and techniques, and these tend to be more complex and subtle and indirect than those of ordinary discourse. Stories, for example, communicate their meaning through character, setting, and action. To understand a story, we must first interact with the form, that is, the characters, settings, and events. Poetry conveys its meanings through figurative language and concrete images. It is therefore impossible to determine what a poem says without first encountering the form, that is, the poetic language.

The literary critic's preoccupation with the *how* of biblical writing is not frivolous. It is evidence of an artistic delight in verbal beauty and craftsmanship, but it is also part of an attempt to understand *what* the Bible says. In a literary text it is impossible to separate what is said (content) from how it is said (form).

SUMMARY

A literary approach to the Bible begins with an awareness of what things make a text literary. The defining features of literature include the concrete presentation of human experience, the presence of literary genres as the form that embodies the meaning, the use of literary resources of language, and the prevalence of artistry.

From what I have said, it is obvious that a literary approach challenges many of the tendencies in traditional biblical scholarship. The emphasis on the unity of a text resists the atomistic analysis found in biblical commentaries and the patchwork that results when scholars undertake excavations into the stages of composition that lie behind a finished text. The premise of literary criticism that literature is a concrete embodiment of human experience takes issue with reducing the Bible to a theological outline with proof texts attached.

The focus on literary technique presupposes self-conscious composition on the part of the human writers, in contrast to theories of divine dictation or the impersonal evolution of texts through various stages of transmission. And the emphasis on variety of literary genres in the Bible challenges a common operating premise that the Bible consists of all one type of material.

By the criteria that I have outlined, how much of the Bible is literary? Eighty percent is not an exaggeration, and even in the predominantly expository parts of the Bible literary techniques appear on virtually every page.

Biblical Narrative

Narrative is the dominant form of the Bible. Above all else, the Bible is a series of events, with many interspersed passages that interpret the meaning of the events. The overall shape of the Bible, moreover, follows the beginning-middle-end pattern of a story. The central character in the Bible's story is God, and the story itself is what biblical scholars call "salvation history"—the story of God's acts of creation, providence, judgment, and redemption.

HOW STORIES WORK

Stories are comprised of three basic elements—setting, character, and plot. Together these yield themes—insights into life that can be stated as propositions.

Settings are physical, temporal, and cultural. They serve two main functions in stories. They are always part of the action, providing a fit container for the actions and characters and allowing the story to come alive in a reader's imagination. Often a setting takes on symbolic importance as well, becoming part of the meaning of a story. In the story of Lot, for example, Sodom is a moral monstrosity as well as a place, and God's turning the city into a wasteland is itself the meaning of the story (God's judgment against sin).

Characters in stories are known to us in a variety of ways: by what the storyteller says about them, by other characters' responses to them, by their words and thoughts, by what they say about themselves, and above all by their actions. Whatever the means of portrayal, a reader's goal should be to get to know the characters in a biblical story as fully as possible.

It is an understood premise of narrative that characters in a story are in some sense universal. They are representative of humanity generally and carry a burden of meaning larger than themselves. On the basis of what happened to them, Bible readers can draw conclusions about people in general.

Plot or action is the backbone of a story. Stories are built around one or more plot conflicts, which can be physical conflict, conflict between people, or moral/spiritual conflict. A plot conflict has a beginning, a discernible development, and a final resolution. This is the essential, inevitable way in which stories are structured, and according to which they must be analyzed.

In the ongoing progression of the plot conflict(s), a reader goes through the action with a central character known as the protagonist. Arrayed against him or her are the antagonists. Common narrative strategies are to show the protagonist in situations of testing and situations that require choice. A discrepancy between what readers know to be true and ignorance on the part of characters in a story is known as irony.

As one moves from story to meaning, the simplest rule of interpretation is that every story is in some sense an example story. We therefore need to determine what it is an example *of*. It is also an understood convention of literary narrative that the world a storyteller creates by the selectivity of details is a picture of the world as the writer understands it, and of what is right and wrong in that world. It is also important to be aware that storytelling is an affective art: it conveys much of its meaning by getting a reader to feel positively or negatively toward characters and events.

The general features of stories that I have noted are the minimal terms for analyzing the stories of the Bible. But the Bible also contains an abundance of specific narrative subtypes, each with its own set of additional conventions.

THE STORY OF ORIGINS

The first story in the Bible, Genesis 1–3, belongs to an important genre of ancient literature known as the story of origins. It is a three-part story.

Genesis 1 is the Bible's creation story. It has only one chief character, God. The story itself is a catalog of God's mighty acts of creation, and it is replete with elements of repetition, balance, and progression.

Genesis 2 narrows the focus from the universe to human life in the Garden of Eden. The unifying motif is God's provisions for human life. It is a picture of how God intended human life to be lived—anytime, anywhere.

Genesis 3 tells about the origin of evil in human experience and the world. The story combines several common narrative types: temptation, fall from innocence, crime and punishment, and initiation (into evil and its consequences). The psychology of guilt is also prominent.

HERO STORIES

Biblical narrative is almost synonymous with the genre "hero story." Hero stories are built around the life and exploits of a protagonist or hero. They spring from one of the most basic literary impulses—the desire to embody the values and typical struggles of a society in the life of a representative and exemplary figure. The main interest of hero stories is the hero's qualities and destiny.

The hero stories of the Bible begin in Genesis ("the book of beginnings"). Noah is a hero of righteousness in an evil age. He is

God's agent of rescue and the father of a new world (Gen. 6–9). One of the longest hero stories in the Bible is the story of the patriarch Abraham (Gen. 12–25). Abraham is both a domestic hero and a spiritual hero of faith in God. His domestic heroism is seen in his quest for a son and in his typical roles (husband, uncle, father, head of a household, and owner of possessions). His spiritual heroism is evident in his obedience to God's call to leave his homeland to become a wanderer, in his faith in God's promise to give him a son, and in his willingness to sacrifice his son Isaac.

Two other heroes complete the images of heroism in the book of Genesis. Jacob is largely unidealized in the story devoted to him (Gen. 25–35), but his life is heroic because it shows how God can work with unpromising material, eventually transforming even a deeply flawed personality. The story of Joseph (Gen. 37–50) is the first example of a significant biblical archetype known as the suffering servant. Heroes who belong to this pattern undergo undeserved suffering and as a result bring about good for other people.

Later Old Testament stories continue the pattern of stories built around the life or acts of a hero. David is one of the most complex heroes in all of literature, both in his roles and personal qualities. His story as a successful warrior and king is the closest parallel in the Bible to the hero stories of ancient literature outside the Bible. Another story of military heroism is the story of Gideon (Judg. 6–8). The story of Daniel presents a nationalistic hero, a hero of integrity and political ability, and a religious hero of uncompromising faith in God. The stories of Elijah (1 Kings 16–21; 2 Kings 1–2) and Elisha (2 Kings 2–9) capture another prominent Old Testament character type, the prophet of God.

Stories built around heroines are few but striking. The book of Ruth is a love story that celebrates Ruth's domestic and religious heroism. Another masterpiece of biblical narrative is the story of

Esther, which portrays the courage of a national and religious heroine. The story of the Israelites' conquest of Sisera's forces (Judg. 4–5) recounts the heroic explots of two women, Deborah and Jael.

The incidence of hero stories continues unabated in the New Testament. The Gospels are hero stories on a grand scale. They are a pure example of narrative built around the life of an exemplary protagonist whose acts and words are treasured and celebrated. The same thing can be said of the book of Revelation, which rightly advertises at the very outset that it will be an unveiling of Jesus Christ in his conquest. And the book of Acts is a small anthology of hero stories, chiefly about Peter and Paul.

This brief survey of hero stories in the Bible shows how widespread the heroic impulse is in the Bible, and how varied its heroic ideal is.

EPIC

Epic is a species within the class of heroic narrative. It is a long narrative of national destiny. Common epic motifs include warfare, conquest, dominion, and kingdom. Supernatural settings, characters, and events have always been a hallmark of epic. Epics are built around a central epic feat performed by the epic hero, a feat that usually involves military conquest.

The most obviously epic work in the Bible is the epic of the Exodus, which spans the narrative portions of Exodus, Numbers, and Deuteronomy. It is built around the epic feat of the Exodus from the land of slavery to the Promised Land. Like other epics, it narrates a decisive moment in national history and is a definitive repository of the religious, moral, and political ideals of the society that produced it.

The Old Testament historical chronicles are also epiclike. They have a national scope and follow the familiar epic motifs of battle, conquest, and dominion. Their heroes are public figures. And the continuous presence of the idea of the covenant lends these stories the epic quality of national and racial destiny that makes them more than simply hero stories.

The epic impulse is also present in the New Testament. The Gospels are so expansive and momentous that they have the world-changing atmosphere of epics. The book of Acts, with its focus on Paul's journeys and quests, recounts bigger-than-life events and the epoch-making story of the early church's expansion over vast geographic stretches. And the book of Revelation is a spiritualized version of virtually every epic motif and stylistic trait that we might name.

TRAGEDY

Literary tragedy is the spectacle of exceptional calamity. It depicts a movement from prosperity to catastrophe. The focus of tragedy is on the tragic hero—a great person of high social standing who in a moment of tragic choice displays a tragic flaw of character (Aristotle called it *hamartia,* the New Testament word translated as "sin"). The plot of tragedy highlights the element of human choice. This means that the hero is always responsible for the downfall, and in biblical tragedy the tragic hero is also deserving of the catastrophe. The tragic pattern consists of six elements that are remarkably constant: dilemma—choice—catastrophe—suffering—perception—death.

The prototypical biblical tragedy is the story of the fall in Genesis 3. Adam and Eve face the dilemma of whether to obey or disobey God's prohibition. They make their tragic mistake, which leads to scenes of suffering and perception.

The masterpiece of biblical tragedy is the story of King Saul (1 Sam. 8–31). Saul's tragedy is a tragedy of weak leadership. His dilemma consisted of his dual allegiance—toward obeying God and taking the path of expediency in order to please the people. The narrative and psychological center of the tragedy is Saul's disobedience of God's command to destroy the Amalekites (1 Sam. 15). It is followed by catastrophe, suffering, perception, and death.

There are other biblical tragedies as well. The story of Samson (Judg. 13–16) fits the tragic pattern exactly. The story of David as told in 1 and 2 Samuel follows the tragic pattern of initial prosperity followed by catastrophe and suffering. In typical tragic fashion, moreover, the hero's downfall is localized in a specific event (the Bathsheba-Uriah debacle). Other brief narratives in the historical books of the Bible are tragic in outline, and some of Jesus' parables are likewise depictions of wrong choices.

Although the spirit of tragedy pervades the Bible (not surprisingly, in a book so devoted to the portrayal of evil and its consequences), there are fewer full-fledged tragedies in the Bible than we might expect. The Bible is an anthology of tragedies averted—averted through the intervention of human repentance and divine forgiveness.

THE GOSPELS
The New Testament Gospels are unique, but that uniqueness has more to do with their content and the nature of their protagonist than with their literary forms. At the level of narrative form, the Gospels are an expanded hero story. They consistently keep the focus on Jesus, and their obvious narrative purpose is to tell the story of the teaching and deeds of Jesus. The organizing principle is loosely (but not strictly) chronological, with virtually all of the space devoted to the three years of Jesus' public ministry. More than a fourth of the accounts is devoted to the trial, crucifixion, and resurrection of Jesus. The plot of the story is not single but episodic.

The hero himself accounts for part of the uniqueness of these stories. He makes claims about himself that conventional heroes do not make—that he has power to forgive sins, that he will lay down his life for the salvation of his followers, that he will rise from the dead, that he is the light of the world. His deeds of power likewise transcend anything we find elsewhere in literature.

While the individual literary forms in the Gospels are not unique, the combination of forms that converge is without exact parallel. Equal space is given to what the hero said and what he did. Within the overall narrative framework, we find continous examples of such common genres as parable, drama or dialogue, sermon or oration, and saying or proverb. Narrative subtypes also abound: annunciation and nativity stories, calling or vocation stories, recognition stories, witness stories, encounter stories, conflict or controversy stories, pronouncement stories (in which a saying of Jesus is linked with an event that correlates with it), miracle stories, and passion stories.

PARABLES

The parables of Jesus loom large in most people's thinking about biblical narrative. These parables are brief fictional stories that embody easily grasped ideas, usually dealing with some aspect of the kingdom of God. Even though a parable often exhibits a single main theme, it is not unusual for additional ideas to be part of the total meaning.

Parables are folk stories that obey the rules of popular storytelling through the centuries. These narrative ingredients include home-spun realism, simplicity of action, suspense, foils (heightened contrasts), repetition (including threefold repetition), end stress, universal character types, and archetypes. Many of the parables include an element of unreality or exaggeration—a "crack" in the dominant realism that teases us into exploring what the stories communicate beyond the simple surface.

Parables are too simple to be meaningful only at the surface level. Their true meaning emerges when we view them as allegories—stories with a double meaning. Contrary to common scholarly lore, there are six impeccable reasons to believe that the parables were intended to be allegories or symbolic stories. One is the etymology of the word "parable," which means "to throw alongside," with the implication of double meaning. The very simplicity of the stories propels us to see a spiritual level of meaning in addition to the realistic surface. Many of the details in the parables carried traditional symbolic meanings (God as father or owner of a vineyard, seed as God's word, etc.). Unrealistic elements in the parables also signal a deeper level of meaning. Furthermore, the religious purpose of the parables emerges only when we start to attach second meanings to the details—when we understand that the seed that is sown is the gospel, for example, and the types of soils are various human responses. Finally, when Jesus interpreted two of his parables (Matthew 13:18-23, 36-43), he attached a corresponding allegorical meaning to virtually every detail in the stories.

A full treatment of a parable falls naturally into four stages of analysis. The process begins by interacting with the stories as literal stories, exploring the narrative ingredients of setting, character, and plot. The second step is to identify the allegorical or symbolic meanings of details that stand for something else. On the basis of this analysis it is possible to state the themes or ideas implicit in the parable. The final step is application—to the original audience and to a modern reader.

Biblical Poetry

The second most prominent literary genre in the Bible is poetry. Poetry is identifiable by two primary features—verse form and the presence of a poetic idiom or style.

PARALLELISM

The verse form of biblical poetry is known as parallelism. It avoids rhyme and consists instead of thought couplets or triplets. Parallelism can be defined as two or more lines that express something in different words but similar grammatical form.

Four main types of parallelism make up biblical poetry. Synonymous parallelism expresses a thought more than once in similar grammatical form or sentence structure:

> The heavens are telling the glory of God;
> and the firmament proclaims his handiwork.[1]

In antithetical parallelism, the second line states the truth of the first in a negative or contrasting way:

> For the Lord knows the way of the righteous,
> but the way of the wicked will perish.[2]

In climactic parallelism, the second line completes the first by repeating part of it and then adding to it:

> Ascribe to the Lord, O heavenly beings,
> ascribe to the Lord glory and strength.[3]

Synthetic ("growing") parallelism consists of a pair of lines that together form a complete unit and in which the second line completes or expands the thought of the first (but without repeating anything in the first line):

> Thou preparest a table before me
> in the presence of my enemies.[4]

Parallelism serves several purposes. It is part of the artistry of biblical poetry, conveying the impression of skillfully handled language. It is also a mnemonic device—an aid to memorization, recitation, or even improvisation in the originally oral composition. Parallelism produces a meditative effect, possessing a retarding element in which we turn the prism of thought or feeling in the light.

POETIC IDIOM

Poets speak a language all their own. This poetic idiom is the heart of poetry; it is much more important than the verse form in which a poem is embodied.

Above all, poets think in images—words naming a sensory thing or action. Poetry avoids the abstraction as much as possible, though in the biblical poetry the verse form of parallelism often leads a poet to combine the concrete with an abstract statement. Poetry requires a reader to experience a series of sensory experiences. Having experienced the image, we need to interpret it—its connotations, its relevance to the topic of the poem, its affective meanings, and whether it is positive or negative in meaning in the context of a given passage.

The next most pervasive element of poetry is comparison. It usually takes the form of either metaphor (an implied comparison) or simile (an explicit comparison that uses the formula "like" or "as"). Both metaphor and simile are based on the principle of correspondence. The very word "metaphor" implies this, for it is based on the Greek words meaning "to carry over."

Metaphor and simile place a double obligation on a reader. One is to experience the literal level of the image. If the poet tells us that "the Lord God is a sun and shield" (Ps. 84:11), we must first experience the physical phenomena of sun and shield. Then we must proceed to the interpretive task of determining *how* God is like sun and shield. Metaphor and simile are based on a principle of transfer of meaning. They secure an effect on one level and then ask us to transfer those meanings (which are usually multiple) to another level—the level of the actual subject of the poem.

Several additional figures of speech round out the poet's repertoire. Personification consists of treating something nonhuman (and frequently inanimate) as though it were a human capable of acting or responding. Hyperbole (conscious exaggeration for the sake of effect) does not express literal truth but emotional truth. Another standard way to express strong feeling is with apostrophe—addressing someone or something absent as though it were present and capable of listening. An allusion is a reference to past literature or history.

LYRIC AS THE BASIC POETIC FORM

Because the Bible is filled with specific types of poems, it is important to note that the concept of "poem" is virtually synonymous with "lyric." Virtually all of the poems in the Bible should be viewed as examples of the genus "lyric" before they are regarded as examples of a particular species.

A lyric poem is a brief poem, often intended to be sung, that expresses the thoughts and especially the feelings of a speaker. In other words, the identifying features of a lyric are three: lyrics are brief, personal or subjective (the speaker speaks in his or her own voice), and reflective or emotional.

Unified impact is important in a lyric, and the best way to see its presence is to employ the scheme of theme and variation, analyzing how a given unit contributes to the controlling theme. The overwhelming majority of lyrics are built on the principle of three-part structure: an opening statement of theme (the stimulus that moves the poet to sing), development of the theme, and concluding resolution. Lyric poets develop their theme by choosing from among four possibilities: repetition, the catalog or list, association (branching out from an initial idea to a related one), and contrast.

THE BOOK OF PSALMS

The best known book of poetry in the Bible is the book of Psalms. It is an anthology of poems collected for use in worship at the temple in Jerusalem. All of the psalms are lyric poems, but a host of subtypes make considerations of genre especially important as a factor in a literary approach to the book of Psalms.

The most numerous category of Psalms is the lament or complaint. It is a fixed form that includes five elements that can appear in any order and that can occur more than once in a given psalm. The ingredients are an invocation or cry to God, the lament or complaint (a definition of the crisis), petition or supplication, a statement of confidence in God, and a vow to praise God.

The second largest category of Psalms is the praise psalm, which follows a three-part format. It begins with a call to praise, which can consist of as many as three ingredients—an exhortation to praise God, the naming of the person or group to whom the command is directed, and identifying the mode of praise (voice, harp, etc.). The development of the praise is usually built on the principle of a catalog of the praiseworthy acts or attributes of God, though occasionally the portrait technique appears. Praise psalms are rounded off with a note of finality, which often takes the form of a brief prayer or wish.

The basis of identifying additional subtypes within the book of Psalms is content rather than form. The dominant categories are nature poems, worship psalms (also called songs of Zion), penitential psalms, historical psalms, royal psalms, meditative psalms, psalms that praise a character type or abstract quality and are known by the label "encomium," royal psalms, imprecatory psalms, and even an epithalamion (a wedding poem, Psalm 45).

THE SONG OF SOLOMON

The Song of Solomon is a collection of love poems that together make up an exalted epithalamion (wedding poem) built around a single courtship and wedding. The poems are pastoral love poems in which the setting is rustic and the lovers are portrayed (at least partly fictionally) as shepherd and shepherdess. A collection of lyrics is not a way of telling a story. Instead the Song of Solomon portrays a series of feelings and moods, structured on a stream-of-consciousness principle.

Both the style and the specific genres of the Song of Solomon are familiar to love poetry both ancient and modern. The style is consciously artificial and highly senuous ("sensory"), metaphoric, hyperbolic, and passionate. Within the general framework of pastoral, specific genres include the invitation to love, praise of the beloved, emblematic blazons (lists of the features of the beloved, with each feature compared to an object in nature), courtship and wedding poems, and songs of separation, longing, and reunion.

NEW TESTAMENT HYMNS

Lyric poems are also common in the New Testament. The nativity story (Luke 1–2) is sprinkled with nativity hymns. We can also find hymn fragments in the Epistles (e.g., Eph. 5:14, 2 Tim. 2:11-13, Heb. 1:3). Hymns of worship punctuate the visions of Revelation (e.g., 4:8, 11; 5:9-10). Three famous Christ hymns are especially noteworthy: John 1:1-18, Philippians 2:5-11, and Colossians 1:15-20.

ENCOMIUM

Spanning both Old and New Testaments is the encomium. While some biblical encomia are written in prose rather than poetry, they are lyric in effect and are usually so stylized that they can easily be printed in the form of Hebrew parallelism.

An encomium is a poem or essay written in praise of either an abstract quality or a generalized character type. Common motifs are an introduction to the subject of praise, the distinguished and ancient ancestry of that subject, a catalog or description of praiseworthy acts and qualities, the superior or indispensable nature of the subject, the rewards that accompany the things being praised, and a conclusion urging the reader to emulate the subject.

Biblical encomia that praise an abstract quality include poems in praise of wisdom in the book of Proverbs (3:13-20; 8), God's law (Ps. 119), love (1 Cor. 13), and faith (Heb. 11). Encomia praising character types include Psalms 1, 15, 112, and 128 (the godly person) and Proverbs 31:10-31 (the virtuous wife). The Song of the Suffering Servant in Isaiah 53 is a parody of the genre, praising the suffering servant for unconventional reasons.

ADDITIONAL POETIC PARTS OF THE BIBLE

In addition to the repositories of poetry that I have noted, it is important to realize that poetry also appears in books of the Bible that we ordinarily assign to another genre as the primary form. The book of Job, a drama, is couched in poetry except for the prose narrative framework. Most of the Old Testament prophetic books are written in a predominantly poetic form. So is Old Testament wisdom literature—the books of Proverbs and Ecclesiastes (where even the prose passages are poetic in effect). Embedded in Old Testament stories we find such varied lyric forms as songs of deliverance (the Song of Moses in Exod. 15 and the Song of Deborah in Judg. 5) and an elegy (David's elegy for Jonathan in 2 Sam. 1).

The New Testament is continuously poetic. Jesus is one of the world's most famous poets. His discourses are imagistic, metaphoric, hyperbolic, impassioned, and filled with paradoxes. The movement of their clauses is replete with parallelism. The New Testament Epistles are only slightly less poetic. And the book of Revelation relies on the staples of poetry—image, symbol, and allusion.

Other Literary Forms in the Bible

BIBLICAL DRAMA

Although no book of the Bible was written for the stage, and although only one book is dramatic in form, the dramatic impulse pervades the Bible. The incidence of directly quoted speeches in the Bible is without parallel in ancient literature and unprecedented until we come to the modern novel. The dramatized scene built out of dialogue between characters in a definite setting is by far the most common mode of biblical narrative. Similarly, the prophetic books are cosmic dramas that take place on a world stage, and the book of Revelation is so filled with elaborately described scenes and dialogues that it is likely to have been influenced by the conventions of Greek drama.

The book of Job is the lone book of the Bible that is structured like a drama. The book poses a problem—why do the righteous suffer?—and then presents the speeches of characters as they debate possible solutions to the problem. Of course, the speeches are longer and more oratorical than we expect in modern drama. As in all drama, the focus of our attention is on character clashes, as Job variously argues with his visitors and with God. To read the dramatic book of Job looking primarily for action is to invite frustration. The pace is leisurely, as the speakers repeat a few common ideas. The poetic style invites us to luxuriate over how an idea is expressed, as we listen to everything at least twice.

The superstructure of this drama is at least threefold. One organizing principle is the hero's quest for understanding and for union with God. A second point of unity is the obtuseness of the friends' wrongheadedness, whose repetitious speeches serve as a static background against which we can measure the intellectual and spiritual progress of Job. A third unifying element in the drama is its irony. In the case of the friends, we witness the irony of orthodoxy—of belief in principles that are generally true but that do not fit the situation of Job. Balancing this is the irony of rebellion against God, as we observe Job make charges against God that we know from the prologue to be untrue.

BIBLICAL PROVERBS
The Bible is one of the most aphoristic or proverbial books in the world. It is filled with concise, memorable sayings from beginning to end.

The literary features of proverbs account for their power. Proverbs are concise and memorable. Their aim is to make an insight permanent. They are simultaneously simple (brief and easily grasped) and profound (dealing with the essential issues of life, and inexhaustible in their application). Often proverbs are both specific and universal: they cover a whole host of similar experiences, and they often use a particularized situation to stand for a broader principle of life (the statement that "in the place where [the tree] falls, there it will lie" [Eccl. 11:3, RSV] is really talking about the principle of finality that characterizes many events in life).

Proverbs are also frequently poetic in form, using the resources of imagery, metaphor, and simile. Some biblical proverbs are descriptive of what is, while others are prescriptive of what should be. The truthfulness of proverbs is truthfulness to human experience. Proverbs are continually being confirmed in our experiences and observations of life. They never go out of date.

Thus defined, the proverb as a literary form is pervasive in the Bible. The books of Proverbs and Ecclesiastes consist wholly of collections of proverbs, sometimes arranged into proverb clusters on a common theme. But the parallelism of biblical poetry tends almost inevitably toward an aphoristic effect. Jesus' discourses rely heavily on the proverb or saying as a basic element. The New Testament Epistles contain an abundance of aphorisms, and the book of James employs the techniques of wisdom literature throughout. Even the stories of the Bible have provided their share of proverbial sayings to the common storehouse of proverbs.

SATIRE

Satire is the exposure, through ridicule or rebuke, of human vice or folly. It consists of three essential elements: an object of attack, a satiric vehicle, and a satiric norm (the stated or implied standard by which the object of attack is criticized). The satiric vehicle is often a story but can be something as specific as a metaphor (as when Jesus calls the Pharisees whitewashed tombs). Satire is often, though not universally, accompanied by a comic or sarcastic tone.

The Bible is a much more satiric book than is commonly acknowledged. The satiric impulse is not confined to books that are mainly satiric. It is present in biblical narrative, for example, where wholly idealized characters are almost unknown and where the character flaws of most characters are satirically exposed. Satire is equally present in the Wisdom Literature, where many of the proverbs attack such human failings as greed, laziness, self-indulgence, and folly.

The largest quantity of satire is found in prophetic writing. The two major types of prophetic oracle are the oracle of salvation and the oracle of judgment. The best literary approach to the oracle of judgment is satire. These passages always have a discernible object of attack and a standard by which the judgment is rendered. The attack, moreover, is embodied in a wide range of literary forms, from the simple prediction of calamity to extended portraits of evil and judgment. A book like Amos is from start to finish a work of satire: it attacks public evils on the basis of clearly stated spiritual and moral standards by means of a kaleidoscopic variety of literary techniques.

Satire pervades the Gospels as well. In the story itself the opponents of Jesus, especially the Pharisees, are portrayed with satiric scorn. The discourses of Jesus are likewise frequently satiric (Matt. 23, for example, is a satiric discourse that attacks the Pharisees with a barrage of satiric devices). And many of the parables that Jesus told are typical satiric pieces that use narrative form to embody an attack on a specific attitude or behavior.

The great masterpiece of biblical satire is the Old Testament book of Jonah. The object of attack is the kind of nationalistic zeal that made God the exclusive property of Israel and refused to accept the universality of God's grace. The protagonist of the story embodies the attitudes that the writer is holding up to satiric attack. The other main character in the story is God, whose universal love and mercy are the standard by which the attitudes of Jonah are exposed as wrong. The irony of the ignominious behavior of the wayward prophet produces latent humor in the story.

EPISTLE

The New Testament Epistles are modifications of the conventional letters of the classical world. Like Greek and Roman letters, the Epistles contain an opening (sender, addressee, greeting), a body, and a closing (greetings and final wishes). But two important additions appear in the New Testament Epistles—the thanksgiving (prayer for spiritual welfare and remembrance or commendation of the spiritual riches of the addressee) and the paraenesis (a list of exhortations, virtues, vices, commands, or proverbs). Whereas the content of ordinary letters in the ancient world might be virtually anything, the New Testament Epistles keep the focus on theological and moral issues.

At the level of style, the Epistles are continuously literary. Figurative language such as imagery, metaphor, and paradox is common. The sentences and clauses are often artfully arranged, with the influence of parallelism so prominent that many a passage could be arranged as a poem. Dramatic apostrophes, rhetorical questions, personifications, question-and-answer constructions, and antitheses, though less frequent, are nonetheless common. The sheer exuberance of these letters produces its own grand style and is often lyric in effect. And, of course, there is the continuous presence of proverbs or aphorisms—striking statements that stay in the memory.

The Epistles are occasional writings, written in response to specific occasions in the life of the early churches. In a manner reminiscent of stories, they give a many-sided picture of everyday life. Because the authors are responding to specific situations that have arisen and questions that have been raised, the Epistles are not (except for the books of Romans, Ephesians, and Hebrews) systematic theological treatises. The points addressed are not necessarily the most important ones; they are simply the ones that have been raised.

ORATORY

Biblical oratory consists of formal, stylized speeches addressed to a specific audience, usually on a noteworthy occasion. Usually the dignity of the occasion produces an elevated style. One whole book—Deuteronomy—is an oratory, being Moses' farewell address to the nation of Israel.

The customary pattern is for orations to be embedded in other material. The Old Testament stories, for example, contain orations delivered in their narrative context—passages like Jacob's blessing of his sons (Gen. 49), Samuel's installation of Saul as king (1 Sam. 12), Solomon's speech and prayer at the dedication of the temple (1 Kings 8), Ezra's speech when the law was reinstituted (Neh. 9). The book of Job is a small collection of orations. The prophetic books frequently have an oratorical cast, whether the speaker is a prophet or God. And God's giving of the law to Moses (Exod.—Num.) is oratorical in nature.

A similar pattern appears in the New Testament. Jesus' discourses are a prime example, with the Sermon on the Mount (Matt. 5–7) being the example par excellence. The book of Acts contains several defense orations (which, incidentally, follow the conventions of classical forensic orations), sermons, and Paul's famous speech in Athens to the Areopagus (Acts 17), which follows all of the rhetorical rules of classical oratory. Finally, the oral nature of the Epistles makes them often produce an oratorical effect.

VISIONARY WRITING

Visionary writing is a major biblical genre. It falls into two subgenres—prophetic writing and apocalyptic writing (with the book of Revelation being the chief example). The underlying literary principles are the same in both categories.

Visionary writing pictures settings, characters, and events that differ from ordinary reality. This is not to say that the events of visionary literature did not happen in past history or will not happen in future history. But the events portrayed by the writer had either not yet happened or do not exist in the ordinary world. They are imagined.

The element of "otherness" pervades visionary writing. Visionary literature transforms the known world or the present state of things into a situation that at the time of writing was as yet only imagined. The simplest form of such transformation is a futuristic picture of the changed fortunes of a person or nation. In a more radical form, visionary literature takes us not simply to a different time but to a different mode of existence. It transports us to realms that transcend earthly reality, usually to the supernatural spheres of heaven or hell.

The strangeness of visionary literature extends to both scenes and actors. The scene is typically cosmic instead of localized. Filling this cosmic stage are actors that we do not meet directly in everyday life—God, the saints in heaven, angels, dragons, monsters, a warrior riding a red horse (Rev. 6:4), flying women with wings like those of a stork (Zech. 5:9). The mingling of the familiar and unfamiliar, a hallmark of visionary literature, takes an even stranger form when inanimate objects and forces of nature suddenly become actors—when the stars refuse to show their light or hail and fire mixed with blood fall on the earth.

All of these imaginary fireworks produce a distinctive structure. Visionary literature is structured as a kaleidoscope of shifting elements—visual scenes, speeches, dialogues, brief snatches of narrative, prayers, hymns, and much besides. Dream or vision provides the organization. Dreams, after all, consist of momentary pictures, fleeting impressions, characters and scenes that play their brief part and then drop out of sight, and abrupt jumps from one action to another.

If fantasy is thus a staple of visionary writing, so is symbolism. The strange events that greet us are pictures of something else. The right question to ask is accordingly this: Given the specific context of a visionary passage, of what historical event or what theological fact is this a picture?

The best aid in interpretation is a keen eye for the obvious. When Isaiah pictured a river that would overflow the entire land of Judah (8:5-8), the surrounding context makes it clear that this is a symbolic picture of the imminent invasion by the armies of Assyria. When the book of Revelation pictures the unsuccessful attempt of a dragon to destroy a child who is to rule all the nations and who miraculously escapes from the dragon by ascending into heaven (12:1-5), we recognize it as a symbolic account of Satan's inability to thwart Jesus during his incarnate life on earth.

The Literary Unity of the Bible

The Bible is an anthology of so many different literary genres and techniques that the effect may finally threaten to confuse us. But literary unity will emerge if we remember the underlying principles.

The overall framework of the Bible is that of a story. It begins with the creation of the world and ends with the consummation of history and the recreation of the world. The plot conflict is a prolonged spiritual battle between good and evil. The central character is God, and every creature and nation interact with this mighty protagonist. Every story, poem, or proverb in the Bible fits into this overarching story.

Furthermore, all of the literary parts of the Bible share the defining traits of literature itself. They present human experience concretely, so that we can share an experience with the author and with characters in a story or poem. The literary parts of the Bible all display technical skill and beauty. They also employ special resources of language, so that we are aware that the writers are doing things with language that go beyond ordinary uses.

Finally, despite the diversity in literary genres found in the Bible, the principle of genre itself helps to organize the picture. Virtually anywhere we turn in the Bible, we are aware that the passage or book belongs to a specific literary genre—a genre that follows its own conventions and that requires a definite set of expectations from the reader.

The Bible is a book for all people and all temperaments, from the prosaic, matter-of-fact to the person who likes far-flung fantasy and visions. The Russian novelist Fyodor Dostoyevsky had one of his fictional characters exclaim, "What a book the Bible is, what a miracle, what strength is given with it to man. It is like a mould cast of the world and man and human nature, everything is there, and a law for everything for all the ages. And what mysteries are solved and revealed" (*Brothers Karamazov*).

NOTES

1. Psalm 19:1, RSV
2. Psalm 1:6, RSV
3. Psalm 29:1, RSV
4. Psalm 23:5, RSV

BIBLIOGRAPHY

Alter, Robert. *The Art of Biblical Narrative,* 1981.
Auerbach, Erich; trans. Willard Trask. "Odysseus' Scar," chapter 1 of *Mimesis: The Representation of Reality in Western Literature,* 1953.

Frye, Northrop. *The Great Code: The Bible and Literature,* 1982.
Gros Louis, Kenneth, ed. *Literary Interpretations of Biblical Narratives,* 1974.
Lewis, C. S. *The Literary Impact of the Authorized Version,* 1963.
Longman III, Tremper *Literary Approaches to Biblical Interpretation,* 1987.
Ryken, Leland. *How to Read the Bible as Literature,* 1984.
————, ed. *The New Testament in Literary Criticism,*1984.
————. *Words of Delight: A Literary Introduction to the Bible,* 1987.
————. *Words of Life: A Literary Introduction to the New Testament,* 1987.

SECTION
FOUR
Bible Texts and Manuscripts

Texts and Manuscripts
of the Old Testament
Mark R. Norton

The ancient manuscripts of the Old Testament are the basic working material used to seek out the original text of the Bible with as great a degree of accuracy as possible. This process is called textual criticism, sometimes designated "lower criticism" to distinguish it from "higher criticism," which is analysis of the date, unity, and authorship of the biblical writings.

The task of the textual critic can be divided into a number of general stages: (1) the collection and collation of existing manuscripts, translations, and quotations; (2) the development of theory and methodology that will enable the critic to use the gathered information to reconstruct the most accurate text of the biblical materials; (3) the reconstruction of the history of the transmission of the text in order to identify the various influences affecting the text; (4) the evaluation of specific variant readings in light of textual evidence, theology, and history.

Both Old and New Testament textual critics undertake a similar task and face similar obstacles. They both seek to unearth a hypothetical "original" text with limited resources that are at varying degrees of deterioration. But the Old Testament textual critic faces a more complex textual history than does his New Testament counterpart. The New Testament was written primarily in the first century A.D., and complete New Testament manuscripts exist that were written only a few hundred years later. The Old Testament, however, is made up of literature written over a thousand-year period, the oldest parts dating to the twelfth century B.C., or possibly even earlier. To make matters even more difficult, until recently, the earliest known Hebrew manuscripts of the Old Testament were medieval. This left scholars with little witness as to the Old Testament's textual development from ancient times to the Middle Ages, a period of over two thousand years.

Until the discovery of the Dead Sea Scrolls in the 1940s and 1950s, secondary Aramaic, Greek, and Latin translations served as the earliest significant witnesses to the early Hebrew Scriptures. Since these are translations, and subject to sectarian and contexual alterations and interpolations, their value to the textual critic, though significant, is limited. The recent discoveries of the Dead Sea Scrolls and other early manuscripts, however, have provided primary witnesses to the Hebrew Old Testament in earlier times. The scholarly assessment of these discoveries is, at present, far from complete, and the discipline of Old Testament textual criticism anxiously awaits a more complete assessment of their significance. In a general sense, however, the Dead Sea Scrolls have affirmed the accuracy of the Masoretic Text that we use today.

Important Old Testament Manuscripts

Most medieval manuscripts of the Old Testament exhibit a fairly standardized form of the Hebrew text. This standardization reflects the work of the medieval scribes known as Masoretes (A.D. 500–900); the text that resulted from their work is called the Masoretic Text. Most of the important manuscripts dated from the eleventh century A.D. or later all reflect this same basic textual tradition. But since the Masoretic Text did not stabilize until well after A.D. 500, many questions about its development in the preceding centuries could not be answered. So the primary task for Old Testament textual critics has been to compare earlier witnesses in order to discover how the Masoretic Text came to be, and how it and earlier witnesses of the Hebrew Bible are related. This leads us to the initial task of textual criticism: the collection of all possible records of the biblical writings.

All the primary sources of the Hebrew Scriptures are handwritten manuscripts, usually written on animal skins, papyrus, or sometimes metal. The fact that they are handwritten is the source of many difficulties for the textual critic. Human error and editorial tampering are often to blame for the many variant readings in Old and New Testament manuscripts. The fact that the ancient manuscripts are written on skins or papyrus is another source of difficulty. Due to natural decay, most of the surviving ancient manuscripts are fragmentary and difficult to read.

There are many secondary witnesses to the ancient Old Testament text, including translations into other languages, quotations used by both friends and enemies of biblical religion, and evidence from early printed texts. Most of the secondary witnesses have suffered in ways similar to the primary ones. They, too, contain numerous variants due to both intentional and accidental scribal errors and are fragmentary as a result of natural decay. Since variant readings do exist in the surviving ancient manuscripts, these must be collected and compared. The task of comparing and listing the variant readings is known as collation.

THE MASORETIC TEXT

The textual history of the Masoretic Text is a significant story in its own right. This text of the Hebrew Bible is the most complete in existence. It forms the basis for our modern Hebrew Bibles and is the prototype against which all comparisons are made in Old Testament textual studies. It is called Masoretic because in its present form it is based on the *Masora,* the textual tradition of the Jewish scholars known as the Masoretes of Tiberias. (Tiberias was the location of their community on the Sea of Galilee.) The Masoretes, whose scholarly school flourished between A.D. 500 and 1000, standardized the traditional consonantal text by adding vowel pointing and marginal notes. (The ancient Hebrew alphabet had no vowels.)

The Masoretic Text, as it exists today, owes much to the Ben Asher family. For five or six generations, from the second half of the eighth century to the middle of the tenth century A.D., this family played a leading role in the Masoretic work at Tiberias. A faithful record of their work can be found in the oldest existing Masoretic manuscripts, which go back to the final two members of that family. The oldest dated Masoretic manuscript is *Codex Cairensis* (A.D. 895), which is attributed to Moses ben Asher. This manuscript contained both the Former Prophets (Joshua, Judges, Samuel, and Kings) and the Latter Prophets (Isaiah, Jeremiah, Ezekiel, and the twelve Minor Prophets). The rest of the Old Testament is missing from this manuscript.

The other major surviving manuscript attributed to the Ben Asher family is the *Aleppo Codex.* According to the manuscript's concluding note, Aaron ben Moses ben Asher was responsible for writing the Masoretic notes and pointing the text. This manuscript contained the entire Old Testament and dates from the first half of the tenth century A.D. It was reportedly destroyed in anti-Jewish riots in 1947, but this proved to be only partly true. A majority of the manuscript survived and will be used as the base for a new critical edition of the Hebrew Bible to be published by the Hebrew University in Jerusalem.

The manuscript known as *Codex Leningradensis,* presently stored in the Leningrad Public Library, is of special importance as a witness to the Ben Asher text. According to a note on the manuscript, it was copied in A.D. 1008 from texts written by Aaron ben Moses ben Asher. Since the oldest complete Hebrew text of the Old Testament (the *Aleppo Codex*) was not available to scholars earlier in this century, *Codex Leningradensis* was used as the textual base for the popular Hebrew texts of today: *Biblia Hebraica,* edited by R. Kittel, and its revision *Biblia Hebraica Stuttgartensia,* edited by K. Elliger and W. Rudolf.

There are quite a number of less important manuscript codices that reflect the Masoretic tradition: the *Petersburg Codex of the Prophets* and the *Erfurt Codices.* There are also a number of manuscripts that no longer exist, but which were used by scholars in the Masoretic period. One of the most prominent is *Codex Hillel,* traditionally attributed to Rabbi Hillel ben Moses ben Hillel about A.D. 600. This codex was said to be very accurate and was used for the revision of other manuscripts. Readings of this codex are cited repeatedly by the early Medieval Masoretes. *Codex Muga, Codex Jericho,* and *Codex Jerushalmi,* also no longer extant, were also cited by the Masoretes. These manuscripts were likely prominent examples of unpointed texts that had become part of a standardizing consensus in the first centuries A.D. These laid the groundwork for the work of the Masoretes of Tiberias.

Despite the completeness of the Masoretic manuscripts of the Hebrew Bible, a major problem still remains for Old Testament textual critics. The Masoretic manuscripts, as old as they are, were written between one and two thousand years after the original autographs. Earlier witnesses to the ancient Hebrew text still needed to be brought forward to testify to the accuracy of the Masoretic Text.

THE DEAD SEA SCROLLS

The most important ancient witnesses to the Hebrew Bible are the texts discovered at Wadi Qumran in the 1940s and 1950s. (*Wadi* is an Arabic word for a river bed that is dry except in the rainy season). Before the Qumran discoveries, the oldest existing Hebrew manuscripts of the Old Testament dated from about A.D. 900. The greatest importance of the Dead Sea Scrolls, therefore, lies in the discovery of biblical manuscripts dating back to only about 300 years after the close of the Old Testament canon. That makes them one thousand years earlier than the oldest manuscripts previously known to biblical scholars. The texts found at Wadi Qumran were all completed before the Roman conquest of Palestine in A.D. 70, and many predate this event by quite some time. Among the Dead Sea Scrolls, the Isaiah scroll has received the most publicity, although the collection contains fragments of all the books in the Hebrew Bible with the exception of Esther.

Because the discovery of the Dead Sea Scrolls is so important for Old Testament textual criticism, a short history and description of these recent discoveries is appropriate. The manuscripts now known as the Dead Sea Scrolls are a collection of biblical and extrabiblical manuscripts from Qumran, an ancient Jewish religious community near the Dead Sea.

Before the Qumran find, few manuscripts had been discovered in the Holy Land. The early church father Origen (third century A.D.) mentioned using Hebrew and Greek manuscripts that had been stored in jars in caves near Jericho. In the ninth century A.D. a patriarch of the eastern church, Timothy I, wrote a letter to Sergius, Metropolitan (Archbishop) of Elam, in which he, too, referred to a large number of Hebrew manuscripts found in a cave near Jericho. For more than one thousand years since then, however, no other significant manuscript discoveries were forthcoming from caves in that region near the Dead Sea.

Scroll Discoveries at Wadi Qumran The history of the Dead Sea manuscripts, both of their hiding and of their finding, reads like a mystery adventure story. It began with a telephone call on Wednesday afternoon, February 18, 1948, in the troubled city of Jerusalem. Butrus Sowmy, librarian and monk of Saint Mark's Monastery in the Armenian quarter of the Old City of Jerusalem, was calling John C. Trever, acting director of the American Schools of Oriental Research (ASOR). Sowmy had been preparing a catalog of the monastery's collection of rare books. Among them he found some scrolls in ancient Hebrew which, he said, had been in the monastery for about forty years. Could ASOR supply him with some information for the catalog?

The following day Sowmy and his brother brought a suitcase containing five scrolls or parts of scrolls wrapped in an Arabic newspaper. Pulling back the end of one of the scrolls Trever discovered that it was written in a clear square Hebrew script. He copied several lines from that scroll, carefully examined three others, but was unable to unroll the fifth because it was too brittle. After the Syrians left, Trever told the story of the scrolls to William H. Brownlee, an ASOR fellow. Trever further noted in the lines he had copied from the first scroll the double occurrence of an unusual negative construction in Hebrew. In addition, the Hebrew script of the scrolls was more archaic than anything he had ever seen.

Trever then visited Saint Mark's Monastery. There he was introduced to the Syrian Archbishop Athanasius Samuel, who gave him permission to photograph the scrolls. Trever and Brownlee compared the style of handwriting on the scrolls with a photograph of the Nash Papyrus, a scroll inscribed with the Ten Commandments and Deuteronomy 6:4 and dated by scholars in the first or second century B.C. The two ASOR scholars concluded that the script on the newly found manuscripts belonged to the same period. When ASOR director Millar Burrows returned to Jerusalem from Baghdad a few days later, he was shown the scrolls, and the three men continued their investigation. Only then did the

Syrians reveal that the scrolls had been purchased the year before, in 1947, and had not been in the monastery for forty years as was first reported.

How had the Syrians come to possess the scrolls? Before that question could be answered, many fragmentary accounts had to be pieced together. Sometime during the winter of 1946–47 three Bedouins were tending their sheep and goats near a spring in the vicinity of Wadi Qumran. One of the herdsmen, throwing a rock through a small opening in the cliff, heard the sound of the rock evidently shattering an earthenware jar inside. Another Bedouin later lowered himself into the cave and found ten tall jars lining the walls. Three manuscripts (one of them in four pieces) stored in two of the jars were removed from the cave and offered to an antiquities dealer in Bethlehem.

Several months later the Bedouins secured four more scrolls (one of them in two pieces) from the cave and sold them to another dealer in Bethlehem. During Holy Week in 1947 Saint Mark's Syrian Orthodox Monastery in Jerusalem was informed of the four scrolls, and Metropolitan Athanasius Samuel offered to buy them. The sale was not completed, however, until July 1947 when the four scrolls were bought by the Monastery. They included a complete Isaiah scroll, a commentary on Habakkuk, a scroll containing a Manual of Discipline of the religious community at Qumran, and the Genesis Apocryphon (originally thought to be the aprocryphal book of Lamech but actually an Aramaic paraphrase of Genesis).

In November and December of 1947 an Armenian antiquities dealer in Jerusalem informed the late E. L. Sukenik, Professor of Archaeology at the Hebrew University in Jerusalem, of the first three scrolls found in the cave by the Bedouins. Sukenik then secured the three scrolls and two jars from the antiquities dealer in Bethlehem. They included an incomplete scroll of Isaiah, the

Hymns of Thanksgiving (containing twelve columns of original psalms), and the War Scroll. (That scroll, also known as "The War of the Children of Darkness," describes a war, actual or spiritual, of the tribes of Levi, Judah, and Benjamin against the Moabites and Edomites.)

On April 1, 1948, the first news release appeared in newspapers around the world, followed by another news release on April 26 by Sukenik about the manuscripts he had already acquired at the Hebrew University. In 1949 Athanasius Samuel brought the four scrolls from Saint Mark's Monastery to the United States. They were exhibited in various places and finally were purchased on July 1, 1954, in New York for $250,000 by Sukenik's son for the nation of Israel and sent to the Hebrew University in Jerusalem. Today they are on display in the "Shrine of the Book" Museum in West Jerusalem.

Because of the importance of the initial discovery of the Dead Sea Scrolls, both archaeologists and Bedouins continued their search for more manuscripts. Early in 1949, G. Lankester Harding, director of antiquities for the Kingdom of Jordan, and Roland G. de Vaux, of the Dominic Ecole Biblique in Jerusalem, excavated the cave (designated cave one or 1Q) where the initial discovery was made. Several hundred caves were explored the same year. So far eleven caves in the Wadi Qumran have yielded treasures. Almost 600 manuscripts have been recovered, about 200 of which are biblical material. The fragments number between 50,000 and 60,000 pieces. About 85 percent of the fragments are leather; the other 15 percent are papyrus. The fact that most of the manuscripts are leather contributed to the problem of their preservation.

Probably the cave next most important to cave one is cave four (4Q), which has yielded about 40,000 fragments of 400 different manuscripts, 100 of which are biblical. Every book of the Old Testament except Esther is represented.

In addition to the biblical manuscripts the discoveries have included Apocryphal works such as Hebrew and Aramaic fragments of Tobit, Ecclesiasticus, and the Letter of Jeremiah. Fragments were also found of Pseudepigraphal books such as 1 Enoch, the Book of Jubilees, and the Testament of Levi.

Many sectarian scrolls peculiar to the religious community that lived at Qumran were also found. They furnish historical background on the nature of pre-Christian Judaism and help fill in the gaps of intertestamental history. One of the scrolls, the Damascus Document, had originally turned up in Cairo, but manuscripts of it have now been found at Qumran. The Manual of Discipline was one of the seven scrolls from cave one. Fragmentary manuscripts of it have been found in other caves. The document gives the group's entrance requirements, plus regulations governing life in the Qumran community. The Thanksgiving Hymns include some thirty hymns, probably composed by one individual.

There were also many commentaries on different books of the Old Testament. The Habakkuk Commentary was a copy of the first two chapters of Habakkuk in Hebrew accompanied by a verse-by-verse commentary. The commentary gives many details about an apocalyptic figure called the "Teacher of Righteousness" who is persecuted by a wicked priest.

A unique discovery was made in cave three (3Q) in 1952. It was a scroll of copper, measuring about eight feet long and a foot wide. Because it was brittle, it was not opened until 1966, and then only by cutting it into strips. It contained an inventory of some sixty locations where treasures of gold, silver, and incense were hidden. Archaeologists have not been able to find any of it. That list of treasures, perhaps from the Jerusalem temple, may have been stored in the cave by Zealots (a revolutionary Jewish political party) during their struggle with the Romans in A.D. 66–70.

During the Six-Day War in June 1967, Sukenik's son, Yigael Yadin of the Hebrew University, acquired a Qumran document called the Temple Scroll. That tightly rolled scroll measures twenty-eight feet and is the longest scroll found so far in the Qumran area. A major portion of it is devoted to statutes of the kings and matters of defense. It also describes sacrificial feasts and rules of cleanliness. Almost half of the scroll gives detailed instructions for building a future temple, supposedly revealed by God to the scroll's author.

Scroll Discoveries at Wadi Murabba'at In 1951 Bedouins discovered more manuscripts in caves in the Wadi Murabba'at, which extends southeast from Bethlehem toward the Dead Sea, about eleven miles south of Qumran. Four caves were excavated there in 1952 under Harding and de Vaux. They yielded biblical documents and important materials, such as letters and coins, from the time of the Second Jewish Revolt under Bar Kochba in A.D. 132–135. Among the biblical manuscripts was a scroll containing a Hebrew text of the Minor Prophets, dating from the second century A.D. This manuscript corresponds almost perfectly to the Masoretic Text, hinting that by the second century, a standard consonantal text was already taking shape. Also found in Wadi Murabba'at were fragments of the Pentateuch (the five books of Moses) and Isaiah.

The Value of the Dead Sea Scrolls Apart from the Dead Sea Scrolls, ancient witnesses to the Hebrew Old Testament that are actually written in the Hebrew language are almost nonexistent. Because of this, the Dead Sea Scrolls may easily be one of the greatest archaeological finds of all time. They take us a thousand years deeper into the history of the Hebrew Old Testament, giving us the ability to assess all the other ancient witnesses with greater understanding.

The most frequently represented Old Testament books among the Dead Sea Scrolls are Genesis, Exodus, Deuteronomy, Psalms, and Isaiah. The oldest text is a fragment of Exodus dating from about 250 B.C. The Isaiah scroll dates from about 100 B.C. These ancient witnesses only confirm the accuracy of the Masoretic Text and the care with which the Jewish scribes handled the Scriptures. Except for a few instances where spelling and grammar differ between the Dead Sea Scrolls and the Masoretic Text, the two are amazingly similar. The differences do not warrant any major changes in the substance of the Old Testament. Yet these discoveries are helping biblical scholars gain a clearer understanding of the text at an earlier time in its history and development.

THE NASH PAPYRUS

Prior to the discovery of the Dead Sea Scrolls, the oldest Hebrew witness to the Old Testament was the Nash Papyrus. This manuscript was acquired in Egypt by W. L. Nash in 1902 and was donated to the Cambridge University Library. This manuscript contains a damaged copy of the Ten Commandments (Exod. 20:2-17), part of Deuteronomy 5:6-21, and also the *Shema* (Deut. 6:4ff.). This is clearly a collection of devotional and liturgical passages, and has been dated to the same period as the Dead Sea Scrolls, between 150 B.C. and A.D. 68.

THE CAIRO GENIZA FRAGMENTS

Near the end of the nineteenth century, many fragments from the sixth to the eighth centuries were found in an old synagogue in Cairo, Egypt, which had been Saint Michael's Church until A.D. 882. They were found there in a geniza, a storage room where worn or faulty manuscripts were hidden until they could be disposed of properly. This geniza had apparently been walled off and forgotten until its recent discovery. In this small room, as many as 200,000 fragments were preserved, including biblical texts in

Hebrew and Aramaic. The fact that the biblical fragments date from the fifth century A.D. makes them invaluable for shedding light on the development of the Masoretic work prior to the standardization instituted by the great Masoretes of Tiberias.

THE SAMARITAN PENTATEUCH

Exactly when the Samaritan community separated from the larger Jewish community is a matter of dispute. But at some point during the postexilic period (c. 540–100 B.C.), a clear division between Samaritans and Jews was marked off. At this point, the Samaritans, who accepted only the Pentateuch as canonical, apparently canonized their own particular version of the Scriptures.

A copy of the Samaritan Pentateuch came to the attention of scholars in 1616. Initially, it caused a great deal of excitement, but most of the early assessments of its value to textual criticism were negative. It differed from the Masoretic Text in some six thousand instances, and many judged this to be the result of sectarian differences between Samaritans and Jews. By some, it was simply viewed as a sectarian revision of the Masoretic Text.

After further assessment, however, it became clear that the Samaritan Pentateuch represented a text of much earlier origin than the Masoretic Text. And although a few of the distinctions of the Samaritan Pentateuch were clearly the result of sectarian concerns, most of the differences were neutral in this respect. Many of them had more to do with popularizing the text, rather than altering its meaning in any way. The fact that the Samaritan Pentateuch had much in common with the Septuagint, some of the Dead Sea Scrolls, and the New Testament, revealed that most of its differences with the Masoretic Text were not due to sectarian differences. More likely, they were due to the use of a different textual base, which was probably in wide use in the ancient Near East until well after the time of Christ. This realization, though not solving any real problems, did much to illustrate the complexity of the Old Testament textual tradition that existed before the Masoretic standard was completed.

THE SEPTUAGINT (LXX)

The Septuagint is the oldest Greek translation of the Old Testament, its witness being significantly older than that of the Masoretic Text. According to tradition, the Septuagint Pentateuch was translated by a team of seventy scholars in Alexandria, Egypt. (Hence its common designation LXX, the Roman numerals for 70.) The Jewish community in Egypt spoke Greek, not Hebrew, so a Greek translation of the Old Testament was sincerely needed by that community of Jews. The exact date of translation is not known, but evidence indicates that the Septuagint Pentateuch was completed in the third century B.C. The rest of the Old Testament was probably translated over a long period of time, as it clearly represents the work of many different scholars.

The value of the Septuagint to textual criticism varies widely from book to book. It might be said that the Septuagint is not a single version but a collection of versions made by various authors, who differed greatly in their methods and their knowledge of Hebrew. The translations of the individual books are in no way uniform. Many books are translated almost literally, while others like Job and Daniel are quite dynamic. So the value of each book for textual criticism must be assessed on a book-by-book basis. The books translated literally are clearly more helpful in making comparisons with the Masoretic Text than the more dynamic ones.

The content of some books is significantly different when comparing the Septuagint and the Masoretic Text. For example, the Septuagint's Jeremiah is missing significant portions found in the Masoretic Text, and the order of the text is significantly different as well. What these differences actually mean is difficult to know with certainty. It has been conjectured that the Septuagint is simply a poor translation and is therefore missing portions of the original Hebrew. But these same differences could also indicate that editorial additions and changes worked their way into the Masoretic Text during its long history of development. It is also possible that there were a number of valid textual traditions at that time, one followed by the Septuagint, and another followed by the Masoretic Text. This illustrates some of the difficulties that arise while doing Old Testament textual criticism.

The Septuagint was the standard Old Testament text used by the early Christian church. The expanding Gentile church needed a translation in the common language of the time—Greek. By the time of Christ, even among the Jews, a majority of the people spoke Aramaic and Greek, not Hebrew. The New Testament writers evidence their inclination to the Septuagint by using it when quoting the Old Testament.

OTHER GREEK VERSIONS

Because of the broad acceptance and use of the Septuagint among Christians, the Jews renounced it in favor of a number of other Greek versions. Aquila, a proselyte and disciple of Rabbi Akiba, produced a new translation around A.D. 130. In the spirit of his teacher, Aquila wrote an extremely literal translation, often to the point of communicating poorly in Greek. This literal approach, however, gained this version wide acceptance among Jews. Only fragments of this version have survived, but its literal nature reveals much about its Hebrew textual base.

Symmachus produced a new version around A.D. 170 designed not only for accuracy, but also to communicate well in the Greek language. His version has survived only in a few Hexapla fragments. A third Greek version came from Theodocian, a Jewish proselyte from the end of the second century A.D. His version was apparently a revision of an earlier Greek version, possibly the

Septuagint. This version has only survived in a few early Christian quotations, though it was once widely used.

The Christian theologian Origen arranged the Old Testament with six parallel versions for comparison in his *Hexapla*. In it, he included the Hebrew text, the Hebrew transliterated into Greek, Aquila's version, Symmachus's version, the Septuagint, and Theodocian's version. Unfortunately, this wonderful compilation has survived only in a few small fragments. Other Greek translations mentioned by Origen and otherwise unknown are the *Quinta*, the *Sexta,* and the *Septima.*

THE ARAMAIC TARGUMS

The Aramaic Targums were Aramaic translations of the Hebrew Old Testament. Since the common language of the Jews during the postexilic period was Aramaic and not Hebrew, a need for Aramaic translations of the Hebrew Bible arose. Hebrew remained the language of scholarly religious circles, and translations for the common people were often spurned by the religious leadership. But over time, the reading of the Scriptures and commentaries in Aramaic became an accepted practice in the synagogues.

The purpose of these translations was to get the message across and to edify the people. Thus, the translations were extremely interpretive. The translators paraphrased, added explanatory glosses, and often boldly reinterpreted the text according to the theological biases of their time. They sought to relate the Bible text to contemporary life and political circumstances. Because of the dynamic approach evident in these translations, their use in textual criticism is limited, but they do add to the welter of evidence to be collected and collated in order to reconstruct the text of the Old Testament.

THE SYRIAC VERSION

Another version worthy of note is the Syriac Version. This version was in common use in the Syriac (eastern Aramaic) church, which designated it the Peshitta, meaning "the simple or plain." What they intended by this designation is difficult to discern. It may indicate that it was intended for popular consumption, or that it avoided adding explanatory glosses and other additions, or perhaps that it was not an annotated text, as was the annotated Syro-Hexapla then in use by the same community.

The literary history of the Syriac Version is not known, though it is clearly complex. Some have identified it as the recasting of an Aramaic Targum in Syriac, while others claim it has a more independent origin. Some connect it to the conversion of the leaders of Adiabene (east of the Tigris River) to the Jewish faith during the first century A.D. Their need for an Old Testament could have brought about the development of a version in their common tongue—Syriac. Still others connect it to Christian origins. Obvious later revisions to the *Peshitta* complicate matters even more. More study needs to be done to assess the nature of this version before it can lend much insight into the history of the Hebrew text.

THE LATIN VERSIONS

Latin was a dominant language in western regions of the Roman Empire from well before the time of Christ. It was in the western regions of southern Gaul and North Africa that the first Latin translations of the Bible appeared. Around A.D. 160 Tertullian apparently used a Latin version of the Scriptures. Not long after this, the Old Latin text seems to have been in circulation, evidenced by Cyprian's use of it before his death in A.D. 258. The Old Latin version was translated from the Septuagint. Due to its early date, it is valuable as a witness to the early Septuagint text, before later editors obscured the nature of the original. It also indirectly gives clues to the nature of the Hebrew text at the time of the Septuagint's translation. Complete manuscripts of the Old Latin text have not survived. After the completion of Jerome's Latin version, the Vulgate, the older text fell into disuse. Enough fragmentary manuscripts of this version do exist, however, to lend significant information to the early Old Testament text.

Around the third century A.D., Latin began to replace Greek as the language of learning in the larger Roman world. A uniform, reliable text was badly needed for theological and liturgical uses. To fill this need, Pope Damasus I (A.D. 336–384) commissioned Jerome, an eminent scholar in Latin, Greek, and Hebrew, to undertake the translation. Jerome began his work as a translation from the Greek Septuagint, considered inspired by many church authorities, including Augustine. But later, and at the risk of great criticism, he turned to the Hebrew text being used in Palestine at that time as the base text for his translation. During the years between A.D. 390 and 405 Jerome wrote his Latin translation of the Hebrew Old Testament. Yet, despite Jerome's return to the original Hebrew, he was heavily dependent on the various Greek versions as aids in translation. As a result the Vulgate reflects the other Greek and Latin translations as much as the underlying Hebrew text. The value of the Vulgate for textual criticism is its pre-Masoretic witness to the Hebrew Bible, though this was compromised to a great extent by the influence of already existing Greek translations.

VARIOUS OTHER VERSIONS

There are various other ancient translations. Most of them were dependent primarily on the Septuagint, including the Coptic versions in Egypt and the related Ethiopic version in Ethiopia. These are valuable as early witnesses to the Septuagint. The Armenian version used the Syriac Peshitta as its textual base and could lend significant information with respect to its development. After the rise of Islam and the spread of the Arabic language throughout much of the Near East, Arabic translations were made for a growing Arabic-speaking population. Translation into Arabic was also undertaken from the Septuagint, but the lateness of these translations (c. A.D. 900) make them of little value to Old Testament textual criticism.

PATRISTIC QUOTATIONS

Additional textual evidence can be drawn from quotations found in the early writers known as the church fathers. The range of such quotations, covering most of the New Testament as well as parts of the Old, provides evidence on the history of transmission of variant readings and text types.

The Transmission of the Old Testament

Reconstruction of the history of the transmission of the text is an important element in evaluating variant readings. Material from a wide variety of sources must be combined in order to arrive at even a tentative reconstruction of the text. A brief sketch of scholarly opinion follows.

The early history of the Old Testament text as reflected in the Dead Sea Scrolls, the Samaritan Pentateuch, the Septuagint, and the ancient Hebrew text shows a remarkable fluidity and diversity. Evidently the standardizing process did not begin at the earliest stages. For example, the materials from the Qumran community, where the Dead Sea Scrolls were found, do not reflect any frustration with varying texts within that community.

Some scholars have attempted to account for such diversity by theories of local texts. They theorize that that various localities in the Near East (e.g., Babylon, Palestine, Egypt) had differing text types which are reflected in the various surviving Hebrew texts and versions. Other scholars account for the diversity by recognizing a precanonical fluidity. They feel that until the process of canonization was complete, accurate reproduction of the manuscripts was not viewed as very important. It should be noted, however, that the basic text that modern scholarship has identified as closest to the original was among the Dead Sea texts (for example, the large Isaiah scroll).

Destruction of the temple in A.D. 70 provided an impetus for standardization of the consonantal text. The texts found at Wadi Murabba'at, copied during the first centuries A.D., reflect the new stage. The scholars initially reporting on the discovery were disappointed to find in these texts so few variations from the standard Masoretic Text. To scholars, the very early texts from the Dead Sea Scroll discoveries had become the standard consonantal text to the exclusion of other variants. Scholars have now gone so far as to identify the only slightly later Wadi Murabba'at texts as a "Proto-Masoretic" standard. This seems to indicate that the Hebrew consonantal text was already approaching a standard in Palestine by the first centuries A.D.

Standardization as practiced by the Masoretes meant identifying one text as normative and copying carefully from that text. It also meant correcting existing texts by the normative text. The Hebrew text, of course, was written with consonants alone, not with consonants *and* vowels as we write English.

The next stage in the transmission of the Old Testament text was standardization of punctuation and vowel patterns. That process, which began fairly early in the New Testament period, extended over a period of one thousand years. A long series of Masoretes provided annotations known as *Masora,* which, in Hebrew, means "tradition." Two different motivations are evident in their work. One was their concern for accurate reproduction of the consonantal text. For that purpose a collection of annotations (on irregular forms, abnormal patterns, the number of times a form or word was used, and other matters) was gathered and inserted in the margins or at the end of the text.

A second concern of the Masoretes was to record and standardize the vocalization of the consonantal text for reading purposes. Up until this point, scribes had been prohibited against inserting vowels to make the vocalization of the text clear. Because of this, a proper reading of the text depended on the oral tradition passed down from generation to generation. The origins of vocalization reflect differences between Babylon and Palestine. The Tiberian Masoretes (scholars working in Tiberias in Palestine) provided the most complete and exact system of vocalization. The earliest dated manuscript from that tradition is a codex of the Prophets from the Karaite synagogue of Cairo dated A.D. 896. Today the standard Hebrew text of the Old Testament, *Biblia Hebraica Stuttgartensia,* an updated version of Kittel's *Biblia Hebraica,* is constructed on the basis of the Tiberian Masoretic tradition.

Standardization of both the consonantal text and vocalization succeeded so well that the manuscripts that have survived display a remarkable agreement. Most of the variants, being minor and attributable to scribal error, do not affect interpretation.

The Methodology of Old Testament Textual Criticism

The search for an adequate methodology to handle the many variant readings found in manuscripts is inseparably intertwined with our understanding of the history of transmission. The basic issue in textual criticism is the method used to decide the relative value of those variant readings. Many factors must be evaluated in order to arrive at a valid decision.

DATING MANUSCRIPTS

The date of a manuscript is important because it places that text within a historical framework, a factor that can often decide the primacy of one variant over another. The process of dating the Dead Sea Scrolls found at Wadi Qumran serves as a good case study for the various methods employed by scholars today.

Early conclusions about the antiquity of the first Dead Sea Scrolls were not accepted by everyone. Some scholars were convinced that the scrolls were of medieval origin. A series of questions relate to the dating problem. When were the texts at Qumran composed? When were they deposited in the caves? Most scholars believe the manuscripts were placed in the caves by members of the Qumran community when Roman legions were besieging Jewish strongholds. That was shortly before the destruction of Jerusalem in A.D. 70.

Careful study of the contents of a document sometimes reveals its authorship and the date when it was written. An example of using such *internal evidence* for dating a non-biblical work is found in the Habakkuk commentary. It gives hints about the people and events in the days of the commentary's author, not in the days of the prophet Habakkuk. The commentator described the enemies of God's people as the *Kittim*. Originally that word denoted Cyprus, but later came to be more generally the Greek islands and the coasts of the eastern Mediterranean. In Daniel 11:30 the term is used prophetically, and most scholars seem to identify the *Kittim* with the Romans. Thus the Habakkuk commentary was probably written about the time of the Roman capture of Palestine under Pompey in 63 B.C.

Another important item to consider when dating a manuscript is its copy date. Although the vast majority of manuscripts are undated, it is often possible to determine when a manuscript was written by paleography, the study of ancient handwriting. That was the method initially employed by Trever when he compared the script of the Isaiah Scroll with the Nash Papyrus, thus dating it to the pre-Christian era. His conclusions were confirmed by the late William F. Albright, then the foremost American archaeologist. During the time of the Babylonian captivity, the square script became the normal style of writing in Hebrew (as well as in Aramaic, a cousin of Hebrew). The evidence of paleography clearly dates the majority of the Qumran scrolls in the period between 200 B.C. and A.D. 200.

Archaeology provides another kind of external evidence. The pottery discovered at Qumran dates from the late Hellenistic and early Roman periods (200 B.C.–A.D. 100). Earthenware articles and ornaments point to the same period. Several hundred coins were found in jars dating from the Graeco-Roman period. A crack in one of the buildings is attributed to an earthquake that, according to Josephus (a Jewish historian who wrote during the first century A.D.), occurred in 31 B.C. The excavations at Khirbet Qumran indicate that the general period of their occupation was from about 135 B.C. to A.D. 68, the year the Zealot revolt was crushed by Rome.

Finally, radiocarbon analysis has contributed to dating the finds. Radiocarbon analysis is a method of dating material from the amount of radioactive carbon remaining in it. The process is also known as carbon-14 dating. Applied to the linen cloth in which the scrolls were wrapped, the analysis gave a date of A.D. 33 plus or minus 200 years. A later test bracketed the date between 250 B.C. and A.D. 50. Although there may be questions concerning the relation of the linen wrappings to the date of the scrolls themselves, the carbon-14 test agrees with the conclusions of both paleography and archaeology. The general period, then, in which the Dead Sea Scrolls can be safely dated is between about 150 B.C. and A.D. 68.

READING MANUSCRIPTS

Modern science has provided a number of aids for deciphering a manuscript. Scientific dating procedures help to determine the age of the writing material. Chemical techniques help clarify writing that has deteriorated. Ultraviolet light enables a scholar to see traces of ink (carbon) in a manuscript even after the surface writing has been effaced.

Each manuscript must be studied as a whole, for each has a "personality." It is important to identify the characteristic errors, characteristic carelessness or carefulness, and other peculiarities of the scribe(s) who copied the material. Then the manuscript must be compared with other manuscripts to identify the "family" tradition with which it agrees. Preservation of common errors or insertions in the text is a clue to relationships. All possible details of date, place of origin, and authorship must be ascertained.

Scribal errors fall into several distinct categories. The first large category is that of *unintentional errors*. (1) Confusion of similar consonants and the transposition of two consonants are frequent errors. (2) Corruptions also resulted from an incorrect division of words (many early manuscripts omitted spaces between words in order to save space). (3) Confusion of sounds occurred particularly when one scribe read to a group of scribes making multiple copies. (4) In the Old Testament, the method of vocalization (addition of vowels to the consonantal text) created some errors. (5) Omissions of a letter, word, or phrase created new readings. (6) Repetition of a letter, word, or even a whole phrase was also common. Omission (called haplography) or repetition (called dittography) could be caused by the eye of a scribe slipping from one word to a similar word or ending. Omissions by *homoioteleuton* (Greek meaning "similar endings") were also quite common. This occurred when two words that were identical, similar, or had identical endings were found close to each other, and the eye of the copyist moved from the first to the second, omitting the words between them. (7) In the Old Testament, errors were at times caused by the use of consonants as vowel letters in some ancient texts. Copyists unaware of this usage of vowel letters would copy them in as aberrant consonants. Normally unintentional errors are fairly easy to identify because they create nonsense readings.

Intentional errors are much more difficult to identify and evaluate. Harmonizations from similar materials occurred with regularity. Difficult readings were subject to improvement by a thinking scribe. Objectionable expressions were sometimes eliminated or smoothed. Occasionally synonyms were employed. Conflation (resolving a discrepancy between two variant readings by including both of them) often appears.

Awareness of these common problems is the first step in detecting and eliminating the more obvious errors and identifying and eliminating the peculiarities of a particular scribe. Then more subtle criteria for identifying the reading most likely to be the original must be employed. Procedures for applying such criteria are similar in both Old Testament and New Testament work.

GENERAL METHODOLOGICAL PRINCIPLES

Through the work of textual critics in the last several centuries, certain basic principles have evolved. The primary principles for the Old Testament can be briefly summarized.

1. The basic text for primary consideration is the Masoretic Text because of the careful standardization it represents. That text is compared with the testimony of the ancient versions. The Septuagint, by reason of age and basic faithfulness to the Hebrew text, carries significant weight in all decisions. The Targums (Aramaic translations) also reflect the Hebrew base but exhibit a tendency to expansion and paraphrase. The Syriac (Peshitta), Vulgate (Latin), Old Latin, and Coptic versions add indirect evidence, although translations are not always clear witnesses in technical details. Use of such versions does enable scholars to use comparative philology in textual decisions and thus expose early errors for which the original reading probably has not survived.

2. The reading that best explains the origin of other variants is preferable. Information from reconstruction of the history of transmission often provides additional insight. Knowledge of typical scribal errors enables the critic to make an educated decision on the sequence of variants.

3. The shorter reading is preferable. The scribes frequently added material in order to solve style or syntax problems and seldom abridged or condensed material.

4. The more difficult reading is more likely to be the original one. This principle is closely related to the third. Scribes did not intentionally create more complex readings. Unintentional errors are usually easy to identify. Thus the easier reading is normally suspect as a scribal alteration.

5. Readings that are not harmonized or assimilated to similar passages are preferable. Copyists had a tendency to correct material on the basis of similar material elsewhere (sometimes even unconsciously).

6. When all else fails, the textual critic must resort to conjectural emendation. To make an "educated guess" requires intimate acquaintance with the Hebrew language, familiarity with the author's style, and an understanding of culture, customs, and theology that might color the passage. Use of conjecture must be limited to those passages in which the original reading has definitely not been transmitted to us.

Conclusion

It should be remembered that textual criticism operates only when two or more readings are possible for a specific word or phrase. For most of the biblical text a single reading has been transmitted. Elimination of scribal errors and intentional changes leaves only a small percentage of the text about which any questions occur. Writing in 1940, textual scholar Sir Frederic Kenyon concluded:

> The interval then between the dates of original composition and the earliest extant evidence becomes so small as to be in

fact negligible, and the last foundation for any doubt that the Scriptures have come down to us substantially as they were written has now been removed. Both the *authenticity* and the *general integrity* of the books of the New Testament may be regarded as finally established.

Similar confidence is expressed in the text of the Old Testament.

The field of textual criticism is complex, requiring the gathering and skillful use of a wide variety of information. Because it deals with the authoritative source of revelation for all Christians, textual argumentation has often been accompanied by emotion.

Yet in spite of controversy, great progress has been made, particularly in the last century. Refinement of methodology has greatly aided our understanding of the accumulated materials. Additional aid has come from accumulations of information in related fields of study such as church history, biblical theology, and the history of Christian thought.

Collection and organization of all variant readings have enabled modern textual critics to give strong assurance that the Word of God has been transmitted in accurate and dependable form. Although variant readings have become obvious through the publication of so many manuscripts, inadequate, inferior, and secondary readings have been largely eliminated. In relatively few places is conjectural emendation necessary. In matters pertaining to the Christian's salvation, clear and unmistakable transmission provides authoritative answers. Christians are thus in debt to the textual critics who have worked, and are working, to provide a dependable biblical text.

BIBLIOGRAPHY

Brownlee, W. H. *The Meaning of the Qumran Scrolls for the Bible,* 1964.
Burrows, M. *The Dead Sea Scrolls,* 1956; and *More Light on the Dead Sea Scrolls,* 1958.

Cross, F. M. *The Ancient Library of Qumran and Modern Biblical Studies,* 1961.

Cross, F. M., and S. Talmon, eds. *Qumran and the History of the Biblical Text,* 1975.

Fitzmeyer, J. A. *The Dead Sea Scrolls: Major Publications and Tools,* 1975.

Kenyon, Frederic G. *Our Bible and the Ancient Manuscripts* (revised), 1958.

LaSor, W. S. *Bibliography of the Dead Sea Scrolls,* 1958.

Milik, J. T. *Ten Years of Discovery in the Wilderness of Judaea,* 1959.

Vaux, R. de *Archaeology and the Dead Sea Scrolls,* 1973.

Vermes, G. *The Dead Sea Scrolls in English,* 1975.

Waltke, Bruce K. and M. O'Connor. *Biblical Hebrew Syntax,* 1990.

Wurthwein, Ernst. *The Text of the Old Testament,* 1979.

Note: Some of the material in this essay was adapted from unpublished articles written for Tyndale House Publishers by Morris A. Weigelt (Old Testament textual criticism) and Paul S. Haik (Dead Sea Scrolls).

Texts and Manuscripts
of the New Testament
Philip W. Comfort

An Introduction to Important New Testament Manuscripts

Because not one original writing (autograph) of any New Testament book still exists, we depend on copies for reconstructing the original text. According to most scholars, the closest copy to an autograph is a papyrus manuscript designated P52, dated around 110–125, containing a few verses of John 18 (31–34, 37–38). This fragment, only twenty to thirty years removed from the autograph, was part of one of the earliest copies of John's Gospel. A few scholars, however, believe that there is an even earlier manuscript, designated P46. This manuscript, known as the Chester Beatty Papyrus II, containing all of Paul's epistles except the Pastorals, has recently been dated in the late first century. If this dating is accurate, then we have an entire collection of Paul's epistles that must have been made only twenty to thirty years after Paul wrote most of the Epistles. We possess many other early copies of various parts of the New Testament; several of the papyrus manuscripts are dated from the late second century to the early fourth century. Some of the most important New Testament papyrus manuscripts are as follows:

THE OXYRHYNCHUS PAPYRI

Beginning in 1898 Grenfell and Hunt discovered thousands of papyrus fragments in the ancient rubbish heaps of Oxyrhynchus,

Egypt. This site yielded volumes of papyrus fragments containing all sorts of written material (literature, business and legal contracts, letters, etc.) as well as over thirty-five manuscripts containing portions of the New Testament. Some of the more noteworthy papyrus manuscripts are P1 (Matthew 1), P5 (John 1, 16), P13 (Hebrews 2–5, 10–12), and P22 (John 15–16).

THE CHESTER BEATTY PAPYRI
(named after the owner, Chester Beatty)

These manuscripts were purchased from a dealer in Egypt during the 1930s by Chester Beatty and by the University of Michigan. The three manuscripts in this collection are very early and contain a large portion of the New Testament text. P45 (second century) contains portions of all four Gospels and Acts; P46 (late first century to early second century) has almost all of Paul's epistles and Hebrews; and P47 (third century) contains Revelation 9–17.

THE BODMER PAPYRI
(named after the owner, M. Martin Bodmer)

These manuscripts were purchased from a dealer in Egypt during the 1950s and 1960s. The three important papyri in this collection are P66 (c. 175, containing almost all of John), P72 (third century, having all of 1 and 2 Peter and Jude), and P75 (c. 200, containing large parts of Luke 3—John 15).

During the twentieth century, nearly a hundred papyrus manuscripts containing portions of the New Testament were discovered. In previous centuries, especially the nineteenth, other manuscripts were discovered—several of which date in the fourth or fifth century. The most noteworthy manuscripts are as follows:

CODEX SINAITICUS—designated $\aleph$ or aleph
This manuscript was discovered by Constantin von Tischendorf in St. Catherine's Monastery situated at the foot of Mount Sinai. It

dates around A.D. 350, contains the entire New Testament, and provides an early and fairly reliable witness to the New Testament autographs.

CODEX VATICANUS—designated B

This manuscript had been in the Vatican's library since at least 1481, but it was not made available to scholars, like Tischendorf and Tregelles, until the middle of the nineteenth century. This codex, dated slightly earlier than Sinaiticus, has both the Old Testament and New Testament in Greek, excluding the last part of the New Testament (from Hebrews 9:15 to the end of Revelation) and the Pastoral Epistles. For the most part, scholars have commended Codex Vaticanus for being one of the most trustworthy witnesses to the New Testament text.

CODEX ALEXANDRINUS—designated A

This is a fifth century manuscript, displaying nearly all of the New Testament. It is known to be a very reliable witness to the General Epistles and Revelation.

CODEX EPHRAEMI RESCRIPTUS—designated C

This is a fifth century document called a palimpsest. (A palimpsest is a manuscript in which the original writing has been erased and then written over.) Through the use of chemicals and painstaking effort, a scholar can read the original writing underneath the overprinted text. Tischendorf did this with a manuscript called Codex Ephraemi Rescriptus, which had the sermons of Ephraemi written over a New Testament text.

CODEX BEZAE—designated D

This is a fifth century manuscript named after Theodore Beza, its discoverer, containing the Gospels and Acts and displaying a text quite different from the manuscripts mentioned above.

CODEX WASHINGTONIANUS

(or, *The Freer Gospels*—named after its owner, Charles Freer)—designated W

This is a fifth century manuscript containing all four Gospels housed in the Smithsonian Institution in Washington, D.C.

Prior to the fifteenth century when Johannes Gutenberg invented movable type for the printing press, all copies of any work of literature were made by hand (hence, the name "manuscript"). At present, we have more than six thousand manuscript copies of the Greek New Testament or portions thereof. No other work of Greek literature can boast of such numbers. Homer's *Iliad,* the greatest of all Greek classical works, is extant in about 650 manuscripts; and Euripides' tragedies exist in about 330 manuscripts. The numbers on all the other works of Greek literature are far less. Furthermore, it must be said that the amount of time between the original composition and the next surviving manuscript is far less for the New Testament than for any other work in Greek literature. The lapse for most classical Greek works is about eight hundred to a thousand years; whereas the lapse for many books in the New Testament is around one hundred years. Because of the abundant wealth of manuscripts and because several of the manuscripts are dated in the early centuries of the church, New Testament textual scholars have a great advantage over classical textual scholars. The New Testament scholars have the resources to reconstruct the original text of the New Testament with great accuracy, and they have produced some excellent editions of the Greek New Testament.

Finally, it must be said that, although there are certainly differences in many of the New Testament manuscripts, not one fundamental doctrine of the Christian faith rests on a disputed reading. Frederic Kenyon, a renowned paleographer and textual critic, affirmed this when he said, "The Christian can take the whole Bible in his hand and say without fear or hesitation that he holds in it the true Word of God, handed down without essential loss from generation to generation throughout the centuries" (*Our Bible and the Ancient Manuscripts,* 55).

A History of the Recovery of the Original Text of the New Testament: An Overview

When we speak of the original text, we are referring to the "published" text—that is, the text as it was in its final edited form and released for circulation in the Christian community. For some books of the New Testament, there is little difference between the original composition and the published text. After the author wrote or dictated his work, he (or an associate) made the final editorial corrections and then released it for distribution. As is the case for books published in modern times, so in ancient times the original writing of the author is not always the same as what is published—due to the editorial process. Nonetheless, the author is credited with the final edited text, and the published book is attributed to the author and considered the autograph. This autograph is the original published text.

Some scholars think it is impossible to recover the original text of the Greek New Testament because they have not been able to reconstruct the early history of textual transmission. Other modern scholars are less pessimistic but still quite guarded in affirming the possiblity. And yet others are optimistic because we possess many early manuscripts of excellent quality and because our view of the early period of textual transmission has been getting clearer and clearer.

When we speak of recovering the text of the New Testament, we are referring to individual books of the New Testament, not to the entire volume per se, because each book (or group of books—such as the Pauline Epistles) had its own unique history of textual transmission. The earliest extant copy of an entire New Testament text is the one preserved in Codex Sinaiticus (written about A.D. 350).

(Codex Vaticanus lacks the Pastoral Epistles and Revelation.) Prior to the fourth century, the New Testament was circulated in its various parts: as a single book or a group of books (such as the four Gospels or the Pauline Epistles). Manuscripts from the late first century to the third century have been found with individual books: such as Matthew (P1), Mark (P88), Luke (P69), John (P5, 22, 52, 66), Acts (P91), Revelation (P18, 47), or containing groups of books, such as the four Gospels with Acts (P45), the Pauline Epistles (P46), the Petrine Epistles and Jude (P72). Each of the books of the New Testament has had its own textual history and has been preserved with varying degrees of accuracy. Nonetheless, all of the books were altered from the original state due to the process of manual copying decade after decade and century after century. And the text of each of the books needs to be recovered.

The recovery of the Greek New Testament has had a long history. The need for recovery arose because the New Testament text was affected with many variations in its early history. In the late first and early second century, the oral traditions and the written word existed side by side with equal status—especially with respect to the material of the Gospels. Often, the text was changed by scribes attempting to conform the written message to the oral tradition or attempting to conform one Gospel account to another. By the end of the second century and into the third century many of the significant variant readings entered into the textual stream.

The early period of textual transmission, however, was not completely marred by textual infidelity and scribal liberty. There were those scribes who copied the text faithfully and reverently— that is, they recognized that they were copying a sacred text written by an apostle. The formalization of canonization did not ascribe this sacredness to the text. Canonization came about as the result of common, historical recognition of the sacredness of various New Testament books. Certain New Testament books, such as the four Gospels, Acts, and Paul's Epistles were considered inspired literature from the onset. As such, certain scribes copied them with reverential fidelity.

Other scribes, however, felt free to make "improvements" in the text—either in the interest of doctrine and harmonization or due to the influence of a competitive oral tradition. The manuscripts produced in such a manner created a kind of "popular text"—i.e., an uncontrolled text. (This text type used to be called the "Western text," but scholars now recognize this as a misnomer.)

The first ones to attempt a recovery of the original text were scribes in Alexandria and/or scribes familiar with Alexandrian scriptoral practices—for in the hellenized world there were many who had come to appreciate the scholarly practices of Alexandria. Beginning as early as the second century, the Alexandrian scribes, associated with or actually employed by the scriptorium of the great Alexandrian library and/or members of the scriptorium associated with the catechetical school at Alexandria (called the Didaskelion) were trained philologists, grammarians, and textual critics. The Alexandrians followed the kind of textual criticism begun by Aristotle, who classified manuscripts as to their date and value; and other scholars followed the practices of Zenodotus, the first librarian, with respect to textual criticism. The Alexandrians were concerned with preserving the original text of works of literature. A great amount of textual criticism was done on the *Iliad* and the *Odyssey* because these were ancient texts existing in many manuscripts. They would make text critical decisions from among many different manuscripts and then produce an archetype. The archetype was the manuscript produced officially and deposited in the library. From this were copied, and with it were collated, further manuscripts as required.

We can presume that the same kind of textual criticism was being applied to the New Testament text by Christian scribes in

Alexandria. From the second century to the fourth century, the Alexandrian scribes worked to purify the text from textual corruption. Speaking of their efforts, Gunther Zuntz wrote:

> The Alexander correctors strove, in ever repeated efforts, to keep the text current in their sphere free from the many faults that had infected it in the previous period and which tended to crop up again even after they had been obelized [i.e., marked as spurious]. These labours must time and again have been checked by persecutions and the confiscation of Christian books, and counteracted by the continuing currency of manuscripts of the older type. Nonetheless they resulted in the emergence of a type of text (as distinct from a definited edition) which served as a norm for the correctors in provincial Egyptian scriptoria. The final result was the survival of a text far superior to that of the second century, even though the revisers, being fallible human beings, rejected some of its own correct readings and introduced some faults of their own (*The Text of the Epistles,* 271-272).

The Alexandrian type of text was perpetuated century after century in a few manuscripts, such as Aleph and B (fourth century), T (fifth century), L (eighth century), 33 (ninth century), 1739 (a tenth century manuscript copied from a fourth century Alexandrian manuscript) and 579 (thirteenth century). Unfortunately, most of the Alexandrian-type manuscripts disappeared for centuries— awaiting discovery fourteen centuries later.

Concurrent with the Alexandrian text was the so-called "Western" text—which is better characterized as the popular text of the second and third centuries. In brief, this popular text was found in any kind of manuscript that was not produced by Alexandrian influences. This text, given to independence, is not as trustworthy as the Alexandrian text type. But because the Alexandrian text is known as a polished text, the "Western," or popular, text sometimes preserved the original wording. When a variant reading has the support of both "Western" texts *and* Alexandrian, it is very likely original; but when the two are divided, the Alexandrian witnesses more often preserve the original wording.

At the end of the third century, another kind of Greek text came into being and then grew in popularity until it became the dominate text type throughout Christendom. This is the text type first instigated by Lucian of Antioch, according to Jerome (in his introduction to his Latin translation of the Gospels). Lucian's text was a definite recension (i.e., a purposely created edition)—as opposed to the Alexandrian text type which came about as the result of a process wherein the Alexandrian scribes, upon comparing many manuscripts, attempted to preserve the best text—thereby serving more as textual critics than editors. Of course, the Alexandrians did do some editing—such as we would call copyediting. The Lucianic text is the outgrowth and culmination of the popular text; it is characterized by smoothness of language, which is achieved by the removal of obscurities and awkward grammatical constructions and by the conflation of variant readings. Lucian (and/or his associates) must have used many different kinds of manuscripts of varying qualities to produce a harmonized, edited New Testament text. The kind of editorial work that went into the Lucianic text is what we would call substantive editing.

Lucian's text was produced prior to the Diocletain persecution (c. 303), during which time many copies of the New Testament were confiscated and destroyed. Not long after this period of devastation, Constantine came to power and then recognized Christianity as the state religion. There was, of course, a great need for copies of the New Testament to be made and distributed to churches throughout the Mediterranean world. It was at this time that Lucian's text began to be propagated by bishops going out from the Antiochan school to churches throughout the east taking the text with them. Lucian's text soon became the standard text of the Eastern church and formed the basis for the Byzantine text—and is thus the ultimate authority for the Textus Receptus.

While Lucian was forming his recension of the New Testament text, the Alexandrian text was taking on its final shape. As was mentioned earlier, the formation of the Alexandrian text type was the result of a process (as opposed to a single editorial recension). The formation of the Alexandrian text involved minor textual criticism (i.e., selecting variant readings among various manuscripts) and copyediting (i.e., producing a readable text). There was far less tampering with the text in the Alexandrian text type than in the Lucian, and the underlying manuscripts for the Alexandrian text type were superior than those used by Lucian. Perhaps Hesychius was responsible for giving the Alexandrian text its final shape, and Athanasius of Alexandria may have been the one who made this text the archetypal text for Egypt.

As the years went by, there were less and less Alexandrian manuscripts produced, and more and more Byzantine manuscripts manufactured. Very few Egyptians continued to read Greek (with the exception of those in St. Catherine's Monastery, the site of the discovery of Codex Sinaiticus), and the rest of the Mediterannean world turned to Latin. It was only those in the Greek-speaking churches in Greece and Byzantium that continued to make copies of the Greek text. For century after century—from the sixth to the fourteenth—the great majority of New Testament manuscripts were produced in Byzantium, all bearing the same kind of text. When the first Greek New Testament was printed (c. 1525), it was based on a Greek text that Erasmus had compiled, using a few late Byzantine manuscripts. This printed text, with minor revisions, became the Textus Receptus.

Beginning in the seventeenth century, earlier manuscripts began to be discovered—manuscripts with a text that differed from that found in the Textus Receptus. Around 1630, Codex Alexandrinus was brought to England. An early fifth-century manuscript, containing the entire New Testament, it provided a good, early witness to the New Testament text (it is an especially good witness to the original text of Revelation). Two hundred years later, a German scholar named Constantin von Tischendorf discovered Codex Sinaiticus in St. Catherine's Monastery (located near Mount Sinai). The manuscript, dated around A.D. 360, is one of the two oldest vellum (treated animal hide) manuscripts of the Greek New Testament. The earliest vellum manuscript, Codex Vaticanus, had been in the Vatican's library since at least 1481, but it had not been made available to scholars until the middle of the nineteenth century. This manuscript, dated slightly earlier (A.D. 350) than Codex Sinaiticus, had both the Old and New Testaments in Greek, excluding the last part of the New Testament (Heb. 9:15 to Rev. 22:21 and the Pastoral Epistles). A hundred years of textual criticism has determined that this manuscript is one of the most accurate and reliable witnesses to the original text.

Other early and important manuscripts were discovered in the nineteenth century. Through the tireless labors of men like Constantin von Tischendorf, Samuel Tregelles, and F. H. A. Scrivener, manuscripts such as Codex Ephraemi Rescriptus, Codex Zacynthius, and Codex Augiensis were deciphered, collated, and published.

As the various manuscripts were discovered and made public, certain scholars labored to compile a Greek text that would more closely represent the original text than did the Textus Receptus. Around 1700 John Mill produced an improved Textus Receptus, and in the 1730s Johannes Albert Bengel (known as the father of modern textual and philological studies in the New Testament) published a text that deviated from the Textus Receptus according to the evidence of earlier manuscripts.

In the 1800s certain scholars began to abandon the Textus Receptus. Karl Lachman, a classical philologist, produced a fresh text (in 1831) that represented the fourth century manuscripts. Samuel Tregelles (self-taught in Latin, Hebrew, and Greek), laboring throughout his entire lifetime, concentrated all of his efforts in publishing one Greek text (which came out in six parts, from 1857 to 1872). As is stated in the introduction to this work, Tregelles' goal was "to exhibit the text of the New Testament in the very words in which it has been transmitted on the evidence of ancient authority." Henry Alford also compiled a Greek text based upon the best and earliest manuscripts. In his preface to *The Greek New Testament* (a multivolume commentary on the Greek New Testament, published in 1849), Alford said he labored for the "demolition of the unworthy and pedantic reverence for the received text, which stood in the way of all chance of discovering the genuine word of God."

During this same era, Tischendorf was devoting a lifetime of labor to discovering manuscripts and producing accurate editions of the Greek New Testament. In a letter to his fiancée he wrote, "I am confronted with a sacred task, the struggle to regain the original form of the New Testament." In fulfillment of his desire, he discovered Codex Sinaiticus, deciphered the palimpsest Codex Ephraemi Rescriptus, collated countless manuscripts, and produced several editions of the Greek New Testament (the eighth edition is the best).

Aided by the work of the previous scholars, two British men, Brooke Westcott and Fenton Hort, worked together for twenty-eight years to produce a volume entitled *The New Testament in the Original Greek* (1881). Along with this publication, they made known their theory (which was chiefly Hort's) that Codex

Vaticanus and Codex Sinaiticus (along with a few other early manuscripts) represented a text that most closely replicated the original writing. They called this text the Neutral Text. (According to their studies, the Neutral Text described certain manuscripts that had the least amount of textual corruption.) This is the text that Westcott and Hort relied upon for compiling their volume.

The nineteenth century was a fruitful era for the recovery of the Greek New Testament; the twentieth century, no less so. Those living in the twentieth century have witnessed the discovery of the Oxyrhynchus Papyri, the Chester Beatty Papyri, and the Bodmer Papyri. To date, there are nearly 100 papyri containing portions of the New Testament—several of which date from the late first century to the early fourth century. These significant discoveries, providing scholars with many ancient manuscripts, have greatly enhanced the effort to recover the original wording of the New Testament.

At the beginning of the twentieth century, Eberhard Nestle used the best editions of the Greek New Testament produced in the nineteenth century to compile a text that represented the majority consensus. The work of making new editions was carried on by his son for several years, and is now under the care of Kurt Aland. The latest edition (the 26th) of Nestle-Aland's *Novum Testamentum Graece* appeared in 1979 (with a corrected edition in 1986). The same Greek text appears in another popular volume published by the United Bible Societies, called the *Greek New Testament* (third, corrected edition—1983). The twenty-sixth edition of the Nestle-Aland text is regarded by many as representing the latest and best in textual scholarship.

The Original Text of the New Testament

In their book *The Text of the New Testament* Kurt and Barbara Aland argue for the position that the Nestle-Aland text, 26th edition (NA^{26}), "comes closer to the original text of the New Testament than did Tischendorf or Westcott and Hort, not to mention von Soden" (32). And in several other passages they intimate that NA^{26} may very well be the original text. This is evident in Kurt Aland's defense of NA^{26} as the new "standard text":

> The new "standard text" has passed the test of the early papyri and uncials. It corresponds, in fact, to the text of the early time. . . . At no place and at no time do we find readings here [in the earliest manuscripts] that require a change in the "standard text." If the investigation conducted here in all its brevity and compactness could be presented fully, the detailed apparatus accompanying each variant would convince the last doubter. A hundred years after Westcott-Hort, the goal of an edition of the New Testament "in the original Greek" seems to have been reached. . . . The desired goal appears now to have been attained, to offer the writings of the New Testament in the form of the text that comes nearest to that which, from the hand of their authors or redactors, they set out on their journey in the church of the first and second centuries ("The Twentieth-Century Interlude in New Testament Textual Criticism" in *Text and Interpretation,* 14).

The Alands should be applauded for speaking about recovering the *original* text, for it is apparent that many modern textual critics have given up any hope of recovering the original text. Other scholars think it can be recovered, and they believe that NA^{26} is quite close to presenting the original text. The reason for this optimism is that we have many early manuscripts and we also have greater understanding about the early history of the text.

There are over forty manuscripts that date before the beginning of the early fourth century—several of these manuscripts are from the second century. Until recently, the dating of certain manuscripts was too conservative because Grenfell and Hunt did not believe the codex existed before the third century and therefore dated many Oxyrhynchus papyri in the third or fourth century which should have been dated in the second or third century.

As was mentioned before, one of the most significant dates is that of P46 (the Chester Beatty Papyrus II, usually dated around 200), containing all of Paul's epistles except the Pastoral Epistles. In a very convincing article, Young Kyu Kim has dated P46 prior to the reign of Domitian (A.D. 81–96).(See *Biblica,* 1988, 248-257). He determined this date because all other literary papyri comparable to the handwriting style of P46 are dated in first century A.D. and because there are no dated parallel papyri from the second or third centuries. If this dating is accurate, we have a copy of the Pauline corpus made within the same decade that the Pauline corpus is believed to have been assembled—i.e., A.D. 75–85. This dating of P46 greatly increases its importance, for this makes P46 the closest manuscript to the original. Even if Kim's dating is too early, it strongly challenges the date of 200 usually assigned to P46. At least, we can say that P46 is late first century to early/middle second century (85–150).

The following manuscripts have been dated in the second century or early third century:

P87, containing a few verses of Philemon, early second century (c. 125) (The handwriting of P87 is very similar to that found in P46.)

P77, containing a few verses of Matthew 23, middle second century (c. 150)

P45 (the Chester Beatty Papyrus I), containing portions of all four Gospels and Acts, middle second century (c. 150)

P32, containing portions of Titus 1 and 2, third quarter of

the second century (c. 175)

P90, containing a portion of John 18, third quarter of the second century (c. 175)

P52, containing a few verses of John 18, early second century (c. 150)—dated earlier by many paleographers (c. 110–125)

P4/64/67, containing portions of Matthew and Luke, c. 200

P1, containing Matthew 1, c. 200

P13, containing Hebrews 2-5, 10-12, c. 200

P27, containing a portion of Romans 8, c. 200

P66 (the Bodmer Papyrus II), containing most of John, c. 175 (but dated by Herbert Hunger, director of papyrological collections in the National Library at Vienna, c. 125-150)

P48, containing a portion of Acts 23, early third century (c. 220)

P75 (the Bodmer Papyrus XIV/XV), containing most of Luke and John, early third century (c. 200)

In addition to the early manuscripts listed above (with Kim's dating), there is another late second century vellum manuscript: 0189, containing a portion of Acts 5. And there are thirty-two other third-century manuscripts, with portions from the passages noted below:

P5, John 1, 16, 20

P9, 1 John 4

P12, Heb. 1

P15, 1 Cor. 7

P16, Phil. 3, 4

P18, Rev. 1

P20, James 2

P22, John 15–16

P23, James 1

P28, John 6

P29, Acts 26

P30, 1 Thess. 4–5, 2 Thess. 1

P37, Matt. 26

P38, Acts 13, 19

P39, John 8

P40, Rom, 1, 2, 3, 4, 6, 9

P47, Rev. 9–17

P49, Eph. 4–5

P53, Matt. 25, Acts 9

P65, 1 Thess. 1–2

P69, Luke 22

P70, Matt. 2, 3, 11, 12, 24

P72, 1 and 2 Peter, Jude

P78, Jude

P80, John 3

P92, Eph. 1, 2 Thess. 1

0162, John 2

0171, Matt. 10, Luke 22

0212, the Diatessaron manuscript containing small portions of each Gospel

0220, Rom. 4 5

The manuscripts listed above, especially the first group (those dated in the late first century, early second century, second century, and early third century), provide the source for recovering the original text of the New Testament. Many of these manuscripts are over two hundred years older than the two great manuscripts discovered in the nineteenth century: Codex Vaticanus (c. 325) and Codex Sinaiticus (c. 350). These were the two great manuscripts that revolutionized New Testament textual criticism in the nineteenth century and were the impetus for the compilation of new critical editions of the Greek New Testament by men such as Tregelles, Tischendorf, Westcott and Hort.

Tregelles, working according to similar principles as Lachmann, compiled a text based on the evidence of the earliest manuscripts. Tischendorf attempted to do the same, even though he was too biased toward his prized discovery, Codex Sinaiticus. Westcott and Hort implemented the same principle when they created their critical edition, even though they were biased toward Codex Vaticanus. Nonetheless, Westcott and Hort made an attempt to print the original text of the Greek New Testament. Some critics in this century deride them or anyone else making such an attempt because they are convinced that it is impossible to recover the original text due to the great divergence of readings that exist in so many different manuscripts.

Other critics will argue that it is not wise to base a recovery of the original text on manuscripts that are all Egyptian in origin. In fact, certain scholars contend that the early papyrus manuscripts represent only the Egyptian New Testament text, not the text of the entire early church. Kurt Aland has effectively argued against this view by pointing out that (1) we are not sure if all of the papyri discovered in Egypt actually originated in Egypt and (2) that the text typically called the Egyptian text (as opposed to the "Western" or Byzantine text) was the text displayed in the writings of early church fathers who lived outside of Egypt—such as Irenaeus, Marcion, and Hippolytus ("The Text of the Church?" *Trinity Journal,* vol. 8, 1987.) Therefore, it is likely that the manuscripts discovered in Egypt were typical of the text existing at that time throughout the entire church.

Furthermore, it must be remembered that the churches of the late first to the third century throughout the Mediterranean area were not isolated from one another. Due to a flourishing commerce, accessible highways, and open seaports (all under Roman rule), there was a regular flow of communication between cities like Carthage and Rome, Rome and Alexandria, Alexandria and Jerusalem. The churches in North Africa and Egypt were not isolated from the rest of the churches to the north. This connection began from the earliest days of the church. Some of the first to become Christians at the day of Pentecost (A.D. 30) were from Egypt and Libya (Acts 2:10); undoubtedly some of them returned home with the gospel. The Ethiopian eunuch, after receiving Jesus as his Savior, must have returned home with the gospel (Acts 8:25ff). Apollos, the Alexandrian, became one of the earliest apostles in Asia (see Acts 18:24).

History tells us that there was a church in Alexandria as early as 100. Around 160–180, Pantaneus became the first known head of a small catechetical school in Alexandria. According to Eusebius, the school had already begun by the time Pantaneus took over the leadership. Clement took over the leadership when Pantaneus left Alexandria, never to return. Clement worked hard to establish the small catechetical school there as the center of Christian study and mission. By 200 Clement had built up a flourishing community of well-educated Alexandrian Christians. But then, due to the savage persecution of 202, Clement fled Alexandria. Origen took over from Clement and established a well-known school of Christian scholars.

History also tells us that there were churches in the rural areas south of Alexandria as early as the first part of the second century. Several of the earliest New Testament manuscripts—those dating from the early second century (see list above) have come from the Fayum and Oxyrhynchus, thereby revealing the existence of Christians in these rural towns as early as 125. This is the area where archeologists have discovered nearly all of our early New Testament manuscripts. The manuscripts have not come from Alexandria because the Alexandrian library was destroyed twice (once accidentally by the Romans, and another time by the Moslems). Furthermore, the water table is too high in Alexandria; papyri could not withstand the moisture.

Rural Middle Egypt, because of its dry climate and low water table, has become a repository of manuscripts produced indigenously and extralocally. And the extant manuscripts, I believe, present a fair sampling of what would have existed in the late first to third centuries throughout the entire Graeco-Roman world. That is to say, if we could find—by some miracle—early manuscripts in Turkey, Israel, Syria, or Greece, they would very likely contain the same samplings of readings found in the so-called Egyptian manuscripts. In other words, the New Testament manuscripts used and read in the churches in Egypt during the early centuries of the church would fairly represent what was being used and read throughout all the churches. Furthermore, it is safe to assume that rural Middle Egypt preserved many manuscripts that had come from Alexandria (and were prepared in the Alexandrian tradition) and other cities, such as Rome or Antioch.

Rural Middle Egypt, the site of our manuscript discoveries, was not isolated from the rest of the world. The numerous nonliterary papyri discovered there have shown that there was regular communication between those living in the Fayum with those living in Alexandria, Carthage, and Rome. And there is evidence that there was general correspondence about works of literature and scriptoral practices. Therefore, among those who produced the early manuscripts we have today, there must have been some scribes who were producing copies of New Testament books much in the same manner as those who lived elsewhere in the Graeco-Roman world. Therefore, we can conclude that the manuscripts discovered in Egypt are legitimate sources for reconstructing the original text of the Greek New Testament.

Examining the Reliability of the Early Text

Some textual critics will argue that an early date for a New Testament manuscript is not necessarily *all that* significant because they believe the early period of textual transmission was inherently "free." Those who espouse this view have argued that the scribes making copies of various books of the New Testament prior to the period of canonization (late third century) used liberty in making the copies. Unlike the Jewish scribes who meticulously made accurate copies of the sacred Old Testament text, the Christian scribes have been characterized as not feeling obligated to produce exact copies of their exemplars because they had not yet recognized the "sacredness" of the text they were copying. This view of the early period, which has become axiomatic among many New Testament textual critics, is not entirely true, for several reasons:

1. Most of the writers of these New Testament books were Jews who believed that the Old Testament, in Hebrew and in Greek, was the inspired Word of God. Because of their Jewish background, they had great respect for the Scriptures, which had become central to their worship and religious life. They were the people of the book. Most of them read the Greek Old Testament, the Septuagint, which was very likely the translation work of Alexandrian Jews.

Some of the Jewish Christian scribes would have emulated Jewish scribal practices. This began with the making of copies of the Septuagint, which they believed was an inspired text, and would have extended to any New Testament books they regarded as authoritative and/or equally inspired. Christians would have been aware of the strict rules that governed the copying of the Old Testament text and the reverence given to the copies.

2. Many of the early copies of various books of the New Testament were copied by scribes who must have believed that they were copying a sacred text—originally composed by their founding

apostles, such as Peter, Matthew, John, and Paul. Certain books were treated as sacred from the onset—such as the four Gospels, Acts, the Pauline Epistles, and 1 Peter—while other books, ones that took a longer time to be "canonized," were perhaps treated with less textual fidelity—books such as 2 Peter and Jude, the Pastoral Epistles, James, and Revelation. Canonization was perceived before it was pronounced for some books as early as the first century. For example, the Pauline Corpus was formed as early as A.D. 75 and recognized as apostolic, authoritative literature. The writer of 2 Peter went so far as to categorize Paul's epistles along with "the other Scriptures" (2 Pet. 3:15-16). The four Gospels were also recognized as being authoritative as early as the second century.

3. Many of the New Testament books were originally produced as works of literature. For example, the four Gospels, Acts, Romans, Ephesians, Hebrews, 1 Peter, and Revelation are clearly literary works. Most of the other New Testament books are "occasional" letters—i.e., letters written primarily to meet the need of the occasion. But not so with the other books, for they were designed from the beginning to be literary works reaching a large audience.

Because they lived in a hellenized world, the New Testament writers spoke Greek, read Greek, and wrote Greek. The kind of Greek they wrote was the common language (koine) of the Graeco-Roman world. Many of the New Testament writers knew other works of Greek literature and cited them. John alludes to Philo. Paul quotes Epimenides, Aratus, and Menander; and his epistolary style is modeled after that first created by such Greek writers as Isocrates and the philosopher Plato. The Gospel writers were typical Greek historiographers. Their works follow the pattern set by the Greek historian Herodotus, who set a high standard of observation and reporting.

The first readers of these works, whether Jewish Christians or Gentile Christians, would have been aware of both the spiritual and literary value of these texts. As such, some of those who were the first to make copies of these books would have done so with great respect for preserving the original text.

4. All the early papyri, without one exception, show that all the early Christians who made copies of the text used special abbreviations to designate divine titles (nomina sacra). The name was written in abbreviated form with a suprascript line over the abbreviation. For example, the Greek word for "Jesus" Ιησους was written as $\overline{IC}$. Other titles that were written as nomina sacra are Lord, Christ, God, Father, Son, and Spirit. Though the creation of the nomina sacra may reflect the Jewish influence of the tetragrammaton (YHWH written for Yahweh), it is an entirely new creation found exclusively in Christian documents. According to C. H. Roberts, the creation of this kind of writing system "presupposes a degree of control and organization. . . . The establishment of the practice would not have been left to the whims of a single community, still less to that of an individual scribe. . . . The system was too complex for the ordinary scribe to operate without rules or an authoritative exemplar" (*Manuscript, Society, and Belief*, 45–46).

The universal presence of the nomina sacra in early Christian documents speaks loudly against the notion that the early period of textual transmission was characteristically "free." Christian scribes were following an established pattern, an "authorized" exemplar. As Roberts said, "The remarkably uniform system of nomina sacra . . . suggests that at an early date there were standard copies of the Christian scriptures" ("Books in the Greco-Roman World," 64).

5. Accompanying the phenomemon of the formation of nomina sacra in Christian documents is the phenomenon of the use of the

codex by all the early Christians. Prior to the middle of the first century, all the Scriptures and other writings were written on scrolls. For example, Jesus used a scroll to read from when he delivered his address from Isaiah 61 in the Nazarene synagogue (Luke 4:18ff). Jews used scrolls and non-Jews used scrolls; everyone in the Graeco-Roman world used scrolls.

Then the codex (a book formed by folding pages and stitching them at the spine) appeared—probably first modeled after parchment notebooks. According to C. H. Roberts's hypothesis, John Mark, while living in Rome, used such a parchment notebook to record the sayings of Jesus (via Peter's preaching). The entire Gospel of Mark, then, was first published as a codex (*Birth of the Codex,* 54ff.). "A gospel circulating in this format determined, partly by way of authority, partly by way of sentiment and symbol, that the proper form for the Christian scriptures was a codex, not a roll" (E. G. Turner's *Greek Papyri,* 11).

Thereafter, all portions of the New Testament were written on codices. The codex was unique to Christianity until the end of the second century. Kenyon wrote, "Among all the papyri discovered in Egypt which can be assigned to the second century, . . . no single pagan [i.e., non-Christian] manuscript is in codex form" (*Books and Readers in Greece and Rome,* 111). This practice (which began either in Rome or Antioch) was a clear break with Judaism and, again, shows a kind of uniformity in the formation and dissemination of the early text.

6. Contrary to the common notion that many of the early New Testament papyri were produced by untrained scribes making personal copies of poor quality, several of the early New Testament papyri were produced with extreme care by educated and professional scribes. Paleographers have been able to classify certain handwriting styles from the first to the fourth century (as well as

beyond). Many of the early New Testament papyri were written in what is called "the reformed documentary hand" (i.e., the scribe knew he was working on a manuscript that was not just a legal document but a literary work). In *The Birth of the Codex*, Roberts wrote:

> The Christian manuscripts of the second century, although not reaching a high standard of calligraphy, generally exhibit a competent style of writing which has been called 'reformed documentary' and which is likely to be the work of experienced scribes, whether Christian or not. . . . And it is therefore a reasonable assumption that the scribes of the Christian texts received pay for their work. (46)

Scriptoral practices in rural Egypt (i.e., the Fayum, Oxyrhynchus, etc.) beginning in the second century were influenced by the work of the professional scribes working in the scriptorium for the great library at Alexandria or perhaps by a Christian scriptorium founded in Alexandria (in association with the catechetical school) in the second century. Eusebius implies that the school began well before the time Pantaneus became in charge of it around 180 (H.E., v. 10. I.). And Zuntz quite convincingly argued that the Pauline corpus was produced by the methods of Alexandrian scholarship and/or in Alexandria itself at the beginning of the second century (*The Text of the Epistles,* 14–15). Functioning as the most ancient of the New Testament textual critics, the Alexandrian scribes selected the best manuscripts and then produced a text that reflected what they considered to be the original text. They must have worked with manuscripts having the same quality as P1, P4/64/67, P27, P46, P75.

Zuntz also argued that by the middle of the second century the Alexandrian bishopric possessed a scriptorium that, by its output, set the standard for the Alexandrian type of biblical manuscript (op. cit.). This standard could have included the coding of nomina sacra, the use of codices, and other literary features. However, in saying that Alexandria set a standard it does not necessarily mean that Alexandria was exerting a kind of textual uniformity throughout Egypt during the second and early third centuries. It was not until the fourth century, when Athanasius became bishop of Alexandria, that Alexandria began to exert control over the Egyptian churches. This may have extended to the production of New Testaments, but certainly would not have reached every church. Prior to the third century, the manuscripts do not give evidence of having been produced at a central scriptorium. Rather, each manuscript was produced by a scriptorium associated with a local church. Nevertheless, it is quite evident that a scriptorial standard had been set by Alexandria, and that certain major Egyptian cities (such as Oxyrhynchus) were influenced by this standard.

Conclusion

Textual critics working with ancient literature universally acknowledge the supremacy of earlier manuscripts over later ones. Textual critics not working with the New Testament would love to have the same kind of early witnesses that biblical scholars possess. In fact, many of them work with manuscripts written 1,000 years after the autographs were composed! We all marvel that the Dead Sea Scrolls have provided a text that is nearly 800 years closer to the originals than the Masoretic manuscripts, and yet many of the Dead Sea manuscripts are still over 600 to 800 years removed from the time of original composition! New Testament textual critics have a great advantage!

The nineteenth century New Testament textual scholars—such as Lachmann, Tregelles, Tischendorf, Westcott and Hort—worked on the basis that the earliest witnesses are the best witnesses. We should continue this line of recovery using the testimony of the earlier witnesses. But textual scholars since the time of Westcott and Hort have been less inclined to produce editions based on the theory that the earliest reading is the best. Most present-day textual critics are more inclined to endorse the maxim: the reading that is most likely original is the one that best explains the variants.

This maxim (or "canon" as it is sometimes called), as good as it is, produces conflicting results. For example, two scholars, using this same principle to examine the same variant unit, will not agree. One will argue that one variant was produced by a copyist attempting to emulate the author's style; the other will claim the same variant has to be original because it accords with the author's style. One will argue that one variant was produced by an orthodox scribe attempting to rid the text of a reading that could be used to promote heterodoxy or heresy; another will claim that the same variant has to be original because it is orthodox and accords with Christian doctrine (thus a heterodox or heretical scribe must have changed it). Furthermore, this principle allows for the possibility that the reading selected for the text can be taken from any manuscript of any date. This can lead to subjective eclecticism.

Modern textual scholars have attempted to temper the subjectivism by employing a method called "reasoned eclecticism." According to Michael Holmes, "Reasoned eclecticism applies a combination of internal and external considerations, evaluating the character of the variants in light of the manuscript's evidence and vice versa in order to obtain a balanced view of the matter and as a check upon purely subjective tendencies" ("New Testament Textual Criticism," in *Introducing New Testament Interpretation* [ed. S. McKnight], 55).

The Alands favor the same kind of approach, calling it the local-genealogical method, which is defined as follows:

It is impossible to proceed from the assumption of a manuscript stemma, and on the basis of a full review and analysis of the relationships obtained among the variety of interelated branches in the manuscript tradition, to undertake a recension of the data as one would do with other Greek texts. Decisions must be made one by one, instance by instance. This method has been characterized as eclecticism, but wrongly so. After carefully establishing the variety of readings offered in a passage and the possibilities of their interpretation, it must always then be determined afresh on the basis of external and internal criteria which of these readings (and frequently they are quite numerous) is the original, from which the others may be regarded as derivative. From the perspective of our present knowledge, this "local-genealogical" method (if it must be given a name) is the only one which meets the requirements of the New Testament textual tradition. (Introduction to *Novum Testamentum Graece,* 26th edition, 43)

The "local-genealogical" method assumes that for any given variation unit any manuscript (or manuscripts) may have preserved the original text. Applying this method produces an extremely uneven documentary presentation of the text. Anyone studying the critical apparatus of NA[26] will detect that there is not an even documentary presentation. The eclecticism is dispersed throughout the text.

"Reasoned eclecticism" and/or the "local-genealogical" method tend to give priority to internal evidence over external evidence. But it has to be the other way around if we are going to recover the original text. This was Westcott and Hort's opinion. With respect to their compilation of *The New Testament in the Original Greek,* Hort wrote, "Documentary evidence has been in most cases allowed to confer the place of honour against internal evidence" (*The Introduction to the New Testament in the Original Greek,* 17).

In this respect, Westcott and Hort need to be revived. Earnest Colwell was of the same mind when he wrote, "Hort Redivivus: A Plea and a Program." Colwell decried the "growing tendency to rely entirely on the internal evidence of readings, without serious consideration of documentary evidence" (152). In this article he calls upon scholars to make an attempt to reconstruct a history of the manuscript tradition. The main thesis of this essay has been to do just that, and in so doing promote the value of the earliest manuscripts in the ongoing endeavor to recover the original text of the New Testament.

BIBLIOGRAPHY

Aland, Kurt, and Barbara Aland. *The Text of the New Testament,* trans. Erroll F. Rhodes, 1987.

Colwell, Earnest. "Hort Redivivus: A Plea and a Program," in *Studies in Methodology in Textual Criticism of the New Testament,* 1969.

Comfort, Philip W. *Early Manuscripts and Modern Translations of the New Testament,* 1990.

Kenyon, Frederic. *Books and Readers in Ancient Greece and Rome,* 1951.

———— *Our Bible and the Ancient Manuscripts,* 1958.

Metzger, Bruce M. *The Text of the New Testament,* 1980.

Roberts, Colin H. "Books in the Graeco-Roman World and in the New Testament" in *Cambridge History of the Bible,* Vol. 1, eds. P. R. Ackroyd and C. F. Evans, 1970.

Roberts, Colin H. *Manuscript, Society, and Belief in Early Christian Egypt,* 1979.

Roberts, Colin H. and T. C. Skeat. *The Birth of the Codex,* 1987.

Turner, Eric G. *Greek Papyri: An Introduction,* 1968.

Westcott, B. F. and F. J. A. Hort, *Introduction to the New Testament in the Original Greek,* 1882.

Zuntz, Gunther. *The Text of the Epistles,* 1953.

SECTION
FIVE
Bible Translation

Biblical Languages
Larry Walker

Christians believe that God has revealed himself through the Bible. Therefore, those who read the Bible can profit from learning as much as possible about the languages in which it was written, of which there are three—Hebrew, Aramaic (a cousin of Hebrew), and Greek.

The connection between language and thought is not a loose one; language is a product and reflection of the human soul. Language is not just a dress for thought to put on or off at pleasure, but the "body" of which thought is the "soul." Each language that God ordained to transmit divine revelation had a "personality" that made it suitable for such a purpose. The two major languages of Scripture, Greek and Hebrew, represent two major language families, Indo-European and Semitic. Their contrasting linguistic traits combine to produce a thorough, progressive, propositional revelation of God. That revelation is characterized by simplicity, variety, and power.

No translation can replace the original languages of the Bible in primary importance for conveying and perpetuating divine revelation. Those languages should be learned not merely from the "outside," with grammar and lexicon, but also from the "inside," with proper appreciation for the uniqueness of each one.

Hebrew

The name "Hebrew" is not applied by the Old Testament to its own language, although the New Testament does use the name that way. In the Old Testament, "Hebrew" means the individual or people who used the language. The language itself is called "the language of Canaan" (Isa. 19:18), or "the language of Judah" (Neh. 13:24).

ORIGIN AND HISTORY

In the Middle Ages a common view was that Hebrew was the primitive language of humankind. Even in colonial America Hebrew was still referred to as "the mother of all languages." Linguistic scholarship has now made such a theory untenable.

Hebrew is actually one of several Canaanite dialects which included Phoenician, Ugaritic, and Moabite. Other Canaanite dialects (for example, Ammonite) existed but have left insufficient inscriptions for scholarly investigation. Such dialects were already present in the land of Canaan before its conquest by the Israelites.

Until about 1974, the oldest witnesses to Canaanite language were found in the Ugarit and Amarna records dating from the fourteenth and fifteenth centuries B.C. A few Canaanite words and expressions appeared in earlier Egyptian records, but the origin of Canaanite has been uncertain. Between 1974 and 1976, however, nearly seventeen thousand tablets were dug up at Tell Mardikh (ancient Ebla) in northern Syria, written in a previously unknown Semitic dialect. Because they possibly date back to 2400 B.C. (perhaps even earlier), many scholars think that language may be the "Old Canaanite" which gave rise to Hebrew. By 1977, when another thousand tablets were unearthed, only about a hundred inscriptions from Ebla had been reported on. Languages change over a long period of time. The English used in the time of Alfred the Great (ninth century A.D.) seems almost like a foreign language to contemporary English speakers. Although Hebrew was no exception to the general principle, like other Semitic languages it remained remarkably stable over many centuries. Poems such as the Song of Deborah (Judg. 5) tended to preserve the language's oldest form. Changes that took place later in the long history of the language are shown in the presence of archaic words (often preserved in poetic language) and a general difference in style. For example, the book of Job reflects a more archaic style than the book of Esther.

Various Hebrew dialects apparently existed side by side in Old Testament times, as reflected in the episode involving the pronunciation of the Hebrew word "shibboleth/sibboleth" (Judg. 12:4-6). It seems that the Israelites east of the Jordan pronounced the initial letter with a strong "sh" sound, while those in Canaan gave it the simple "s" sound.

Scholars have also identified features of Hebrew which could be described as reflecting the northern or southern parts of the country.

FAMILY

Hebrew belongs to the Semitic family of languages; these languages were used from the Mediterranean Sea to the mountains east of the Euphrates River valley, and from Armenia (Turkey) in the north to the southern extremity of the Arabian peninsula. Semitic languages are classified as *Southern* (Arabic and Ethiopic), *Eastern* (Akkadian), and *Northwestern* (Aramaic, Syriac, and Canaanite [Hebrew, Phoenician, Ugaritic, and Moabite]).

CHARACTER

Hebrew, like the other early Semitic languages, concentrates on observation more than reflection. That is, things are generally observed according to their appearance as phenomena, not analyzed as to their inward being or essence. Effects are observed but not traced through a series of causes.

Hebrew's vividness, conciseness, and simplicity make the language difficult to translate fully. It is amazingly concise and direct. For example, Psalm 23 contains fifty-five words; most translations require about twice that many to translate it. The first two lines with slashes separating the individual Hebrew words in the original read:

> The Lord/(is) my shepherd/
> I shall want/not

Thus eight English words are required to translate four Hebrew words.

Hebrew does not use separate, distinct expressions for every shade of thought. Someone has said, "The Semites have been the quarries whose great rough blocks the Greeks have trimmed, polished, and fitted together. The former gave religion; the latter philosophy."

Hebrew is a pictorial language in which the past is not merely described but verbally painted. Not just a landscape is presented but a moving panorama. The course of events is reenacted in the mind's sight. (Note the frequent use of "behold," a Hebraism carried over to the New Testament.) Such common Hebraic expressions as "he arose and went," "he opened his lips and spoke," "he lifted up his eyes and saw," and "he lifted up his voice and wept" illustrate the pictorial strength of the language.

Many profound theological expressions of the Old Testament are tightly bound up with Hebrew language and grammar. Even the most sacred name of God himself, "the LORD" (Jehovah or Yahweh), is directly related to the Hebrew verb "to be" (or perhaps "to cause to be"). Many other names of persons and places in the Old Testament can best be understood only with a working knowledge of Hebrew.

GRAMMAR

Many figures of speech and rhetorical devices in the Old Testament are more intelligible if one is familiar with the structure of Hebrew.

Alphabet and Script   The Hebrew alphabet consists of twenty-two consonants; signs for vowels were devised and added late in the language's history. The origin of the alphabet is unknown. The oldest examples of a Canaanite alphabet were preserved in the Ugaritic cuneiform alphabet of the fourteenth century B.C.

The old style of writing the letters is called the Phoenician or paleo-Hebrew script. It is the predecessor of the Greek and other Western alphabets. The script used in modern Hebrew Bibles (Aramaic or square script) came into vogue after Israel's exile into Babylon (sixth century B.C.). The older style was still used sporadically in the early Christian era on coins and for writing God's name (as in the Dead Sea Scrolls). Hebrew has always been written right to left.

Consonants   The Canaanite alphabet of the Phoenician and Moabite languages had twenty-two consonants. The older Canaanite language reflected in Ugaritic had more consonants. Arabic also preserves some Old Canaanite consonants found in Ugaritic but missing in Hebrew.

Vowels   In the original consonantal Hebrew script, vowels were simply understood by the writer or reader. On the basis of tradition and context, the reader would supply whatever vowels were needed much as is done in English abbreviations ("bldg." for "building"; "blvd." for "boulevard"). After the Christian era began, and after the collapse of the nation, the dispersion of the Jews and the destruction of Jerusalem led to Hebrew's becoming a "dead language," no longer widely spoken. Loss of traditional pronunciation and understanding then became more of a possibility, so

Jewish scribes felt a need for permanently establishing the vowel sounds.

First, vowel letters called "mothers of reading" (*matres lectionis*) were added. These were consonants used especially to indicate long vowels. These were added before the Christian era as the Dead Sea Scrolls reveal.

Later (about the fifth century A.D.), the scribes called Masoretes added vowel signs to indicate short vowels. At least three different systems of vowel signs were employed at different times and places. The text used today represents the system devised by Masoretic scribes who worked in the city of Tiberias. The vowels, each of which may be long or short, are indicated by dots or dashes placed above or below the consonants. Certain combinations of dots and dashes represent very short vowel sounds or "half-vowels."

Linkage Hebrew joins together many words that in Western languages would be written separately. Some prepositions (*be-*, "in"; *le-*, "to"; *ke-*, "like") are prefixed directly to the noun or verb which they introduce, as are the definite article *ha-*, "the" and the conjunction *wa-*, "and." Suffixes are used for pronouns, either in the possessive or accusative relationship. The same word may simultaneously have both a prefix and a suffix.

Nouns Hebrew has no neuter gender; everything is masculine or feminine. Inanimate objects may be either masculine or feminine, depending on the formation or character of the word. Usually, abstract ideas or words indicating a group are feminine. Nouns are derived from roots and are formed in various ways, either by vowel modification or by adding prefixes or suffixes to the root. Contrary to Greek and many western languages, compound nouns are not characteristic of Hebrew.

The Hebrew plural is formed by adding *-im* for masculine nouns (*seraphim, cherubim*), and *-oth* for feminine nouns.

Three original case endings indicating nominative, genitive, and accusative have dropped away during the evolution of Hebrew. To compensate for the lack of case endings, Hebrew resorts to various indicators. Indirect objects are indicated by the preposition *le-*, "to"; direct objects by the objective sign *eth*; the genitive relationship by putting the word before the genitive in the "construct state," or shortened form.

Adjectives   Hebrew is deficient in adjectives. "A double heart" is indicated in the original Hebrew by "a heart and a heart" (Ps. 12:2) and "two differing weights" is actually "a stone and a stone" (Deut. 25:13); "the whole royal family" is "the seed of the kingdom" (2 Kings 11:1).

Adjectives that do exist in Hebrew have no comparative or superlative forms. Relationship is indicated by the preposition "from." "Better than you" is expressed literally in Hebrew "good from you." "The serpent was more subtle than any other beast" is literally "the serpent was subtle from every beast" (Gen. 3:1). The superlative is expressed by several different constructions. The idea "very deep" is literally "deep, deep" (Eccl. 7:24); the "best song" is literally "song of songs" (compare "king of kings"); "holiest" is literally "holy, holy, holy" (Isa. 6:3).

Verbs   Hebrew verbs are formed from a root usually consisting of three letters. From such roots, verbal forms are developed by change of vowels or by adding prefixes or suffixes. The root consonants provide the semantic backbone of the language and give a stability of meaning not characteristic of Western languages. The vowels are quite flexible, giving Hebrew considerable elasticity.

Hebrew verb usage is not characterized by precise definition of tenses. Hebrew tenses, especially in poetry, are largely determined by context. The two tense formations are the perfect (completed action), and imperfect (incomplete action). The imperfect is ambiguous.

It represents the indicative mood (present, past, future) but may also represent such moods as the imperative, optative, and jussive or cohortative. A distinctive usage of the perfect tense is the "prophetic perfect," where the perfect form represents a future event considered so sure that it is expressed as past (for example, see Isa. 5:13).

STYLE
Hebrew diction is characterized by a picturesque quality.

Vocabulary   Most Hebrew roots originally expressed some physical action or denoted some natural object. The verb "to decide" originally meant "to cut"; "to be true" originally meant "to be firmly fixed"; "to be right" meant "to be straight"; "to be honorable" meant "to be heavy."

Abstract terms are alien to the character of Hebrew; for example, biblical Hebrew has no specific words for "theology," "philosophy," or "religion." Intellectual or theological concepts are expressed by concrete terms. The abstract idea of sin is represented by such words as "to miss the mark" or "crooked" or "rebellion" or "trespass" ("to cross over"). Mind or intellect is expressed by "heart" or "kidneys," emotion or compassion by "bowels" (see Isa. 63:15 KJV). Other concrete terms in Hebrew are "horn" for strength or vigor, "bones" for self and "seed" for descendants. A mental quality is often depicted by the part of the body thought of as its most appropriate embodiment. Strength can be represented by "arm" or "hand," anger by "nostril," displeasure by "falling face," acceptance by "shining face," thinking by "say."

Some translators have attempted to represent a Hebrew word always by the same English word, but that leads to serious problems. Sometimes there is considerable disagreement on the exact shade of meaning of a Hebrew word in a given passage. A single root frequently represents a variety of meanings, depending on usage and context. The word for "bless" can also mean "curse, greet, favor, praise." The word for "judgment" is used also for "justice, verdict, penalty, ordinance, duty, custom, manner." The word for "strength" or "power" also means "army, virtue, worth, courage."

Further ambiguity arises from the fact that some Hebrew consonants stand for two different original consonants that have merged in the evolution of the language. Two words which on the surface appear to be identical may be traced back to two different roots. For an example of this phenomenon in English, compare "bass" (a fish) with "bass" (a vocalist).

Syntax Hebrew syntax is relatively uncomplicated. Few subordinating conjunctions ("if," "when," "because," etc.) are used; sentences are usually coordinated by using the simple conjunction "and." English translations of biblical texts generally try to show the logical connection between successive sentences even though it is not always clear. In Genesis 1:2–3:1, all but three of the 56 verses begin with "and," yet the RSV translates that conjunction variously as "and" (1:3), "so" (1:27), "thus" (2:1), "but" (2:6), and "now" (3:1).

Hebrew style is enlivened by use of direct discourse. The narrator does not simply state that "such and such a person said that . . ." (indirect discourse). Instead, the parties speak for themselves (direct discourse), creating a freshness that remains even after repeated reading.

Poetry Hebrew poetry uses a variety of rhetorical devices. Some of them—such as assonance, alliteration, and acrostics—can be appreciated only in the original Hebrew. But parallelism, the most important characteristic of Hebrew poetry, is evident even in English translation. Among the many forms of parallelism possible, four common categories exist: (1) synonymous, a repeating style where parallel lines say the same thing in different words; (2) antithetic, a contrasting style where contrary thoughts are expressed;

(3) completive, with a completing parallel line filling out the thought of the first; (4) climactic, in which an ascending parallel line picks up something from the first line and repeats it. Numerous other forms of parallelism enrich Hebrew poetry. The possible varations of parallelism are almost endless.

Figures of Speech Hebrew abounds in expressive figures of speech based on the Hebrew people's character and way of life. Certain odd but well-known expressions found in English literature come from the Hebrew style, like "apple of his eye" (Deut. 32:10; Ps. 17:8; Prov. 7:2; Zech. 2:8) and "skin of my teeth" (Job 19:20). Some of the more striking Hebrew modes of expression are hard to transfer into English, such as "to uncover the ear," meaning "to disclose, reveal." Others are more familiar, like "to stiffen the neck" for "to be stubborn, rebellious"; "to bend or incline the ear" for "to listen closely."

LEGACY

English and a number of other modern languages have been enriched by Hebrew.

Words English contains a number of Hebrew "loan words." Some of these have had wide influence ("amen," "hallelujah," "jubilee"). Many Hebrew proper nouns are used in modern languages for persons and places, such as David, Jonathan/John, Miriam/Mary, Bethlehem (the name of several towns and cities in the United States).

Expressions Many common Hebrew expressions have been unconsciously accepted into English figures of speech, as in "mouth of the cave" and "face of the earth." Some figures, such as "east of Eden," have been used as titles for books and films.

Aramaic

A secondary Old Testament language is Aramaic, found in sections of the book of Daniel (2:4b–7:28) and Ezra (4:8–6:18;

7:12–26). Aramaic phrases and expressions also appear in Genesis (31:47), Jeremiah (10:11), and the New Testament.

OLD TESTAMENT USE

Genesis 31:47 reflects usage of Hebrew and Aramaic by two individuals who were contemporaries. Jacob, the father of the Israelites, and Laban, the Aramean, referred to the same memorial or "witness heap" by their own language: Laban called it his own Aramaic expression, but Jacob used the Hebrew counterpart.

Aramaic is linguistically very close to Hebrew and similar in structure. Aramaic texts in the Bible are written in the same script as Hebrew. In contrast to Hebrew, Aramaic uses a larger vocabulary, including many loan words, and a greater variety of connectives. It also contains an elaborate system of tenses, developed through the use of participles with pronouns or with various forms of the verb "to be." Although Aramaic is less euphonious and poetical than Hebrew, it is probably superior as a vehicle of exact expression.

Aramaic has perhaps the longest continuous living history of any language known. It was used during the Bible's patriarchal period and is still spoken by a few people today. Aramaic and its cognate, Syriac, evolved into many dialects in different places and periods. Characterized by simplicity, clarity, and precision, it adapted easily to the various needs of everyday life. It could serve equally well as a language for scholars, pupils, lawyers, or merchants. Some have described it as the Semitic equivalent of English.

The origin of Aramaic is unknown, but it seems to have been closely related to Amorite and possibly to other ancient Northwest Semitic dialects barely known to scholars. Although an Aramean kingdom as such never really existed, various Aramean "states" developed into influential centers. A few short Aramean inscriptions from that era (tenth to eighth centuries B.C.) have been found and studied.

By the eighth century B.C., King Hezekiah's representatives requested the spokesmen of the Assyrian king Sennacherib to "speak to your servants in Aramaic, since we understand it. Don't speak to us in Hebrew in the hearing of the people on the wall" (2 Kings 18:26). By the Persian period, Aramaic had become the language of international trade. During their captivity, the Jews probably adopted it for convenience—certainly in commerce—while Hebrew became confined to the learned and to religious leaders.

Gradually, especially after the Babylonian exile, Aramaic influence pervaded the land of Palestine. Nehemiah complained that children from mixed marriages were unable to speak Hebrew (Neh. 13:24). The Jews seem to have continued using Aramaic widely during the Persian, Greek, and Roman periods. Eventually the Hebrew Scriptures were translated into Aramaic paraphrases, called Targums, some of which have been found among the Dead Sea Scrolls.

NEW TESTAMENT USE

In popular thought, Aramaic was the common language of Palestine during the time of Jesus. Yet that is by no means certain, and probably is an oversimplification of the linguistic situation of that time. Names used in the New Testament reflect Aramaic (Bartholomew, Bar-jonah, Barnabas), Greek (Andrew, Philip), and Latin (Mark), as well as Hebrew. There is no question that Aramaic was widely used, as were Greek and Hebrew. Latin was probably limited to military and governmental circles. Mishnaic Hebrew, a common kind of everyday Hebrew dialect was also used in Jesus' day; Mishnaic Hebrew documents have been discovered among the Dead Sea Scrolls.

What was the "Hebrew" referred to in certain New Testament passages (John 5:2; 19:13, 17, 20; 20:16; Rev. 9:11; 16:16)? The languages used for the inscription put on Jesus' cross were "Hebrew, Latin, and Greek" (John 19:19-20). Later, the apostle Paul was said to speak "Hebrew" (Acts 22:2; 26:14). The exact dialect he spoke may be debated, but as a Pharisee he was undoubtedly able to read the Hebrew of the Old Testament. The Greek word for "Hebrew" is sometimes translated "Aramaic" and may be a general term for Semitic, or for a blend of Hebrew-Aramaic (as Yiddish is German-Hebrew). At any rate, Aramaic served as a transition from Hebrew to Greek as the language spoken by Jews in Jesus' day. In that sense Aramaic connects Old Testament Hebrew with New Testament Greek.

Greek

The Greek language is beautiful, rich, and harmonious as an instrument of communication. It is a fitting tool both for vigorous thought and for religious devotion. During its classic period, Greek was the language of one of the world's greatest cultures. During that cultural period, language, literature, and art flourished more than war. The Greek mind was preoccupied with ideals of beauty. The Greek language reflected artistry in its philosophical dialogues, its poetry, and its stately orations.

The Greek language was also characterized by strength and vigor. It was capable of variety and striking effects. Greek was a language of argument, with a vocabulary and style that could penetrate and clarify phenomena rather than simply tell stories. Classical Greek elaborately developed many forms from a few word roots. Its complex syntax allowed intricate word arrangements to express fine nuances of meaning.

ANCIENT HISTORY

Although the antecedents of Greek are obscure, the first traces of what could be called antecedents of ancient Greek appear in

Mycenaean and Minoan documents that use three different scripts: Minoan hieroglyphic (the earliest), linear A, and linear B (the latest). Linear B, generally considered "pre-Greek," is written in a syllabic script found on clay tablets discovered on the island of Crete and on the Greek mainland (1400–1200 B.C.)

Mycenaean civilization and script ended suddenly with the Dorian invasions (1200 B.C.), and writing seems to have disappeared for several centuries. Later, about the eighth century B.C., Greek writing appeared in a different script. That script was based on an alphabet presumably borrowed from the Phoenicians and then adapted to the Greek speech sound system and direction of writing. Greek was first written from right to left like the West Semitic languages, then in a back-and-forth pattern, and finally from left to right. Several dialects appeared during the archaic period (eighth to sixth centuries B.C.): Dorian, Ionian, Achaean, and Aeolic.

During the classical period (fifth to fourth centuries B.C.), Greek culture reached its literary and artistic zenith. Classical (or Attic) Greek was characterized by subtlety of syntax and an expressive use of particles (short, uninflected parts of speech, often untranslatable). As the city of Athens attained cultural and political control, the Attic dialect also gained in prestige. With the Macedonian conquests, Attic Greek, combined with influences from other dialects (especially Ionic), became the international language of the eastern Mediterranean area.

HELLENISM AND THE KOINE DIALECT

The conquests of Alexander the Great encouraged the spread of Greek language and culture. Regional dialects were largely replaced by "Hellenistic" or "koine" (common) Greek. Koine Greek is a dialect preserved and known through thousands of inscriptions reflecting all aspects of daily life. The koine dialect added many vernacular expressions to Attic Greek, thus making it more cosmopolitan. Simplifying the grammar also better adapted it to a worldwide culture. The new language, reflecting simple, popular speech, became the common language of commerce and diplomacy. The Greek language lost much of its elegance and finely shaded nuance as a result of its evolution from classic to koine. Nevertheless, it retained its distinguishing characteristics of strength, beauty, clarity, and logical rhetorical power.

It is significant that the apostle Paul wrote his letter to Christians in Rome in the Greek language rather than in Latin. The Roman Empire of that time was culturally a Greek world, except for governmental transactions.

THE SEPTUAGINT

During the centuries immediately before Christ, the eastern Mediterranean had been undergoing not only Hellenization, but also "Semitization." Both influences can be observed in the Greek translation of the Old Testament.

Translation of the Hebrew Scriptures into Greek was an epochal event. The Septuagint (the earliest Greek translation of the Old Testament) later had a strong influence on Christian thought. A necessary consequence of Hebrew writers using the Greek language was that a Greek spirit and Greek forms of thought influenced Jewish culture. The Jews soon appropriated from the rich and refined Greek vocabulary some expressions for ideas that were beyond the scope of Hebrew terminology. Also, old Greek expressions acquired new and extended meanings in this translation of the Old Testament by Greek-speaking Jews.

The Greek Old Testament has been very significant in the development of Christian thought. Often the usage of a Greek word in the Septuagint provides a key to its meaning in the New Testament. The Old Testament dialect of "Jewish-Greek" is at times seen in New Testament passages translated very literally; at other times, the New Testament translation of Old Testament texts is very loose.

NEW TESTAMENT GREEK

Although most New Testament authors were Jewish, they wrote in Greek, the universal language of their time. In addition, the apostle John seems to have been acquainted with some Greek philosophy, which influenced his style. John used "Word" (Greek *logos*) in reference to Christ (John 1:1), and several other abstract expressions. John may have been influenced by the Egyptian center of Alexandria, where Greek philosophy and Hebrew learning had merged in a unique way.

The apostle Paul also was acquainted with Greek authors (Acts 17:28; 1 Cor. 15:33; Tit. 1:12). Thus Greek orators and philosophers influenced Paul's language as well as Hebrew prophets and scholars.

Exactly which dialect of Hebrew or Aramaic Jesus spoke is debated. It is certainly possible that Jesus also spoke Greek. The fact remains that the Gospels were originally written as Greek texts. The records in Greek of Jesus' teachings and accomplishments prepared the way for the gospel to spread throughout a Greek-speaking culture.

The dignity and restraint of koine Greek used by Christian writers was neither so artificial and pedantic as some classical writings, nor so trivial and vulgar as spoken koine.

Greek words took on richer, more spiritual meaning in the context of Scripture. Influenced by the simplicity and rich vividness of Semitic style, the New Testament was not written in a peculiar "Holy Ghost" language (as some medieval scholars believed) but in koine (common) Greek—largely by Semitic-thinking authors. Tens of thousands of papyri unearthed in Egypt in the early twentieth century furnish lexical and grammatical parallels to biblical language, revealing that it was part of the linguistic warp and woof of that era. Yet New Testament Greek was nevertheless "free," often creating its own idiom. Christian writers influenced Greek thought by introducing new expressions in order to convey their message about Jesus Christ.

SEMITIC INFLUENCE

Because New Testament Greek combines the directness of Hebrew thought with the precision of Greek expression, Greek's subtle delicacy often interprets Hebrew concepts. The Semitic influence is strongest in the Gospels, the book of Revelation, and the letter of James. Books like Luke and Hebrews exhibit a more typical Greek style. The New Testament epistles blend the wisdom of Hebrew and the dialectic philosophy of Greek. Sermons recorded in the New Testament combine the Hebrew prophetic message with Greek oratorical force.

In addition to direct quotes and allusions from the Septuagint, a pervasive Semitic influence on New Testament Greek has been noted in many areas. For example, the syntax of New Testament Greek contains many examples of Semitic style.

VOCABULARY

The Greek New Testament vocabulary is abundant and sufficient to convey just the shade of meaning the author desires. For example, the New Testament uses two different words for "love" (for two kinds of love), two words for "another" (another of the same, or another of a different kind), and several words for various kinds of knowledge. Significantly, some words are omitted, such as *eros* (a third kind of love) and other words commonly employed in the Hellenistic culture of that time.

Moreover, Greek words often took on new meanings in the context of the gospel, arising from a combination of new teachings with an exalted morality. The writers did not hesitate to use such words as "life," "death," "glory," and "wrath" in new ways to express new thoughts. Sometimes the literal meaning of a word almost disappears, as when the authors use "water," "washing," and "baptism" for Christ's spiritually purifying power. New Testament vocabulary also contains words found elsewhere only in the Greek Old Testament, such as "circumcision," "idolatry," "anathema," "Diaspora," and "Pentecost." Loan words from Hebrew or Aramaic include *alleluia* and *amen* (Hebrew), and *abba, mammon,* and *corban* (Aramaic).

For understanding the meaning of a New Testament word, then, a lexicon of classical Greek is helpful but not sufficient. One must also know how the word is used in the Greek Old Testament, in Hellenistic writings, and in the inscriptions and documents representing the language of everyday life. Papyrus documents provide many illustrations of the meaning of New Testament words. For example, the Greek word for "contribution" (1 Cor. 16:1), at one time thought limited to the New Testament, is commonly used with the same meaning in the papyri. Many Greek words once defined on the basis of classical Greek have been given sharper meaning in the light of their use in the papyri.

GRAMMAR

As in other Indo-European languages, the meaning of Greek words is affected by the addition and alteration of various prefixes and suffixes (the process known as "inflection"). Although its system of inflection is simplified compared to classical Greek, New Testament Greek is more inflected than many languages. Greek meaning is thus much less susceptible to ambiguity than English.

In contrast to Hebrew, Greek has a neuter gender as well as masculine and feminine. The many and precise Greek prepositions are subtle, having various meanings depending on their context.

New Testament Greek uses only about half of the particles used in classical Greek.

The Greek verb system, much more complicated than that of Hebrew, is capable of nuances of meaning difficult to express even in English. Each Greek verb has five aspects, which grammarians call tense, mood, voice, person, and number.

Tense   Greek verb tense deals primarily with "kind of action," rather than "time of action" as in English. In Greek there are three basic kinds of action: "durative," expressed by the present, imperfect, and (sometimes) future tenses; "simple" or punctiliar, expressed by the aorist and (often) future tenses; and "completed," expressed by the perfect tense (results of past action continue into the present) and pluperfect tense (results are confined to the past).

Greek tenses are often hard to translate into English; the time of action as well as the verb stem's basic meaning (such as whether it takes an object) must be subtly blended with the kind of action into a single idea.

Mood   The mood shows how a verb's action should be understood. Is the action real? (Use the indicative mood.) Is the action demanded by someone? (Use the imperative mood.) Does the action depend on other conditions? (Use the subjunctive or optative mood.) Is the action basically descriptive of another substantive? (Use a participle.) Is the action basically substantive? (Use an infinitive.) In grammar, a substantive is a word or group of words functioning as a noun; the last two examples are not strictly moods, but they are used that way by grammarians. The moods give a Greek writer a rich choice of verbal expression.

Voice   A verb's voice describes whether action is directed outward (active), inward (middle), or back upon the sentence's subject (passive).

Person The person of a verb tells who is doing the acting, whether I (first person), you (second person), or another (third person).

Number Verb number shows whether the action is performed by one person (singular) or more than one person (plural).

STYLE

The New Testament contains a variety of writing styles in its use of Greek. The Gospels especially exhibit Semitic features. Matthew uses a style less picturesque than Mark's and in some respects close to the style of Luke, Acts, Hebrews, James, and 1 Peter. Luke's style varies from that of both Mark and Matthew; it is elegant. The rather simple style of John contains many Semitisms.

Among the apostle Paul's letters, differences of style have been noted. The least literary and most direct in expression are his letters to the Thessalonians. The Pastorals (1 and 2 Timothy, Titus) have a style nearer to the koine than most of the other epistles—not so Jewish, and not so much influenced by the Septuagint as his other letters.

The letter to the Hebrews combines elegance with Jewish-Greek style. James's letter, though high in cultural quality, is not as sensitive in style as Hebrews. Less elegant is 1 Peter, which is strongly influenced by the Septuagint and thus reflects Semitic style.

The letter of Jude contains elevated, somewhat ponderous diction, and shows the influence of Jewish style. 2 Peter, resembling Jude in its high style, is even more influenced by the Septuagint.

The book of Revelation has a generally simple style, but shows considerable Semitic influence in its use of parallelism and redundancy. Linguistic scholars have identified a number of apparent grammatical mistakes in the Greek of Revelation.

Conclusion

To Christians, the message conveyed by the Bible is simple and direct, yet capable of communicating to people in the most complex cultural circumstances. Although every human language has its limitations, the biblical languages have proved to be a remarkably adequate vehicle for conveying God's message in all its power and richness.

BIBLIOGRAPHY

Bauer, Hans and Pontus Leander. *Hebraischen Sprache*, 1962.

Bergstrasser, G. *Hebraische Grammatik*, 1962.

Blass, F. and A. Debrunner. *A Greek Grammar of the New Testament and Other Early Christian Literature*, 1961.

Cohen, Simon. "The Hebrew Language." Ed. Isaac Landman, *The Universal Jewish Encyclopedia*, Vol. 5, 1941.

Kautzsch, E. *Gesenius' Hebrew Grammar*, 1910.

Kutscher, Raphael. *A History of the Hebrew Language*, 1982.

Robertson, A. T. *A Grammar of the Greek New Testament in Light of Historical Research*, 1934.

Terry, Milton S. *Biblical Hermeneutics*, n.d.

Bible Translation
Raymond Elliott

Translation is the process of beginning with something (written or oral) in one language (the source language) and expressing it in another language (the receptor language).

The goals of translation may be summed up under four headings: accuracy, appropriateness, naturalness, and form.

For "accuracy," the message or content which the author intended to communicate in the source document must be transmitted so that the reader of the translation receives the same message.

"Appropriateness" refers to expressing that message in a style which reflects the attitude and intention of the author.

"Naturalness" means translating so that the reader feels his language has been used as he would use it, in a way that allows him to read for meaning.

The "form" in which the original was written should be reflected in the translation if it can be done without distorting the accuracy, appropriateness, and naturalness. (See "Artistic Use of Language" later in this chapter.)

All translation, including Bible translation, involves at least two languages. For convenience, we will refer to the language in which the document already exists as the source language. The language into which translation is being made will be called the receptor language.

The problems that arise in the process of translating have their basis in the similarities and differences between languages, as well as in the specific nature of the documents being translated. The principles of translation have been developed over the years in the process of dealing with the problems.

The first major section of this article deals with factors of language structure that affect any and all kinds of translation. The other major section will deal with problems related specifically to the documents that make up the Bible. Following this, there will be brief mention of the way in which translation relates to other subjects such as inspiration, interpretation, revision, dialect differences, paraphrases, versions, and styles intended for special audiences.

Language Factors of Translation

Today, there are more versions of the Bible in English than in any other language. Most Bible translation now being done in the world, however, is destined for other languages.

The language factors mentioned below are pertinent to all languages, but they will be illustrated by examples from only a few languages.

SOUNDS

The human vocal mechanism is capable of producing hundreds of different sounds. At birth every person is capable of learning to use all of them. In the process of growing up, most people learn only the sounds and structures of their own language, quite unaware of the structures of other languages.

In this article we are dealing with translation from written sources, not from spoken sources, so we are concerned only with reading the source documents and not with speaking the languages in which those documents were written. So usually, in Bible translation, we are not concerned with the sounds of the source language.

With the receptor language, however, the situation may be quite different. If a translation is to be made for a language that has previously had no written form, the sound system of the receptor language must be mastered as a basis for devising an alphabet for writing it.

The need for analysis of the receptor language sound system is often the first major translation problem to be faced. The principle involved in solving it is that the sounds of the receptor language must be analyzed in terms of that language's own structure. Fortunately, excellent training courses are available to prepare translators for language analysis.

WORDS AND WORD PARTS
Sounds combine with elements of meaning to produce words, phrases, clauses, sentences, paragraphs, and even larger units of discourse.

Words are the basic building blocks for language structure. They simultaneously form two different kinds of units: (a) grammatical, that is, the way words combine with each other, and (b) semantic, that is, the kinds of meaning patterns which result.

All of us easily recognize word parts if we focus on them (build-ing, part-s, pro-duce, relation-ship, re-present), yet we are usually unaware that we put these parts together in very rigidly defined ways. Present-ship, pro-build, s-relation are examples of things we "cannot" do in English.

Every language has its own inventory of word parts of many different shapes and sizes, and each language has its own rules about the ways these parts can or cannot be put together to form words.

The author of the source document has already put the word parts together in the way he wanted to use them. It is possible, of course, for the translator to misuse the analysis of word parts in the source document and arrive at shades of meaning the author never intended.

The situation with the receptor language may be quite different, especially if it has previously had no written form. Keeping track of word parts and taking note of the kinds of combinations they are allowed to form is a crucial part of learning the language and gaining creative fluency.

One problem may be a temptation to "invent" new words by combining word parts to fill up gaps in the receptor language where needed words seem to be missing. An important principle is to resist that temptation, since such invented words often are meaningless to the local people or carry a wrong meaning entirely. Natural local ways of expressing most concepts are already a part of the language, and it is well worth the patient effort required to find them.

In some other regards, however, careful attention to word parts in the source language is both necessary and crucial. For example, one of the important but complex features of Greek, the source language of the New Testament, is a case system affecting the use of nouns, pronouns, adjectives, and the article "the." This case system consists of word endings that supply information that may or not be carried by nouns in other languages. A Greek noun ending may indicate (a) whether the word is singular or plural, (b) whether its gender is masculine, feminine, or neuter, (c) something about the grammatical function of the word within its sentence, and (d) information about semantic categories that may be implicit in the word.

The Greek case system also requires that any article, pronoun, or adjective used along with or referring to a noun must in turn use endings that either convey the same information as that carried by the noun's case ending, or that at least do not conflict with it. One illustration of this occurs in 2 Peter 3:1, where the word "letter" has an ending that identifies it as singular number, feminine gender, and accusative case. It functions as the object of the verb "write." In the same noun phrase with "letter" are two other words, "this" and "second," both of which have endings showing that they too are singular, feminine, and accusative.

There are many other languages that have case endings in nouns, and many that do not. Even among those languages having features similar to those of Greek, their features may not be used for exactly the same functions as in Greek. While Greek structure includes word endings representing five different cases, Spanish and English have only a few vestiges of case endings (most of which involve only pronouns), while a language such as Finnish includes thirty-one cases.

Another illustration of the importance of source language word parts is found in Greek verbs whose parts may represent not only their basic "dictionary meaning" but also such things as (a) who is performing the action, (b) whether just one or more than one person is doing it, (c) when it is done, (d) whether it is a single event or a process, (e) whether it is an actual happening, a command, or something wished for, or (f) whether the subject of the verb is an active or a passive participant in the activity.

The translation of a single Greek word may thus often require a phrase or even a sentence or more in another language. For example, the single word "enter" in Mark 6:10 tells us (1) that those who are performing the action are the people Jesus is speaking to, (2) that there are more than one of them, (3) that the action is viewed as a single event, but also (4) that it is viewed as something which is yet to happen. Since all this information is carried in the Greek form of a single word "enter," all these factors must be taken into consideration in the course of translating the passage in which it is used.

WORDS

Each language has its own inventory of words, as well as its own characteristic ways of classifying them, and its own rules for the kinds of combinations they form, the functions they perform, and the kinds of meanings they express. As with word parts, there are the same possibilities and problems involved in attempting to match the words used in one language with equivalent words in another.

Greek has a class of "verbal" words called participles that function either as if they were nouns or as if they were adjectives. Yet, because of the basically verblike meanings of their stems, they frequently have to be translated as if they were verbs whose subjects and objects, among other elements, may have to be deduced from the contexts in which they occur. A Greek participle can seldom be adequately translated by a single word in another language.

For example, in 2 Timothy 2:15 a participle "straight-cutting" is masculine accusative singular, referring both to the previous pronoun "yourself" and to the previous noun "worker." The type of action expressed is "continuing" or "habitual," and its grammatical object is the "word of truth." The meaning of the word has to do with cutting a straight path toward a goal, as, for example, cutting a road through the woods. In this reference it can be interpreted with the "word of truth" either functioning as the grammatical goal object or as the means of reaching that goal. Depending upon the interpretation chosen, the phrase will mean either "cutting straight through to the word of truth" or "using the word of truth to cut straight through" to the minds and hearts of the people for whom Timothy is responsible. Again, the single Greek word carries much more information than can be represented by a single English word.

WORDS IN RELATION TO THE "REAL WORLD"

No one language ever quite matches any other language in the way its vocabulary relates to objects and events and concepts. For example, some languages classify relatives very carefully depending on whether they are related on the father's side of the family or on the mother's. English, while it has the word "cousin," does not have a single word, as some languages do, to indicate "daughter of mother's sister," nor does it distinguish that relationship as distinct from "daughter of father's sister."

In some cultures the vocabulary for kinship carefully distinguishes between relatives "born before I was" and those "born after I was." In some languages it is important to use one term for a man's mother-in-law and another term for a woman's mother-in-law. And in languages where kin terms are also used to signify social roles and ranking of greater versus lesser degrees of respect, the choice of the correct term to represent a "simple" relationship may be a complex matter.

Luke 1–2 tells us that John the Baptist was born before Jesus. Therefore, in some cultures it is to be expected that Jesus will reflect this fact by the way he speaks to or speaks about John, as in Matthew 3:15. But John clearly states, in 3:11, that Jesus deserves greater status than John. Within some cultures, it may also be assumed that the person who does the baptizing has higher rank than the person being baptized. These considerations may affect the forms chosen in some languages to represent the way John and Jesus spoke to or about each other, as well as the way the followers of John would quote him in speaking to Jesus, as in Matthew 11:3.

If respect is automatically or exclusively accorded to anyone born before another, the choice of terms may have to be different from that made in a cultural situation where civil, religious, economic, or political status can outrank chronological age. Relationships and terminology that governed the choice of terms in Hebrew and Greek, then, may not coincide with those required by the receptor language.

A similar statement can be made about other types of vocabulary categories. For example, in a culture that has only five basic color terms (black, white, red, green, and brown), it may not be easy to find a way to say "purple." And if the color purple does not represent the concept of royalty, then simply saying that the soldiers put purple robes on Jesus (John 19:2) might not communicate the mockery involved.

When Jesus called Herod a fox (Luke 13:32), we understand that he was describing him as deceitful. That would not be understood in the same way in a culture where the fox is an omen of disaster.

In translating for people to whom "hardness of heart" means "bravery" (i.e., a hard heart being one which fear cannot enter), it is confusing, as well as inaccurate, to state that Jesus scolded his disciples for their "hardness of heart" (Mark 16:14).

The translation principle in focus here is that the vocabulary of a language reflects categories and relationships relevant to the culture of the people who speak it, and these are different with each culture and each language.

TWO SIMPLE WORDS: "OF" AND "THE"

The word "of" is very common in English, and it is used to represent a wide variety of relationships between words. In only the first chapter of the Gospel of Mark, nine different English translations use the word "of" between eighteen and thirty-one times. The word represents such relationships as possession, kinship, location, names of geographical places and features, the material from which something is made, political jurisdictions, the doer of an action, and so on. But there is no word "of" in Greek at all! Greek has other ways of expressing those relationships that are translated by "of" in English.

Spanish has a word for "of" (de), but it is used for some purposes where it would not sound right in English. The Nebaj Ixil language of Guatemala does not have a word "of," but the ways it expresses the equivalent of English "of" and Spanish *de* are different from the corresponding devices used in Greek.

Another common English word is "the." The article in English is much simpler than in Spanish which has four forms: *el, los, la, las*. These distinguish between singular and plural as well as between masculine and feminine.

In Ixil the article is similar to English "the" with two exceptions: (1) To specify plural, Ixil can add a suffix to the word for "the." (2) Ixil uses "the" in a number of constructions for which English does not use it, and vice versa.

In Greek the article "the" is spelled seventeen different ways, some of the forms being used to distinguish singular from plural, others distinguish between masculine, feminine, or neuter gender, and some show grammatical functions such as subject of sentence, object, possessor, or location.

However, Chuj, a Mayan language spoken in Guatemala, divides all nouns into fourteen different categories such as male, female, baby, wooden, metal, round, animal, and so on. It has a different form of the word "the" for each of these categories! Once a noun has been introduced in speaking or writing, the noun does not have to be mentioned again in the same paragraph: the correct form of "the" serves as a pronoun in referring to it again.

Thus, even such simple words as "the" and "of" differ remarkably from one language to another in the complex interplay between grammar and meaning. Nothing about the source documents can be taken for granted in the translation process, and the normal structures of the receptor languages must be employed with care to insure accurate, appropriate, and natural translation.

The problem for the translator is to find, in the receptor language, those forms that will appropriately represent the structures of the source language—first as to meaning, style, and naturalness, then as much as possible as to form.

LARGER GRAMMATICAL UNITS

We realize that neither the sounds nor the words of one language can be translated into another language on a one-to-one basis. But we may be tempted to assume that the order of words in phrases, sentences, or paragraphs can be transferred into the receptor language in order to "retain the form of the original" or to "stay as close to the original as possible."

We are aware that there are times when this is not possible, but we often treat such times as if they were only occasional exceptions to a goal that was usually desirable or attainable. In reality, it is rare to find two unrelated languages whose larger grammatical structures can routinely be equated with each other.

Naturally, the more closely related two languages are, the more nearly alike their grammars will be. But even closely related languages may exhibit surprising differences in the structure or meaning of the same language features.

The examples below represent the general facts of life with which the translator is constantly at work, rather than just the rare exceptions. Therefore, the problems of equivalence and the principles to be followed in solving them apply with equal force to each level of language structure.

PHRASES

One result of the Greek noun case system noted above is the relative flexibility of word order allowed by Greek on the phrase level. The noun phrase in 2 Peter 3:1 "this second letter" (mentioned above) actually occurs as the first, fourth and seventh words in that Greek sentence. This word order ("This now beloved second to-you I-write letter") is perfectly natural and easily understood in Greek. English requires changing the word order to something like, "Beloved, I now write this second letter to you."

In terms of linguistic family relationships, Greek and English and Spanish are distant cousins. Where English usually puts an adjective before a noun, Spanish usually puts the noun first with the adjective following.

In Nebaj Ixil, a Mayan language of Guatemala which is not related to English, Spanish, or Greek, there are many hundreds of adjectives, but most of them are not allowed to occur in a noun phrase at all! They are usually used in separate clauses, so that where English can use a phrase to say "the tall cedars," and use a sentence such as "I cut down the tall cedars of Lebanon" (Isa. 37:24), Ixil would require a series of separate clauses such as "Lebanon has cedars; they are tall; I cut them down."

CLAUSES

Each of the following clauses communicates the age of Noah (Gen. 5:32), yet each uses a different clause structure and each reflects a somewhat different cultural attitude toward age:

> *English:* Noah was five hundred years old.
> *Spanish:* Noah had five hundred years.
> Greek has a construction similar to that of Spanish.
> *Hebrew:* Noah was the son of five hundred years.
> *Ixil:* There were five hundred (of) Noah's years.

In English the years are one of Noah's characteristics, in Spanish they are his possession, in Hebrew Noah is their product, and the Ixil expression simply states their existence.

In an English transitive clause the most usual phrase pattern in the clause is Subject—Verb—Object, but for Spanish and Ixil the expected order is Verb—Subject—Object. For Greek the case system allows much variation in word and phrase order.

Many other examples could be listed to illustrate that even at the clause level it may be futile and misleading to try to duplicate in one language the patterns of another.

SENTENCES

Ephesians 1:3-14 is often cited as an example of the long sentences Greek allows. This sentence is one main independent clause (which does not contain a verb) linked to a series of dependent clauses by a normal series of appositional phrases, participial phrases, prepositional phrases, relative pronouns, and adverbial conjunctions—all of which combine to urge ascribing praise to God and mention some of the reasons why it is appropriate to do so!

The first verse of Matthew consists entirely of eight nouns in Greek. The second verse clearly begins a new sentence. In structure, verse one has a kind of stair-step arrangement of relationships:

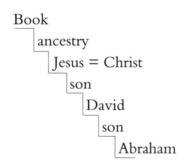

Because this verse does not contain a verb, some commentators conclude that it must be a kind of title, even though it is not adequate as a title for the entire book. In fact, it is a perfectly good Greek sentence just as it stands. Most other languages will require the addition of other words to express the relationships already signalled by the Greek nouns.

At the sentence level also, the translator desires not so much to duplicate the structure as to communicate the content of the original by linguistic devices which are natural to the receptor language.

PARAGRAPHS AND OTHER STRUCTURING DEVICES

A paragraph may be composed of only one long sentence as Ephesians 1:3-14, of a single short sentence, or even of a phrase or word. More common is a paragraph in which a series of sentences develop a short episode, theme, or relationship.

Greek is a language that uses many conjunctions. Mark begins many paragraphs with the conjunction "and," at times when such usage would not be natural to English. Two of the most commonly used sentence-joining conjunctions in the New Testament cannot occur as the first word in a Greek sentence. Here again, other languages often do not use conjunctions in the way that Greek does.

Paragraph structure varies, even within the same language, with different types of content. The introductory paragraphs to both Luke and Acts are different from those of Paul's letters. John begins his Gospel and first letter in a way distinct from Matthew and Mark or the letters of Peter.

Paul's prayers, as in Ephesians 1:17-21 and 3:16-19, and praise or benediction, as in Ephesians 3:20-21 or Romans 16:25-27, are extremely concise. They could rarely be adequately expressed as tersely in other languages, or by the same linguistic devices as those employed in Greek.

Reporting conversation differs from language to language. Some languages customarily use indirect quotations, as in Mark 6:8, "And He instructed them that they should take nothing . . ." and only rarely use direct quotations, as in Mark 6:9, "And do not put on two tunics" (NASB).

In other languages the usual pattern is to use direct quotation almost exclusively. In some languages, either the choice is a matter of personal preference or it is determined by the type of conversation being reported or by the nature of the audience. If the speaker knows his listeners have not heard the story before, for example, he may insert signals which help keep the cast of characters straight.

Such signals might not be thought necessary for hearers already familiar with the story.

Interestingly, some quotations in the Gospels such as "He cried out, saying . . ." are not typical of Greek at all. They reflect common usage among Hebrew speakers who have retained in Greek some patterns of their own language.

Romans 12:1 is a good example of the use of Greek "therefore" to draw a forceful conclusion from reasons which have already been stated. Romans 1:16-20 contains a series of statements introduced by six occurrences of "for" in which each supports the statement which has just preceded it.

In my personal experience, I had once worked long and hard to unravel one of the passages where Paul developed a theme on the basis of logical reasoning and deduction. But the response of the Christian leaders, when they heard my translation, was devastating: "What is he talking about?" I then began the paragraph by having Paul say: "Now I want to talk to you about . . . ," and I filled in the subject which was the theme of the passage. With the addition of this one feature of expected receptor language structure, the paragraph communicated beautifully.

Thus, on the paragraph level as well as at every other level, the translator must employ the normally expected forms of the receptor language if they are to reflect the content and development of the source document in a natural, accurate, and adequate way.

DISCOURSE STRUCTURE

At the discourse level the translator attempts to "get inside" the heart and mind of the author in order to understand (1) what he intends to say and (2) how he develops the presentation of the way he says it. The author has already used those discourse devices of the source that will accomplish his purpose; now the translator must choose appropriate devices in the receptor language to express the corresponding attitudes and relationships.

Discourse types include narrative, argument, instruction, emotional appeal, persuasion, etc. It is of vital importance to the translator to understand how each discourse type works in the source language as well as in the receptor language. A few examples will make clear the crucial nature of many small details.

A friend of ours was aware that, in the language in which he was translating, there were more than a dozen ways of reporting "he said," either in introducing or in closing a quotation. When speakers of the language were questioned about the meanings of the various forms, the response was, "They're all the same; they all mean 'he said.'" Analysis of discourse structures, however, revealed that each of the various options performed a specific function in the development of the story and in the roles played by the characters in relation to each other. For example, one type of closing quotation formula implied that the speaker will not appear further in the story. When that formula was used for Jesus' closing words in Mark 5, and then Jesus was quoted again in Mark 6, the obvious implication was that a different person named Jesus was being introduced in Mark 6.

In another language, there were four different ways of saying "and" in tying sentences and paragraphs together. Analysis eventually showed that one word for "and" was used only to indicate that "we are continuing with the same characters in the same relationship to each other and the author's point of view has not shifted yet." Another "and" meant "This person is now in focus, and not that person—but the main character remains unchanged." Still another "and" signalled "Now we are going back to pick up the main thread of the story."

In some languages, this type of control is handled by the choice of pronouns rather than by conjunctions. In one language, for example, one word meaning "he" refers only to the main character while other words for "he" show how the other characters relate to him. Or the manipulation of active versus passive verbs may serve to keep the main character as the grammatical subject of all the main verbs, even when he is not the one performing the action.

Verb tense may show the author's attitude. In one language, a story is told in the past tense until the climax, which shifts to present. Or, a shift of tense may signal "This is the moral of my story."

The Nebaj Ixil language has a series of one-syllable particles that indicate the author's attitude or the response he wishes from his reader or hearer. One such particle indicates sympathy with an action or character, while another particle signals disdain. One adds emphasis, another limits the scope of the action, and yet another casts doubt upon a statement another person has made.

If the author's intention is to report information, it will govern his choice of the small, seemingly meaningless bits and syllables. If he wants to persuade, or to deceive, his choices will be governed by that.

Since the devices available and the functions they serve are different in every language, there is no substitute for understanding the devices the receptor language has available and using them in ways natural to the receptor language for the type of content being translated.

These considerations are crucial for the translation of every passage of Scripture. Mastery of both the source and receptor languages, as well as of the content of what is being translated, is vital if the reader is to understand clearly the author's message.

GRAMMAR AND MEANING

Words in grammatical arrangements communicate meaning. Certain combinations of words can communicate special or restricted meanings that are different from the meaning that might be arrived at by merely adding up the meanings of the individual words. To say "He really bit my head off," for example, indicates a severe scolding, not decapitation.

The significance of a passage often involves considerations that are not literally present in the text at all. In 2 Peter 3:1 following the noun phrase "my second letter" ("letter" here is feminine singular) are the words "in which." "Which" obviously refers to "letter"—but "which" is plural! So the following statement in the verse refers to both "my second letter" and the first one. The plural form of "which" is the only clue to that fact in the passage.

In Matthew 21:28-32 Jesus tells a story of a man who told his sons to work in a vineyard. One son replied, "I, sir!" but did not go. His answer has universally been treated as affirmative even though he only said "I" (not "aye") in addition to "sir."

Mark 6:39 says that Jesus told the apostles to have the crowd sit in party-groups "on the green grass." "Grass" is a generalization that conveyed information as specific as Mark needed. It was not necessary to specify the number or condition of the blades of grass. Yet languages differ from each other in the types of generalizations they normally employ.

FIGURES OF SPEECH

Each language differs from every other language in the way it groups things together, specifies certain ones out of a group, describes, compares, suggests, and generalizes. Many of these categories of thought are expressed by figures of speech. Biblical examples of several types follow.

Simile: a comparison, such as "I can see people, but they look like trees, walking" (Mark 8:24, NRSV).

Metaphor: a direct comparison of characteristics, as when Jesus called his disciples "little flock" in Luke 12:32.

Metonymy: to rename something, as Jesus did when he referred to Herod as "that fox" in Luke 13:32.

Synecdoche: this is the mention of only a part of something, when the whole is actually meant, as in Acts 11:30 when famine relief was sent by the "hand" of Barnabas and Saul. It can also refer to the whole when only a part is meant, as in John 1:19 where "the Jews of Jerusalem sent priests and Levites." "Jews" here did not refer to the entire nation but only its leaders.

Euphemism: speaking about a delicate, unpleasant, or forbidden subject in a way that sounds better or is more socially acceptable. A Hebrew custom of referring to sexual intercourse under the guise of "knowing" a person (Gen. 4:1, KJV) is reflected also in Matthew 1:25. Death is referred to as being "asleep" (1 Thess. 4:13).

The Bible is rich in figures of speech. Some are composed very deliberately, while some had already become part of everyday speech. Either way, the translator must know not only "what is said" but also "what is meant."

Figures of speech in other languages may contain the same elements but use those elements to communicate different meanings. Likewise, expressions that sound quite different may communicate the same meaning. The most natural way for Ixil people to express "My anger will be aroused" (Exod. 22:24) is to say "My head will come." Instead of "Phinehas . . . has turned my anger away" (Num. 25:11), they would say "My head has lowered because of Phinehas."

It is a happy exception to the rule when "the same" figure of speech can be used in the receptor language as was used in the source language. More often the result of "borrowing" a figure produces a different meaning or no meaning at all.

When the same figure cannot be used, (1) a different figure may be found to communicate both the content and the effect of the figure in the source language, or (2) the significance of the figure may be translated literally into the receptor language with no attempt to retain the figure itself. If Peter were speaking in some languages, he would not be able to urge people to "gird up the loins of your mind" (1 Pet. 1:13, KJV). He might have to say, "Be mentally alert and prepared to respond to the Lord's direction."

ARTISTIC USE OF LANGUAGE

Literary forms that are carefully designed to bring about artistic effects may employ sounds as in rhyming and alliteration, or timing as in cadence and meter, or meaning as in using different grammatical forms of the same word in a passage, or combinations of these or other features.

Art forms that are valued, or even possible, within a given culture vary greatly from one language to another. Language features at every level may be involved. Word-parts such as noun and verb endings affect rhyming, for example. The number of syllables in a word affects meter and cadence, and some languages tend to have longer words than others. Inversion of normal grammatical order in poetry may not be allowed in some receptor languages.

Greek and Hebrew occasionally indulge in punning, but it is usually impossible to transfer the same puns into other languages.

Parallelism is a common form of Hebrew poetry. A statement is made, then followed by another that amplifies it or points out its opposite. This requires a highly developed synonymy and a degree of balance in meter. This is one artistic form that is natural to the Ixil language, for example; it is often used in prayers.

The art forms in Scripture are used to communicate style as well as the message and are not just "art for the sake of art." The Bible translator determines the meaning first, but he is not free from the impact of artistic use of form, and he attempts to reproduce it where possible. But it is usually not possible, for example, in the case of an acrostic, such as Psalm 119. This Psalm has twenty-two sections, each having eight lines. Each line of the first section begins with the first letter of the Hebrew alphabet, *aleph*. Each line of the second section begins with the second letter, *beth,* and so on through the twenty-two letters of the Hebrew alphabet. The total effect of this Hebrew acrostic is bound to be missed in any other language.

Due to the virtual impossibility of duplicating in another language these art forms that are dependent upon a combination of factors such as meaning, rhyming, meter, or homonymy, every translation of passages that employs the artistic use of language features represents some degree of compromise. But the translation should still reflect some attempt by the translator to convey some representation of the artistic devices used by the author.

Bible Translation in Particular

HISTORICAL, GEOGRAPHICAL, AND CULTURAL SETTINGS

Isaac, Shechem, circumcision, phylacteries, fishing nets, sheep, sand, north—these are only a few of the terms or concepts that are not familiar to one or another group of people today.

Eskimos may not know of sand and sheep. Landlocked mountain people may be unfamiliar with fishing. Many cultures are not aware of Jewish religious terms and historical figures. "Where the sun rises" may be the only term for "east" in some areas of the world.

Sometimes the missing vocabulary can be replaced by a descriptive phrase. But to translate "sheep," for example, as "a four-footed animal whose hair is used in making cloth" both ignores the role of the sheep in the Jewish sacrifical system and creates awkward problems for the natural flow of the translation.

The role of sheep in Jewish sacrifices might be captured by "a four-footed animal used by the Jews as a sin offering," but this is not particularly pertinent in Psalm 23, where the emphasis is on caring for rather than sacrificing the sheep. Where some such problems may not be resolved in the translation itself, there may be no alternative to using supplementary materials such as footnotes or a dictionary. Or it may be necessary to rely entirely on teaching.

Other possible solutions, each with its own restrictions, include: (1) borrowing a term from a neighboring language, (2) using a local word for a similar item or function, (3) using a phrase to describe the concept, or (4) transliterating a source-language word, in the same way, for example, that "phylacteries" and "baptism" have been carried over into English.

MONEY

The terms shekel, dracma, or farthing do not give us, today, a clear idea of their buying power in ancient times. Dollars and cents differ from the British pounds, shillings, and pence. And all monetary units are constantly changing in relative value.

In some Scripture passages the time involved in earning the money can make the terms meaningful. For example, a denarius in one of Jesus' parables (Matt. 20:2) represents a day's wage for a laborer. In the incident of the feeding of the five thousand, Philip's statement (John 6:7) becomes significant: "Eight months' wages would not buy enough bread for each one to have a bite!" (NIV).

A talent was worth perhaps fifteen years' wages. In Matthew 18:24, the same man who asked to be excused from a debt of ten thousand talents (the tragi-comically unimaginable sum of the wages that might be earned in fifteen thousand years "be patient with me and I will pay back everything!") refused to forgive the man who owed him the value of one hundred denarii—the wages of approximately three months.

In any passage dealing with money, the translator must communicate not only the relative value of the amounts but also a feeling for what those amounts meant to the people described in the Bible.

PROBLEM PASSAGES

Some words or combinations of words have formerly been unknown outside the Scriptures, so that even translators themselves had no clue to their meanings. There are fewer such words now, mainly because archeological evidence has filled in so many gaps. When the meaning of a passage is not known, usually an educated guess is made in the translation, and a marginal note indicates the nature of the problem.

Sometimes the meaning of each of the words is known, and the grammar may be clear, but the specific sequence of words does not make sense to us. One such passage is Mark 9:49, "Everyone will be salted with fire."

In a different category are phrases that mean nothing to us in our culture but were clear to readers long ago. Modern readers stumble at the combination of images in 1 Peter 1:13 (KJV), which has been translated into English as a command: "Gird up the loins of your mind!" Yet this was easily understood in its original setting: men engaged in active work had to take off their long flowing robes or tie them up around their waists so they could work unimpeded by them. Adding the words "of your mind" to "gird up your loins" indicates that a mental attitude is in focus. The thought might be translated, "Be mentally ready for the work facing you!"

AFFIRMATION OF TRUTH

For some cultures, translation of Paul's series of statements in Romans 9:1, "I speak the truth in Christ—I am not lying, my conscience confirms it in the Holy Spirit," will convince readers that Paul is lying, since only a person who is lying would use such a series of claims to be telling the truth. Faithfully preserving the source-language form of these statements would thus communicate a meaning just the opposite of what Paul intends.

One solution might be a simple affirmation: "I am telling the truth." The following statements are then more likely to be accepted as true. What Paul meant would be translated, but the way he said it would not. Another possible solution is to retain the form of the original with a footnote or marginal reference explaining Paul's intent. Still another suggestion is to trust the Holy Spirit to interpret the truth to the reader. The Holy Spirit is able to do this, and sometimes does. But the many differences of opinion on matters both small and great among Christians indicate that he does not always do so.

To translate in such a way that the readers are quite likely to misunderstand the message is to translate in an irresponsible way. This principle applies to all translation problems and potential solutions—not only to Romans 9:1.

TRANSLATION AND INTERPRETATION

"One should merely translate, and not interpret." Statements such as this are still heard from time to time. The work of the translator would be easier if that were possible. But the differences in languages are such that a one-to-one string of word equivalences does not constitute a translation.

There is a quite restricted sense, however, in which it is necessary to "translate without interpreting." The book of Revelation, some say, is the easiest book to translate but the hardest to interpret. The language and style of Revelation is relatively simple. For example, it may be quite easy to say in the receptor language, "I saw a beast coming out of the sea. He had ten horns and seven heads" (13:1). But if the translator attempts to include the significance of the beast, the horns, and the heads, then he is interpreting beyond the intentions of the author. Even so, in some cultures, "horns" are associated only with evil, so that in a passage such as Revelation 5:6 where a "good" character is represented as having "horns," an apparent clash of values results from a literal translation. Careful teaching may be the only answer to such a problem in such a cultural setting.

In some of the parables, also, what is stated is easily grasped, but how the extended figure is to be understood in its context is a matter of interpretation, not specifically of translation.

Decisions about interpretation and application will hinge on the translator's conception of the extent to which the symbolism is intended to reveal or to conceal the purpose and meaning of the author.

TRANSLATION AND PARAPHRASE

"Paraphrase" has been both misused and greatly criticized in recent times. Dictionaries define "paraphrase" as a rewording for the purpose of clarification. A paraphrase, then, is assumed to be in the same language as the source it is restating, and to reflect the same content, if not the same form, as that original source.

Two translations made from the same source may differ, but the results are not paraphrases of each other. Rather they are simply separate, and possibly divergent, translations from the same source.

From the considerations presented earlier in this article, it is easy to understand how translations may differ in legitimate ways. They can be equally valid expressions of what the translators understood about the author's intentions.

A paraphrase, however, is properly so called only when it expresses, in different words, the content of something already in the language. If the meaning of the paraphrase is not the same as the meaning of the document being paraphrased, then it is not a paraphrase at all!

It is thus erroneous to apply the word "paraphrase" to a translation for the purpose of implying that it has changed the meaning of the original.

Another problem with such misuse of the word "paraphrase" is that it encourages the question: "How does translation *A* compare or contrast with translation *B?*" The proper question is rather:

"How successfully does either translation *A* or translation *B* express the content and the intent of the source document in the receptor language?" This is the vital concern, not how one translation differs from another.

DIALECT DIFFERENCES

Americans are generally aware that people in Brooklyn, Boston, and Birmingham (Alabama) do not speak English in precisely the same way. They may also be aware that the same is true of English speakers in New York, London, and Brisbane.

Opinions differ as to whether separate translations are needed for Boston and Birmingham, but most informed people will agree that the differences between New York and London are sufficient reason for separate versions.

In many areas of the world, the dialect problem is much more severe than these examples of national or international difference might suggest.

Fifty thousand speakers of the Ixil language in Guatemala constitute a linguistic "island" surrounded by eight other language areas. This language has three dialects. The word in one dialect center that means "younger brother" means "woman's child" in the neighboring dialect center twelve miles away.

A river gorge or a mountain range often constitutes a language boundary or a dialect boundary. In one case, for example, "He did not go" on one side of a mountain river means "Did he go?" on the other side of the river.

A dialect boundary in the Aguacatec language of Guatemala runs through the middle of a small town, with people on each side of the line affirming that the people on the other side do not speak the language correctly.

Apart from such geographical differences of dialect, there are also social or cultural dialect differences. In time such differences come to be identified (sometimes incorrectly) as superior versus inferior, or as educated versus ignorant, or as formal versus informal, or as polite versus impolite, or as cultured versus uncultured, or as standard versus regional.

In one country, for example, the Scriptures had always been published in a specialized literary dialect. Scholars refused to produce a translation in the language of the common people on the grounds that "it could then be understood by just anyone," and would thus no longer be the exclusive province of the literary class.

In some countries a "Christian" dialect has grown up around nonstandard use of a language by a foreigner (at times a missionary). The result is that only those who have been in contact with the foreigner over a long period of time can understand his special vocabulary.

For a community or language area to which Christianity has only recently been introduced, it may be necessary to be more explicit in some aspects of the translation for new Christians than for people who have had knowledge of Bible history and Bible characters in their culture for a long period of time.

TRANSLATION AND REVISION

Languages are constantly undergoing a process of change. Ideally, every translation should be revised each time any word or structure has changed to the extent that it no longer accurately or adequately reflects the intent or content of the source. Practically, however, due to the expense involved in editing, setting type, printing, and distribution, it is not common to make changes in a translation until a large number of changes can be made at one time. Emotionally, some people react to any such changes as if they constituted "tampering with God's Word" rather than representing a prayerful and careful concern that the reader benefit from the most accurate and appropriate expression of God's Word possible.

God's Word does not change, but languages and word meanings do. The only way God's Word can continue to communicate is to update the translation periodically.

In a very real sense the wording of the Scriptures not only stimulates Christian experience but is the product of it. As "babes in Christ" grow to maturity and as a foreign translator grows in mastery of and creativity in the receptor language, it is quite true that the Christians, the translator, and the translation "grow up" together. After a period of some twenty years, better ways of expressing the content of Scripture should be available.

TRANSLATION AND INSPIRATION

Is a Bible translation the inspired Word of God? Yes—to the extent that the translation relays to the reader what God directed the authors to write. No—to the extent that it misses the meaning of what God originally communicated.

Missing the meaning can happen in different ways: one can add to the original or omit something from it; he can translate so that no meaning (i.e., confusion) or the wrong meaning is transmitted. All efforts at translation are in danger of committing errors of each type.

Experience teaches us that even a partially defective translation can still transmit a great deal of the content of what God expressed through the original writings of Scripture. It also teaches us that neither the translator nor his readers are thereby free from the effects of those elements that were not correctly or adequately transmitted.

Does God through the Holy Spirit help the translator today? The answer is, emphatically, yes! Does this guarantee that the work of the translator will be free from any error or misinformation? Experience says no. Perhaps some translators could be said to be more "inspired" than others to the extent that they are more able to appropriate the guiding impulses of the Holy Spirit. I prefer to say that some translations reflect God's message more accurately and more adequately than do others. It is easy to lose sight of the fact that any version not the original Hebrew or Greek is a translation prepared by one or more human beings!

"Some say that translation is a science; some say it is an art; others say it is impossible." Each of these statements is partly true.

If we neglect science, we do not know what content and style the source documents intended to express, nor do we know what forms in the receptor language can appropriately be used to express that same content and intent.

If we neglect art, we fail to have insight into the attitudes of the authors and are unable to blend into the translation both the content and the feel of a passage in an appropriate way. We might have the "words" and still miss the "music."

Neither art nor science can substitute for the other, but they make excellent—and crucial—companions!

Translation is impossible—if we mean that even an appreciable proportion of the same sound, grammar, and meaning combinations in any given source language can be duplicated acceptably in any given receptor language.

Translation is quite possible, on the other hand, if we mean by translation that we represent the content of the source document in such a way that the full effect and intent of the author is made available to the reader. This requires that the translator bring to bear upon his task all the resources of both art and science that he can command, trusting the Holy Spirit of God to direct the way they are used.

BIBLIOGRAPHY

Beekman, John and John Callow. *Translating the Word of God,* 1974.
De Ward, Jan and Eugene Nida. *From One Language to Another,* 1986.
Nida, Eugene. *Toward a Science of Translation,* 1964.
Nida, Eugene and Charles Taber. *The Theory and Practice of Translation,* 1974.
Schwarz, W. *Principles and Problems of Biblical Translation,* 1955.

History of the English Bible
Philip W. Comfort

As the gospel spread and churches multiplied in the early centuries of the Christian era, Christians in various countries wanted to read the Bible in their own language. As a result, many translations were made in several different languages—as early as the second century. For example, there were translations done in Coptic for the Egyptians, in Syriac for those whose language was Aramaic, in Gothic for the Germanic people called the Goths, and in Latin for the Romans and Carthagenians. The most famous Latin translation was done by Jerome around 400. This translation, known as the Latin Vulgate (*vulgate* meaning "common"—hence, the Latin text for the common man), was used extensively in the Roman Catholic church for centuries and centuries.

Early Translations: Caedmon's, Bede's, Alfred the Great's

The gospel was brought to England by missionaries from Rome in the sixth century. The Bible they carried with them was the Latin Vulgate. The Christians living in England at that time depended on monks for any kind of instruction from the Bible. The monks read and taught the Latin Bible. After a few centuries, when more monasteries were founded, the need arose for translations of the Bible in English. The earliest English translation, as far as we know, is one done by a seventh century monk named Caedmon, who made a metrical version of parts of the Old and New Testaments. Another English churchman, named Bede, is said to have translated the Gospels into English. Tradition has it that he was translating the Gospel of John on his deathbed in 735. Another translator was Alfred the Great (reigned 871–899), who was regarded as a very literate king. He included in his laws parts of the Ten Commandments translated into English, and he also translated the Psalms.

Other Early Versions: Lindisfarne Gospels, Shoreham's Psalms, Rolle's Psalms

All translations of the English Bible prior to the work of Tyndale (discussed later) were done from the Latin text. Some Latin versions of the Gospels with word-for-word English translations written between the lines, which are called interlinear translations, survive from the tenth century. The most famous translation of this period is called the Lindisfarne Gospels (950). In the late tenth century, Aelfric (c. 955–1020), abbot of Eynsham, made idiomatic translations of various parts of the Bible. Two of these translations still exist. Later, in the 1300s, William of Shoreham translated the Psalms into English and so did Richard Rolle, whose editions of the Psalms included a verse-by-verse commentary. Both of these translations, which were metrical and therefore called Psalters, were popular when John Wycliffe was a young man.

Wycliffe's Version

John Wycliffe (c. 1329–1384), the most eminent Oxford theologian of his day, and his associates were the first to translate the entire Bible from Latin into English. Wycliffe has been called the "Morning Star of the Reformation" because he boldly questioned papal authority, criticized the sale of indulgences (which were supposed to release a person from punishment in purgatory), denied the reality of transubstantiation (the doctrine that the bread and wine are changed into Jesus Christ's body and blood during Communion), and spoke out against church hierarchies. The pope reproved Wycliffe for his heretical teachings and asked that Oxford University dismiss him. But Oxford and many government leaders stood with Wycliffe, so he was able to survive the pope's assaults.

Wycliffe believed that the way to prevail in his struggle with the church's abusive authority was to make the Bible available to the people in their own language. Then they could read for themselves about how each one of them could have a personal relationship with God through Christ Jesus—apart from any ecclesiastical authority. Wycliffe, with his associates, completed the New Testament around 1380 and the Old Testament in 1382. Wycliffe concentrated his labors on the New Testament, while an associate, Nicholas of Hereford, did a major part of the Old Testament. Wycliffe and his coworkers, unfamiliar with the original Hebrew and Greek, translated the Latin text into English.

After Wycliffe finished the translation work, he organized a group of poor parishioners, known as Lollards, to go throughout England preaching Christian truths and reading the Scriptures in their mother tongue to all who would hear God's Word. As a result the Word of God, through Wycliffe's translation, became available to many Englishmen. He was loved and yet hated. His ecclesiastical enemies did not forget his opposition to their power or his successful efforts in making the Scriptures available to all. Several decades after he died, they condemned him for heresy, dug up his body, burned it, and threw his ashes into the Swift River.

One of Wycliffe's close associates, John Purvey (c. 1353–1428), continued Wycliffe's work by producing a revision of his translation in 1388. Purvey was an excellent scholar; his work was very well received by his generation and following generations. Within less than a century, Purvey's revision had replaced the original Wycliffe Bible.

As was stated before, Wycliffe and his associates were the first Englishmen to translate the entire Bible into English from Latin. Therefore, their Bible was a translation of a translation, not a translation of the original languages. With the coming of the Renaissance came the resurgence of the study of the classics—and with it the resurgence of the study of Greek, as well as Hebrew. Thus, for the first time in nearly a thousand years (500–1500—the approximate time when Latin was the dominant language for scholarship, except in the Greek church) scholars began to read the New Testament in its original language, Greek. By 1500, Greek was being taught at Oxford.

Tyndale's Translation

William Tyndale was born in the age of the Renaissance. He graduated in 1515 from Oxford, where he had studied the Scriptures in Greek and in Hebrew. By the time he was thirty, Tyndale had committed his life to translating the Bible from the original languages into English. His heart's desire is exemplified in a statement he made to a clergyman when refuting the view that only the clergy were qualified to read and correctly interpret the Scriptures. Tyndale said, "If God spare my life, ere many years, I will cause a boy that driveth the plough to know more of the Scripture than thou dost" (Brian Edwards, *God's Outlaw*, 61).

In 1523 Tyndale went to London seeking a place to work on his translation. When the bishop of London would not give him hospitality, he was provided a place by Humphrey Monmouth, a cloth merchant. Then, in 1524, Tyndale left England for Germany because the English church, which was still under the papal authority of Rome, strongly opposed putting the Bible into the hands of the laity. Tyndale first settled in Hamburg, Germany. Quite possibly, he met Luther in Wittenberg soon thereafter. Even if he didn't meet Luther, he was well acquainted with Luther's writings and Luther's German translation of the New Testament (published in 1522). Throughout his lifetime, Tyndale was harrassed for propagating Luther's ideas. Both Luther and Tyndale used the same Greek text (one compiled by Erasmus in 1516) in making their translations.

Tyndale completed his translation of the New Testament in 1525. Fifteen thousand copies, in six editions, were smuggled into England between the years 1525 and 1530. Church authorities did their best to confiscate copies of Tyndale's translation and burn them, but they couldn't stop the flow of Bibles from Germany into England. Tyndale himself could not return to England because his life was in danger since his translation had been banned. However, he continued to work abroad—correcting, revising, and reissuing his translation until his final revision appeared in 1535. Shortly thereafter, in May of 1535, Tyndale was arrested and carried off to a castle near Brussels. After being in prison for over a year, he was tried and condemned to death. He was strangled and burnt at the stake on October 6, 1536. His final words were so very poignant: "Lord, open the king of England's eyes."

After finishing the New Testament, Tyndale had begun work on a translation of the Hebrew Old Testament, but he did not live long enough to complete his task. He had, however, translated the Pentateuch (the first five books of the Old Testament), Jonah, and some historical books. While Tyndale was in prison, an associate of his named Miles Coverdale (1488–1569) brought to completion an entire Bible in English—based largely on Tyndale's translation of the New Testament and other Old Testament books. In other words, Coverdale finished what Tyndale had begun.

Coverdale's Version

Miles Coverdale was a Cambridge graduate who, like Tyndale, was forced to flee England because he had been strongly influenced by Luther to the extent that he was boldly preaching against Roman Catholic doctrine. While he was abroad, Coverdale met Tyndale and then served as an assistant—especially helping Tyndale translate the Pentateuch. By the time Coverdale produced a complete translation (1537), the king of England, Henry VIII, had broken all ties with the pope and was ready to see the appearance of an English Bible. Perhaps Tyndale's prayer had been answered—with a very ironic twist. The king gave his royal approval to Coverdale's translation, which was based on the work done by Tyndale, the man Henry VIII had earlier condemned.

Thomas Matthew's Version and the Great Bible

In the same year that Coverdale's Bible was endorsed by the king (1537), another Bible was published in England. This was the work of one called Thomas Matthew, a pseudonym for John Rogers (c. 1500–1555), a friend of Tyndale. Evidently, Rogers used Tyndale's unpublished translation of the Old Testament historical books, other parts of Tyndale's translation, and still other parts of Coverdale's translation, to form an entire Bible. This Bible also received the king's approval. Matthew's Bible was revised in 1538 and printed for distribution in the churches throughout England. This Bible, called the Great Bible because of its size and costliness, became the first English Bible authorized for public use.

Many editions of the Great Bible were printed in the early 1540s. However, its distribution was limited. Furthermore, King Henry's attitude about the new translation changed. As a result, the English Parliament passed a law in 1543 restricting the use of any English translation. It was a crime for any unlicensed person to read or explain the Scriptures in public. Many copies of Tyndale's New Testament and Coverdale's Bible were burned in London.

Greater repression was to follow. After a short period of leniency (during the reign of Edward VI, 1547–1553), severe persecution came from the hands of Mary. She was a Roman Catholic who was determined to restore Catholicism to England and repress Protestantism. Many Protestants were executed, including John Rogers, the Bible translator. Coverdale was arrested, then released. He fled to Geneva, a sanctuary for English Protestants.

The Geneva Bible and the Bishops' Bible

The English exiles in Geneva chose William Whittingham (c. 1524–1579) to make an English translation of the New Testament for them. He used Theodore Beza's Latin translation and consulted the Greek text. This Bible became very popular because it was small and moderately priced. The preface to the Bible and its many annotations were affected by a strong evangelical influence, as well as by the teachings of John Calvin. Calvin was one of the greatest thinkers of the Reformation, a renowned biblical commentator, and the principal leader in Geneva during those days.

While the Geneva Bible was popular among many English men and women, it was not acceptable among many leaders in the Church of England because of its Calvinistic notes. These leaders, recognizing that the Great Bible was inferior to the Geneva Bible in style and scholarship, initiated a revision of the Great Bible. This revised Bible, published in 1568, became known as the Bishops' Bible; it continued in use until it was superseded by the King James Version of 1611.

The King James Version

After James VI of Scotland became the king of England (known as James I), he invited several clergymen from Puritan and Anglican factions to meet together with the hope that differences could be reconciled. The meeting did not achieve this. However, during the meeting one of the Puritan leaders, John Reynolds, president of Corpus Christi College, Oxford, asked the king to authorize a new translation because he wanted to see a translation that was more accurate than previous translations. King James liked this idea because the Bishops' Bible had not been successful and because he considered the notes in the Geneva Bible to be seditious. The king initiated the work and took an active part in planning the new translation. He suggested that university professors work on the translation to assure the best scholarship, and he strongly urged that they should not have any marginal notes besides those pertaining to literal renderings from the Hebrew and Greek. The absence of interpretive notes would help the translation be accepted by all the churches in England.

More than fifty scholars, trained in Hebrew and Greek, began the work in 1607. The translation went through several committees before it was finalized. The scholars were instructed to follow the Bishops' Bible as the basic version, as long as it adhered to the original text, and to consult the translations of Tyndale, Matthew, and Coverdale, as well as the Great Bible and the Geneva Bible when they appeared to contain more accurate renderings of the original languages. This dependence on other versions is expressed in the preface to the King James Version: "Truly, good Christian reader, we never thought from the beginning that we should need to make a new translation, nor yet to make of a bad one a good one . . . but to make a good one better, or out of many good ones one principal good one."

The King James Version, known in England as the Authorized Version because it was authorized by the king, captured the best of all the preceding English translations and far exceeded all of them. This is aptly expressed by J. H. Skilton:

> The Authorized Version gathered to itself the virtues of the long and brilliant line of English Bible translations; it united

high scholarship with Christian devotion and piety. It came into being at a time when the English language was vigorous and young, and its scholars had a remarkable mastery of the instrument [talent] which Providence had prepared for them. Their version has justifiably been called "the noblest monument of English prose." (J. H. Skilton, "English Versions of the Bible," *New Bible Dictionary*, 325–33)

Indeed, the King James Version has become an enduring monument of English prose because of its gracious style, majestic language, and poetic rhythms. No other book has had such a tremendous influence on English literature, and no other translation has touched the lives of so many English-speaking people for centuries and centuries, even until the present day.

The Eighteenth and Nineteenth Centuries: New Discoveries of Earlier Manuscripts and Increased Knowledge of the Original Languages

The King James Version became the most popular English translation in the seventeenth and eighteenth centuries. It acquired the stature of becoming the standard English Bible. But the King James Version had deficiencies that did not go unnoticed by certain scholars. First, knowledge of Hebrew was inadequate in the early seventeenth century. The Hebrew text they used (i.e., the Masoretic Text) was adequate, but their understanding of the Hebrew vocabulary was insufficient. It would take many more years of linguistic studies to enrich and sharpen understanding of the Hebrew vocabulary. Second, the Greek text underlying the New Testament of the King James Version was an inferior text. The King James translators basically used a Greek text known as the Textus Receptus (or, the "Received Text"), which came from the work of Erasmus, who compiled the first Greek text to be produced on a printing press. When Erasmus compiled this text, he used five or six very late manuscripts dating from the tenth to the thirteenth centuries. These manuscripts were far inferior to earlier manuscripts.

The King James translators had done well with the resources that were available to them, but those resources were insufficient, especially with respect to the New Testament text. After the King James Version was published, earlier and better manuscripts were discovered. Around 1630, Codex Alexandrinus was brought to England. A fifth century manuscript containing the entire New Testament, it provided a fairly good witness to the New Testament text, especially the original text of Revelation. Two hundred years later, a German scholar named Constantin von Tischendorf discovered Codex Sinaiticus in St. Catherine's Monastery. The manuscript, dated around A.D. 350, is one of the two oldest manuscripts of the Greek New Testament. The earliest manuscript, Codex Vaticanus, had been in the Vatican's library since at least 1481, but it was not made available to scholars until the middle of the nineteenth century. This manuscript, dated slightly earlier (A.D. 325) than Codex Sinaiticus, is one of the most reliable copies of the Greek New Testament.

As these manuscripts (and others) were discovered and made public, certain scholars labored to compile a Greek text that would more closely represent the original text than did the Textus Receptus. Around 1700 John Mill produced an improved Textus Receptus, and in the 1730s Johannes Albert Bengel, known as the father of modern textual and philological studies in the New Testament, published a text that deviated from the Textus Receptus according to the evidence of earlier manuscripts.

In the 1800s certain scholars began to abandon the Textus Receptus. Karl Lachman, a classical philologist, produced a fresh text in 1831 that represented the fourth century manuscripts. Samuel Tregelles, self-taught in Latin, Hebrew, and Greek, laboring throughout his entire lifetime, concentrated all of his efforts in publishing one Greek text, which came out in six parts, from 1857 to 1872. Tischendorf devoted a lifetime of labor to discovering manuscripts and producing accurate editions of the Greek New Testament. He not only discovered Codex Sinaiticus, he also deciphered the palimpsest Codex Ephraemi Rescriptus, collated countless manuscripts, and produced several editions of the Greek New Testament (the eighth edition is the best). Aided by the work of these scholars, two British men, Brooke Westcott and Fenton Hort, worked together for twenty-eight years to produce a volume entitled *The New Testament in the Original Greek* (1881). This edition of the Greek New Testament, based largely on Codex Vaticanus, became the standard text that was responsible for dethroning the Textus Receptus.

The English Revised Version and the American Standard Version

By the latter part of the nineteenth century, the Christian community had been given three very good Greek New Testament texts. Tregelles', Tischendorf's, and Westcott and Hort's. These texts were very different from the Textus Receptus. And as was mentioned earlier, the scholarly community had accumulated more knowledge about the meaning of various Hebrew words and Greek words. Therefore, there was a great need for a new English translation based upon a better text—and with more accurate renderings of the original languages.

A few individuals attempted to meet this need. In 1871 John Nelson Darby, leader of the Plymouth Brethren movement, produced a translation called the *New Translation,* which was largely based on Codex Vaticanus and Codex Sinaiticus. In 1872 J. B. Rotherham published a translation of Tregelles' text, in which he attempted to reflect the emphasis inherent in the Greek text. This translation is still being published under the title *The Emphasized*

Bible. And in 1875 Samuel Davidson produced a New Testament translation of Tischendorf's text.

The first major corporate effort was initiated in 1870 by the Convocation of Canterbury, which decided to sponsor a major revision of the King James Version. Sixty-five British scholars, working in various committees, made significant changes in the King James Version. The Old Testament scholars corrected mistranslations of Hebrew words and reformatted poetic passages into poetic form. The New Testament scholars made thousands of changes based upon better textual evidence. Their goal was to make the New Testament revision reflect not the Textus Receptus, but the texts of Tregelles, Tischendorf, and Westcott and Hort. When the complete Revised Version appeared in 1885, it was received with great enthusiasm. Over 3 million copies sold in the first year of its publication. Unfortunately, its popularity was not long lasting because most people continued to prefer the King James Version over all other translations.

Several American scholars had been invited to join the revision work, with the understanding that any of their suggestions not accepted by the British scholars would appear in an appendix. Furthermore, the American scholars had to agree not to publish their own American revision until after fourteen years. When the time came (1901), the American Standard Version was published by several surviving members of the original American committee. This translation, generally regarded as superior to the English Revised Version, is an accurate, literal rendering of very trustworthy texts both in the Old Testament and the New.

The Twentieth Century: New Discoveries and New Translations

The nineteenth century was a fruitful era for the Greek New Testament and subsequent English translations; it was also a century in which Hebrew studies were greatly advanced. The twentieth century has also been fruitful—especially for textual studies. Those living in the twentieth century have witnessed the discovery of the Dead Sea Scrolls (see "Texts and Manuscripts of the Old Testament" in section 4), the Oxyrhynchus Papyri, the Chester Beatty Papyri, and the Bodmer Papyri (see "Texts and Manuscripts of the New Testament" in section 4). These amazing discoveries, providing scholars with hundreds of ancient manuscripts, have greatly enhanced the effort to recover the original wording of the Old and New Testaments. At the same time, other archaeological discoveries have validated the historical accuracy of the Bible and helped Bible scholars understand the meaning of certain ancient words. For example, the Greek word *parousia* (usually translated "coming") was found in many ancient documents dated around the time of Christ; very often the word indicated the visitation of royalty. When this word was used in the New Testament concerning Christ's second coming, the readers would think of his coming as being the visitation of a king. In Koine Greek, the expression *entos humon* (literally, "inside of you") often meant "within reach." Thus, Jesus' statement in Luke 17:21 could mean "The kingdom is within reach."

As earlier and better manuscripts of the Bible have emerged, scholars have been engaged in updating the Bible texts. Old Testament scholars have still used the Masoretic Text but have noted significant differences found in the Dead Sea Scrolls. The current edition used by Old Testament scholars is called *Biblia Hebraica Stuttgartensia*. New Testament scholars, for the most part, have come to rely upon an edition of the Greek New Testament known as the Nestle-Aland text. Eberhard Nestle used the best editions of the Greek New Testament produced in the nineteenth century to compile a text that represented the majority consensus. The work of making new editions was carried on by his son for several years and is now under the care of Kurt Aland. The latest edition (the 26th) of Nestle-Aland's *Novum Testamentum Graece* appeared in 1979, with a corrected edition in 1986. The same Greek text appears in another popular volume published by the United Bible Societies, called the *Greek New Testament* (third, corrected edition—1983).

Early Twentieth Century Translations in the Language of the People

The thousands and thousands of papyri that were discovered in Egypt around the turn of the century displayed a form of Greek called Koine Greek. Koine (meaning "common") Greek was everyman's Greek; it was the common language of almost everybody living in the Graeco-Roman world from the second century B.C. to the third century A.D. In other words, it was the "lingua franca" of the Mediterranean world. Every educated person back then could speak, read, and write in Greek just like every educated person in modern times can speak a little English, read some English, and perhaps write in English. Koine Greek was not literary Greek (i.e., the kind of Greek written by the Greek poets and tragedians); it was the kind of Greek used in personal letters, legal documents, and other nonliterary texts.

New Testament scholars began to discover that most of the New Testament was written in Koine Greek—the language of the people. As a result, there was a strong prompting to translate the New Testament into the language of the people. Various translators chose to divorce themselves from the traditional Elizabethan English as found in the King James Version (and even in the English Revised Version and American Standard Version) and produce fresh renderings in the common idiom.

THE TWENTIETH CENTURY NEW TESTAMENT

The first of these new translations was *The Twentieth Century New Testament* (1902). The preface to a new edition of this translation provides an excellent description of the work:

> *The Twentieth Century New Testament* is a smooth-flowing, accurate, easy-to-read translation that captivates its readers from start to finish. Born out of a desire to make the Bible readable and understandable, it is the product of the labors of a committee of twenty men and women who worked together over many years to construct, we believe under divine surveillance, this beautifully simple rendition of the Word of God. (Preface to the new edition [1961] published by Moody Press)

THE NEW TESTAMENT IN MODERN SPEECH

A year after the publication of *The Twentieth Century New Testament,* Richard Weymouth published *The New Testament in Modern Speech* (1903). Weymouth, who had received the first Doctor of Literature degree from the University of London, was headmaster of a private school in London. During his life, he spent time producing an edition of the Greek text (published in 1862) that was more accurate than the Textus Receptus, and then he labored to produce an English translation of this Greek text (called *The Resultant Greek Testament*) in a modern speech version. His translation was very well received; it has gone through several editions and many printings.

THE NEW TESTAMENT: A NEW TRANSLATION

Another new and fresh translation to appear in the early years of this century was one written by James Moffatt, a brilliant Scottish scholar. In 1913 he published his first edition of *The New Testament: A New Translation.* This was actually his second translation of the New Testament; his first was done in 1901, called *The Historical*

New Testament. In his *New Translation* Moffatt's goal was "to translate the New Testament exactly as one would render any piece of contemporary Hellenistic prose." His work displays brilliance and marked independence from other versions; unfortunately it was based on Hermann von Soden's Greek New Testament, which, as all scholars now know, is quite defective.

THE COMPLETE BIBLE: AN AMERICAN TRANSLATION

The earliest American modern speech translation was produced by Edgar J. Goodspeed, a professor of New Testament at the University of Chicago. He had criticized *The Twentieth Century New Testament,* Weymouth's version, and Moffatt's translation. As a consequence, he was challenged by some other scholars to do better. He took up the challenge and in 1923 published *The New Testament: An American Translation.* When he made this translation he said that he wanted to give his "version something of the force and freshness that reside in the original Greek." He said, "I wanted my translation to make on the reader something of the impression the New Testament must have made on its earliest readers, and to invite the continuous reading of the whole book at a time" (*New Chapters in New Testament Study,* 113). His translation was a success. An Old Testament translation followed, produced by J. M. Powis Smith and three other scholars. *The Complete Bible: An American Translation* was published in 1935.

The Revised Standard Version

The English Revised Version and the American Standard Version had gained a reputation of being accurate study texts but very "wooden" in their construction. The translators who worked on the Revised Versions attempted to translate words consistently from the original language regardless of its context and sometimes even followed the word order of the Greek. This created a very unidiomatic version. This called for a new revision.

The demand for revision was strengthened by the fact that several important biblical manuscripts had been discovered in the 1930s and 1940s—namely, the Dead Sea Scrolls for the Old Testament and the Chester Beatty Papyri for the New Testament. It was felt that the fresh evidence displayed in these documents should be reflected in a revision. The revision showed some textual changes in the book of Isaiah due to the Isaiah scroll and several changes in the Pauline Epistles due to the Chester Beatty Papyrus P46. There were other significant revisions. The story of the woman caught in adultery (John 7:52–8:11) was not included in the text but in the margin because none of the early manuscripts contain this story, and the ending to Mark (16:9-20) was not included in the text because it is not found in the two earliest manuscripts, Codex Vaticanus and Codex Sinaiticus.

The organization that held the copyright to the American Standard Version, called the International Council of Religious Education, authorized a new revision in 1937. The New Testament translators generally followed the seventeenth edition of the Nestle Text (1941), while the Old Testament translators followed the Masoretic Text. Both groups, however, adopted readings from other ancient sources when they were considered to be more accurate. The New Testament was published in 1946, and the entire Bible with the Old Testament, in 1952.

The principles of the revision were specified in the preface to the Revised Standard Version:

> The Revised Standard Version is not a new translation in the language of today. It is not a paraphrase which aims at striking idioms. It is a revision which seeks to preserve all that is best in the English Bible as it as been known and used throughout the years.

This revision was well received by many Protestant churches and soon became their "standard" text. The Revised Standard Version was later published with the Apocrypha of the Old Testament (1957), in a Catholic Edition (1965), and in what is called the *Common Bible,* which includes the Old Testament, the New Testament, the Apocrypha, and the deuterocanonical books, with international endorsements by Protestants, Greek Orthodox, and Roman Catholics. Evangelical and fundamental Christians, however, did not receive the Revised Standard Version very well—primarily because of one verse, Isaiah 7:14, which reads, "Therefore the Lord himself will give you a sign. Look, the young woman is with child and shall bear a son, and shall name him Immanuel." Evangelicals and fundamentalists contend that the text should read "virgin," not "young woman." As a result, the Revised Standard Version was panned, if not banned, by many evangelical and fundamental Christians.

The New English Bible

In the year that the New Testament of the Revised Standard Version was published (1946), the Church of Scotland proposed to other churches in Great Britain that it was time for a completely new translation of the Bible to be done. Those who initiated this work asked the translators to produce a fresh translation in modern idiom of the original languages; this was not to be a revision of any foregoing translation, nor was it to be a literal translation. The translators, under the direction of C. H. Dodd, were called upon to translate the meaning of the text into modern English. The preface to the New Testament (published in 1961), written by C. H. Dodd, explains this more fully:

> The older translators, on the whole, considered that fidelity to the original demanded that they should reproduce, as far as possible, characteristic features of the language in which it was

written, such as the syntactical order of words, the structure and division of sentences, and even such irregularities of grammar as were indeed natural enough to authors writing in the easy idiom of popular Hellenistic Greek, but less natural when turned into English. The present translators were enjoined to replace Greek constructions and idioms by those of contemporary English.

This meant a different theory and practice of translation, and one which laid a heavier burden on the translators. Fidelity in translation was not to mean keeping the general framework of the original intact while replacing Greek words by English words more or less equivalent. . . . Thus we have not felt obliged (as did the Revisers of 1881) to make an effort to render the same Greek word everywhere by the same English word. We have in this respect returned to the wholesome practice of King James's men, who (as they expressly state in their preface) recognized no such obligation. We have conceived our task to be that of understanding the original as precisely as we could (using all available aids), and then saying again in our own native idiom what we believed the author to be saying in his.

The entire *New English Bible* was published in 1970; it was well received in Great Britain and in the United States (even though its idiom its extremely British) and was especially praised for its good literary style. The translators were very experimental, producing renderings never before printed in an English version and adopting certain readings from various Hebrew and Greek manuscripts never before adopted. As a result, *The New English Bible* was both highly praised for its ingenuity and severely criticized for its liberty.

The *Good News Bible:* Today's English Version

The New Testament in Today's English Version, also known as *Good News for Modern Man,* was published by the American Bible Society in 1966. The translation was originally done by Robert Bratcher, a research associate of the Translations Department of the American Bible Society, and then further refined by the American Bible Society. The translation, heavily promoted by several Bible societies and very affordable, sold more than 35 million copies within six years of the time of printing. The New Testament translation, based upon the first edition of the *Greek New Testament* (the United Bible Societies, 1966), is an idiomatic version in modern and simple English. The translation was greatly influenced by the linguistic theory of dynamic equivalence and was quite successful in providing English readers with a translation that, for the most part, accurately reflects the meaning of the original texts. This is explained in the preface to the New Testament:

> This translation of the New Testament has been prepared by the American Bible Society for people who speak English as their mother tongue or as an acquired language. As a distinctly new translation, it does not conform to traditional vocabulary or style, but seeks to express the meaning of the Greek text in words and forms accepted as standard by people everywhere who employ English as a means of communication. Today's English Version of the New Testament attempts to follow, in this century, the example set by the authors of the New Testament books, who, for the most part, wrote in the standard, or common, form of the Greek language used throughout the Roman Empire.

Because of the success of the New Testament, the American Bible Society was asked by other Bible societies to make an Old

Testament translation following the same principles used in the New Testament. The entire Bible was published in 1976, and is known as the *Good News Bible:* Today's English Version.

The Living Bible

In 1962 Kenneth Taylor published a paraphrase of the New Testament Epistles in a volume called *Living Letters.* This new dynamic paraphrase, written in common vernacular, became well received and widely acclaimed—especially for its ability to communicate the message of God's Word to the common man. In the beginning its circulation was greatly enhanced by the endorsement of the Billy Graham Evangelistic Association, which did much to publicize the book and distributed thousands of free copies. Taylor continued to paraphrase other portions of the Bible and publish successive volumes: *Living Prophecies* (1965), *Living Gospels* (1966), *Living Psalms* (1967), *Living Lessons of Life and Love* (1968), *Living Books of Moses* (1969), and *Living History of Moses* (1970). The entire *Living Bible* was published in 1971 (the *Living New Testament* was printed in 1966).

Using the American Standard Version as his working text, Taylor rephrased the Bible into modern speech—such that anyone, even a child, could understand the message of the original writers. In the preface to *The Living Bible* Taylor explains his view of paraphrasing:

> To paraphrase is to say something in different words than the author used. It is a restatement of the author's thoughts, using different words than he did. This book is a paraphrase of the Old and New Testaments. Its purpose is to say as exactly as possible what the writers of the Scriptures meant, and to say it simply, expanding where necessary for a clear understanding by the modern reader.

Even though many modern readers have greatly appreciated the fact that *The Living Bible* made God's Word clear to them, Taylor's paraphrase has been criticized for being too interpretive. But that is the nature of paraphrases—and the danger as well. Taylor was aware of this when he made the paraphrase. Again, the preface clarifies:

> There are dangers in paraphrases, as well as values. For whenever the author's exact words are not translated from the original languages, there is a possibility that the translator, however honest, may be giving the English reader something that the original writer did not mean to say.

The Living Bible has been very popular among English readers worldwide. More than 35 million copies have been sold by the publishing house Taylor specifically created to publish *The Living Bible*. The company is called Tyndale House Publishers—named after William Tyndale, the father of modern English translations of the Bible.

The *New American Standard Bible*

There are two modern translations that are both revisions of (or based on) the American Standard Version (1901): the Revised Standard Version (1952) and the *New American Standard Bible* (1971). The Lockman Foundation, a nonprofit Christian corporation committed to evangelism, promoted this revision of the American Standard Version because "the producers of this translation were imbued with the conviction that interest in the American Standard Version 1901 should be renewed and increased" (from the preface). Indeed, the American Standard Version was a monumental work of scholarship and a very accurate translation. However, its popularity was waning, and it was fast disappearing from the scene. Therefore, the Lockman Foundation organized a team of thirty-two scholars to prepare a new revision. These scholars, all committed to the inspiration of Scripture, strove to produce a literal translation of the Bible in the belief that such a translation "brings the contemporary reader as close as possible to the actual wording and grammatical structure of the original writers" (ibid.).

The translators of the *New American Standard Bible* were instructed by the Lockman Foundation "to adhere to the original languages of the Holy Scriptures as closely as possible and at the same time to obtain a fluent and readable style according to current English usage" (Sakae Kubo and Walter Specht, *So Many Versions?* 171). After the *New American Standard Bible* was published (1963 for the New Testament and 1971 for the entire Bible), it received a mixed response. Some critics applauded its literal accuracy, while others sharply criticized its language for hardly being contemporary or modern.

On the whole, the *New American Standard Bible* became respected as a good study Bible that accurately reflects the wording of the original languages yet is not a good translation for Bible reading. Furthermore, it must be said that this translation is now nearly thirty years behind in terms of textual fidelity—especially the New Testament, which, though it was originally supposed to follow the 23rd edition of the Nestle text, tends to follow the Textus Receptus.

The New International Version

The New International Version is a completely new rendering of the original languages done by an international group of more than a hundred scholars. These scholars worked many years and in several committees to produce an excellent thought-for-thought translation in contemporary English for private and public use. The New International Version is called "international" because it was prepared by distinguished scholars from English-speaking countries such as the United States, Canada, Great Britain, Australia, and New Zealand, and because "the translators sought to use vocabulary common to the major English-speaking nations of the world" (ibid., 191-192).

The translators of the New International Version sought to make a version that was midway between a literal rendering (as in the *New American Standard Bible*) and a free paraphrase (as in *The Living Bible*). Their goal was to convey in English the thought of the original writers. This is succinctly explained in the original preface to the New Testament:

> Certain convictions and aims guided the translators. They are all committed to the full authority and complete trustworthiness of the Scriptures. Therefore, their first concern was the accuracy of the translation and its fidelity to the thought of the New Testament writers. While they weighed the significance of the lexical and grammatical details of the Greek text, they have striven for more than a word-for-word translation. Because thought patterns and syntax differ from language to language, faithful communication of the meaning of the writers of the New Testament demanded frequent modifications in sentence structure and constant regard for the contextual meanings of words.
>
> Concern for clarity of style—that it should be idiomatic without being idiosyncratic, contemporary without being dated—also motivated the translators and their consultants. They have consistently aimed at simplicity of expression, with sensitive attention to the connotation and sound of the chosen word. At the same time, they endeavored to avoid a sameness of style in order to reflect the varied styles and moods of the New Testament writers.

The New Testament of the New International Version was published in 1973, and the entire Bible, in 1978. This version has been phenomenally successful. Millions and millions of readers have adopted the New International Version as their "Bible." Since 1987 it has outsold the King James Version, the best-seller for centuries—a remarkable indication of its popularity and acceptance in the Christian community. The New International Version, sponsored by the New York Bible Society (now the International Bible Society) and published by Zondervan Publishers, has become a standard version used for private reading and pulpit reading in many English-speaking countries.

Two Modern Catholic Translations:
The Jerusalem Bible and *The New American Bible*

In 1943 Pope Pius XII issued the famous encyclical encouraging Roman Catholics to read and study the Scriptures. At the same time, the pope recommended that the Scriptures should be translated from the original languages. Previously, all Catholic translations were based on the Latin Vulgate. This includes Knox's translation, which was begun in 1939 and published in 1944 (the New Testament) and in 1955 (the whole Bible).

The first complete Catholic Bible to be translated from the original languages is *The Jerusalem Bible,* published in England in 1966. *The Jerusalem Bible* is the English counterpart to a French translation entitled *La Bible de Jerusalem.* The French translation was "the culmination of decades of research and biblical scholarship" (from the preface to *The Jerusalem Bible*), published by the scholars of the Dominican Biblical School of Jerusalem. This Bible, which includes the Apocrypha and deuterocanonical books, contains many study helps—such as introductions to each book of the Bible, extensive notes on various passages, and maps. The study helps are an intricate part of the whole translation because it is the belief of

Roman Catholic leadership that laypeople should be given interpretive helps in their reading of the sacred text. The study helps in
The Jerusalem Bible were translated from the French, whereas the
Bible text itself was translated from the original languages with the
help of the French translation. The translation of the text produced
under the editorship of Alexander Jones is considerably freer than
other translations, such as the Revised Standard Version, because
the translators sought to capture the meaning of the original
writings in a "vigorous, contemporary literary style" (from the
preface to *The Jerusalem Bible*).

The first American Catholic Bible to be translated from the
original languages is *The New American Bible* (not to be confused
with the *New American Standard Bible*). Although this translation
was published in 1970, work had begun on this version several
decades before. Prior to Pope Pius's encyclical, an American
translation of the New Testament based on the Latin Vulgate was
published—known as the Confraternity Version. After the
encyclical, the Old Testament was translated from the Hebrew
Masoretic Text and the New Testament redone, based on the
twenty-fifth edition of the Greek Nestle-Aland text. *The New
American Bible* has short introductions to each book of the Bible and
very few marginal notes. Kubo and Specht provide a just description of the translation itself:

> The translation itself is simple, clear, and straightforward and
> reads very smoothly. It is good American English, not as
> pungent and colorful as the NEB [*New English Bible*]. Its
> translations are not striking but neither are they clumsy. They
> seem to be more conservative in the sense that they tend not
> to stray from the original. That is not to say that this is a literal
> translation, but it is more faithful. (*So Many Versions?* 165)

Jewish Translations

In the twentieth century some very important Jewish translations of the Bible were published. The Jewish Publication Society created a translation of the Hebrew Scriptures called *The Holy Scriptures According to the Masoretic Text, A New Translation* (published in 1917). The preface to this translation explains its purpose:

> It aims to combine the spirit of Jewish tradition with the results of biblical scholarship, ancient, medieval and modern. It gives to the Jewish world a translation of the Scriptures done by men imbued with the Jewish consciousness, while the non-Jewish world, it is hoped, will welcome a translation that presents many passages from the Jewish traditional point of view.

In 1955 the Jewish Publication Society appointed a new committee of seven eminent Jewish scholars to make a new Jewish translation of the Hebrew Scriptures. The translation called the New Jewish Version was published in 1962. A second, improved edition was published in 1973. This work is not a revision of *The Holy Scriptures According to the Masoretic Text*; it is a completely new translation in modern English. The translators attempted "to produce a version that would carry the same message to modern man as the original did to the world of ancient times" (Kubo and Specht, *So Many Versions?* 108).

Revisions, Revisions, Revisions

The last part of the twentieth century (the 1980s and 1990s) seems to be a time for new revisions, not new translations. The general consensus among the consumers is, "We have enough translations, don't give us any more." Most of the publishers seem to be getting the message. Therefore, instead of publishing new translations, they are issuing new, revised editions of existing translations.

The New Revised Standard Version published in 1990 is an excellent example of this current trend. In the preface to this revision, Bruce Metzger, chairperson of the revision committee, wrote:

> The New Revised Standard Version of the Bible is an authorized revision of the Revised Standard Version, published in 1952, which was a revision of the American Standard Version, published in 1901, which, in turn, embodied earlier revisions of the King James Version, published in 1611.
>
> The need for issuing a revision of the Revised Standard Version of the Bible arises from three circumstances: (a) the acquisition of still older Biblical manuscripts, (b) further investigation of linguistic features of the text, and (c) changes in preferred English usage.

The three criteria specified by Metzger for the New Revised Standard Version are essentially the same principles behind all revisions of Bible translations.

In the 1980s several significant revisions appeared: the New King James Version (1982); *The New Jerusalem Bible* (1986); *The New American Bible,* Revised New Testament (1986); and the *Revised English Bible* (1989), which is a radical revision of *The New English Bible.* Other translations, such as the New International Version and Today's English Version, were also revised in 1980s but not publicized as such. Inevitably, more revisions, and perhaps some new translations, will appear in the 1990s.

BIBLIOGRAPHY

Comfort, Philip. *Complete Guide to Bible Versions,* 1991.
Edwards, Brian. *God's Outlaw,* 1981.
Kubo, Sakae, and Walter Specht. *So Many Versions?* rev. ed., 1983.
Skilton, J. H. "English Versions of the Bible" in the *New Bible Dictionary,* ed. J. D. Douglas, 1962.

Versions of the Bible
Victor Walter

To get a picture of how the Bible has come to different peoples in the world, spread out a map of the eastern hemisphere and imagine Palestine as the center of a pool. Think of God's revelation of himself through the prophets, the Christ, and the apostles as a pebble dropped into the center of that body of water. In your mind's eye watch the advance of the concentric circles out across that world pool from Palestine and call out the languages covered by the fast-spreading ripple: to the south, Coptic, Arabic, Ethiopic; to the west, Greek, Latin, Gothic, English; to the north, Armenian, Georgian, Slavonic; and eastward toward the rising sun, Syriac. The farther the Bible moved from its Hebrew/Aramaic/Greek center in Palestine, the later the date of its translation into yet another language.

That pebble of God's revelation, the Bible, was produced in the Middle East predominantly in two of Palestine's languages. The Old Testament was written in Hebrew with the exception of portions of the books of Daniel and Ezra, which may have been written in Aramaic, the language of the captivity. Probably the entire New Testament was written in common Greek (koine) which was the dominant language of the eastern half of Caesar's domain and understood almost everywhere else in the Roman Empire. Therefore every person who did not speak Hebrew or Greek was apt to remain untouched by God's written revelation until someone translated the Bible into his language.

The process of Bible translation began even before the birth of Christ, with translations of the Old Testament being made into Greek and Aramaic. Many of the dispersed Jews who lived prior to the coming of Christ did not know Hebrew and therefore required a translation in Greek or Aramaic. The most popular Greek translation of the Old Testament was the Septuagint. It was used by many Jews, and then by many Christians. In fact, the Septuagint was the "Bible" for all the first generation Christians, including those who wrote various books of the New Testament.

The early Christian missionaries carrying a text of the Septuagint (or Hebrew Bible) and the Greek New Testament (or portions thereof), which they themselves could read, moved ever outward from those early churches at Jerusalem and Antioch about which we read in the book of Acts. They moved out among peoples whose language they learned to speak. Such missionaries orally translated or paraphrased Bible passages necessary for instruction, preaching, and liturgy. Converts were made. New churches sprang up. Feeling an urgent need for the Bible to be put in the language of the new believers, missionaries would soon set about translating the whole Bible into their language. The impulse behind our modern Wycliffe Bible Translators has always been at the heart of missions, and in that way the major Bible versions were born.

Bible translation was thus spontaneous, invariably informal and oral at first, and sharply evangelistic in its motivation. The early church enthusiastically encouraged and undertook translating efforts. Even as late as the birth of the Slavonic version in the mid-ninth century, popes Adrian II (867–872) and John VIII (872–882) endorsed the project. But an amazing change came in the Western church in regard to Bible translation. Latin took over as the dominant language—such that no one read Greek anymore. Then, as learning became the province of only the wealthy nobility and prelates (churchmen of high rank, such as bishops), as the splendors of classical civilization were lost in the ferment of feudalism in Europe, and as the Roman Catholic hierarchy—headed by the pope—claimed a firm grip on Western Christendom, the Bible was removed from the hands of the laity. Therefore, as long as the priests could read the Latin texts and speak the liturgy in Latin (at least at a minimal level), there was no longer significant motivation for translations into the vernacular.

Latin came to be considered almost a sacred language and translations of the Bible into the vernacular were viewed with suspicion. Pope Gregory VII (1073–1085) gave voice to such suspicions when, only two hundred years after Adrian II and John VIII had called for a Slavonic translation, Gregory attempted to stop its circulation. He wrote to King Vratislaus of Bohemia in 1079:

> For it is clear to those who reflect upon it that not without reason has it pleased Almighty God that holy scripture should be a secret in certain places lest, if it were plainly apparent to all men, perchance it would be little esteemed and be subject to disrespect; or it might be falsely understood by those of mediocre learning, and lead to error.

Meanwhile in Palestine and northern Africa, the inexorable march of Islam changed the religious texture of the Mediterranean's eastern and southern littorals. Within one hundred years of Mohammed's death in 632 (b. 570), over nine hundred churches had been destroyed and the Koran became the "bible" in the great circle from the walls of embattled Byzantium round to the west—to the Spanish end of Europe.

Cramped by official opposition in the West and hindered by Islamic conquest in the Mid East, Bible translations slowed to a trickle for half a millennium. Translation efforts did not regain vitality until the Protestant Reformation of the early sixteenth century, at which time missionaries took advantage of movable-type printing (invented by Johannes Gutenberg) to produce multiple translations of the Bible. Erasmus expressed the desire of all Bible translators in the preface of his freshly published Greek New Testament (1516):

> I wish that even the weakest woman should read the Gospel–should read the Epistles of Paul. And I wish these were translated into all languages, so that they might be read and understood, not only by Scots and Irishmen, but also by Turks and Saracens. To make them understood is surely the first step. It may be that they might be ridiculed by many, but some would take them to heart. I long that the husbandman should sing portions of them to himself as he follows the plough, that the weaver should hum them to the tune of his shuttle, that the traveller should beguile with their stories the tedium of his journey.

But what materials were used by the early translators and copyists who worked so painstakingly over their Bible translations? At the time of Christ and through the first two centuries of the church, the most popular writing materials were ink on papyrus (the ubiquitous glued-together strips of the Nile River reed). Until the first century, "books" were actually scrolls with long sheets of papyrus paper glued end to end and rolled up on paired spindles. Then, later in the first century, another form of a book was created—called the codex (the precursor to the modern form of a book with folded sheets and stitched spine). Christians were among the first to use this form for books. In A.D. 332 the first Christian emperor, Constantine I, ordered fifty Bibles for the churches of his new capital city, Constantinople. He ordered those from Eusebius, Bishop of Caesarea, and specified that they were not to be scrolls, but codexes (or codices). They were also to be not of papyrus, but of vellum, carefully prepared sheep or antelope skins; for it was right about this time, in the late third and early fourth centuries, that codexes and vellum almost universally replaced scrolls and papyrus.

For centuries scribes laboriously copied Bibles all in capital letters; the earliest surviving manuscripts of Bible versions are of that type, called "uncials." In the ninth and tenth centuries it became the fashion to write in lower-case letters; surviving manuscripts of that type are called "minuscules" or "cursives." (There were, however, occasional cursive manuscripts as far back as the second century before Christ.) Minuscules dominate the surviving Biblical manuscripts from the tenth through the sixteenth centuries.

It was in 1454 that Johannes Gutenberg made manuscript writing obsolete by using movable type for the first time. His first printed book appeared in 1456, a splendid Latin Bible. Our printed Bibles today contain chapter and verse divisions that were a relatively late development. Chapter divisions began in the Latin Vulgate and are variously credited to Lanfranc, Archbishop of Canterbury (died 1089), to Stephen Langton, Archbishop of Canterbury (died 1228), or to Hugo de Sancto Caro of the thirteenth century. Verse numbers first appeared in the fourth edition of the Greek New Testament issued at Geneva in 1551 by Robert Etienne (Stephanus) and in the Athias Hebrew Old Testament of 1559–1561.

Earliest Versions of the Old Testament

The first version to be considered, the Samaritan Pentateuch, cannot rightly be termed a translation because it is a Hebrew version of the first five books of the Old Testament, the Books of the Law. These books comprise the total canon of Scripture for the

Samaritan community, which still survives and is now centered in modern Nablus in Palestine.

The Samaritan Pentateuch reflects a textual tradition different from that of traditional Judaism, whose Hebrew text goes back through the centuries to the work of the Masoretes. The Masoretes were a body of scribes charged with Old Testament text preservation, beginning about A.D. 600 and extending to the first half of the tenth century. It was they who devised a pointing system to indicate the vowels missing from consonantal Hebrew. It is this so-called Masoretic text that forms (as the "received text") the basis for the King James Old Testament.

The Samaritan Pentateuch, on the other hand, goes back to the fourth century before Christ. According to textual scholars, the Samaritan Pentateuch differs from the "received" or Masoretic Hebrew text in about six thousand places. About one thousand of those differences need to be taken seriously. Where the text of the Samaritan Pentateuch agrees with the Septuagint or one of the other ancient versions against the Hebrew of the Masoretic text, its witness must be regarded as important. The two oldest manuscripts of the Samaritan Pentateuch outside of Nablus are both codexes. One copy in the John Rylands Library in Manchester, England, bears a date corresponding to A.D. 1211 or 1212; the other is somewhat older than 1149 and is presently in the University Library at Cambridge, England. Two minor translations of the Samaritan Pentateuch also exist; one is the Aramaic Samaritan Targum from early Christian times, the other an Arabic translation from about the eleventh century.

The second Old Testament version, the Septuagint, is an actual translation from the Hebrew into the Greek. It is the first translation of the Old Testament known. It was the Bible of Jesus and the apostles, the version from which most Old Testament quotations in the New Testament come, and the Bible of the early church as far as the Old Testament was concerned.

The story of its production, from which it draws its name, is told in "The Letter of Aristeas" (written around 150–100 B.C.). Aristeas purportedly was an official of Egypt's Ptolemy Philadelphus (285–247 B.C.). Ptolemy was attempting to gather all of the world's books into his great Alexandrian library. The Old Testament was not on hand in translation, the letter says, so Ptolemy sent to the high priest in Jerusalem for texts and scholars to translate. Texts and six elders of each tribe were sent. After being royally entertained by Ptolemy, these seventy-two elders were cloistered and in exactly seventy-two days produced the full Greek translation of the Old Testament, called Septuagint ("Seventy") and usually abbreviated LXX in Roman numerals.

The truth of the matter is probably more prosaic. The Septuagint is a translation done for hellenized Jews of the diaspora who, no longer understanding Hebrew, wished to hear and teach the Bible in their language. Scholars argue over the date of the translation, placing portions as early as 250 B.C. and other parts as late as 100 B.C. Most concur that it was translated in segments by many translators over a couple of centuries and then was gathered together into one library of scrolls or one codex. The Septuagint follows a different order from English Bibles and usually includes up to fifteen apocryphal or noncanonical books. A table of contents would look something like this (the numbers in parentheses indicate the apocryphal texts):

Genesis
Exodus
Leviticus
Numbers
Deuteronomy

Joshua

Judges

Ruth

I Samuel

II Samuel

I Kings

II Kings

I Chronicles

II Chronicles

I Esdras (1)

II Esdras (being Ezra and Nehemiah together)

Psalms

Proverbs

Ecclesiastes

Song of Solomon

Job

Wisdom of Solomon (2)

Wisdom of ben Sira (3) or Ecclesiasticus

Esther—with additions (4)

Judith (5)

Tobit (6)

Hosea

Amos

Micah

Joel

Obadiah

Jonah

Nahum

Habakkuk

Zephaniah

Haggai

Zechariah

Malachi

Isaiah

Jeremiah

Baruch (7)

Lamentations

Epistle of Jeremiah (8)

Ezekiel

Daniel—which begins with Susanna (9), inserts The Song
of the Three Children (10) after 3:23, and adds Bel and the
Dragon (11)

I Maccabees (12)

II Maccabees (13)

III Maccabees (14)

IV Maccabees (15)

Since the best of scribes occasionally inadvertently made errors
in copying a text, the tendency was for any text to deteriorate.
Careful scholars, then as now, compared manuscripts in an effort
to recapture the original. By the third century A.D., therefore, there
were four rival versions of the Septuagint in wide usage: (1) the
traditional Septuagint the Christians took over and the Jews consequently abandoned; (2) a Jewish retranslation done by Aquila in
the second century A.D. that translated the Hebrew very literally;
(3) a free Jewish revision of the traditional Septuagint by
Theodotian; and (4) a translation in more idiomatic Greek by
Symmachus.

Then came the greatest textual scholar of all antiquity, Origen
of Alexandria (c. A.D. 185–255), who produced antiquity's most
massive Bible, the *Hexapla*. In his effort to find the best text of the
Septuagint, Origen wrote out six parallel columns containing first
the Hebrew, second the Hebrew transliterated into Greek characters, third the text of Aquila, fourth the text of Symmachus, fifth

his own corrected Septuagint text, sixth the text of Theodotian. Jerome used this great Bible at Caesarea in his work on the Vulgate (after 382—see below). Almost four centuries after Origen's death, a Mesopotamian Bishop, Paul of Tella, also used the *Hexapla* in the library at Caesarea (616–617) to make a translation into Syriac of Origen's fifth column, the corrected Septuagint. Then in 638 the Islamic hordes swept through Caesarea and the *Hexapla* disappeared. Other than a few fragments, only Bishop Paul's Syriac translation of Origen's fifth column remains.

An eighth century copy of Bishop Paul's Syriac *Hexapla* Septuagint is extant in a Milan museum. Other famous uncial manuscripts of the Septuagint are the codexes: Vaticanus, early fourth century, now in the Vatican Library; Sinaiticus, mid-fourth century; and Alexandrinus, probably from the fifth century—both of the latter are in London's British Museum. These copies are intensely studied because they bear a Greek witness to Hebrew texts far earlier than the Masoretic or "received text."

The third Old Testament version is the Aramaic. Biblical Aramaic, called Chaldee up through the nineteenth century, was the language of the conquerors that gradually became the household speech of the conquered. When the Jewish exiles began to return to Palestine from Babylon in 536 B.C., they brought Aramaic with them. Many scholars believe that when Ezra and the Levites "explained the meaning of the passage" as the Book of the Law was read (Neh. 8:8, TLB), they were paraphrasing the Hebrew into Aramaic so all could understand. Aramaic remained as the living language in Palestine up to the Bar-Kochba revolt against the Romans (A.D. 132–135), and Hebrew became increasingly a religious language for synagogue and temple specialists. As priests and scribes read the Law and Prophets, the custom of following the reading with an Aramaic translation spread. Such translations were called targums.

Rabbinical leadership was very loath to formalize and write down the targums, but inevitably they were collected and standardized. The earliest standardized targum was that of the Law done by someone known as Onkelos, sometime in the second or third century A.D. Targums on the historical and prophetic books were crystallized in the third and fourth centuries A.D., with the most important one called the Targum Jonathan ben Uzziel. Evidently no targums of the wisdom literature (Proverbs, Ecclesiastes, Job, some Psalms) were completed earlier than the fifth century A.D. Finally rabbinical Aramaic targums included all of the Old Testament except Daniel, Ezra, and Nehemiah. Meanwhile, the Islamic conquest of the entire Middle East gave people a new common language, Arabic. Rabbis were apt to find themselves beginning to produce informal oral Arabic targums, and Aramaic faded from the synagogue into religious history.

Complete Bible Versions of Christendom

As the church gathered the New Testament together and added it to the Old, there began the process of Bible translation which has marked the growth of Christianity from Jerusalem through Judea to Samaria and on toward the "uttermost part" of the world.

LATIN VERSIONS

Like the Aramaic targums of Jewish worshipers, the Old Latin Bible was an informal growth. In the early days of the Roman Empire and of the church, Greek was the language of Christians. Even the first bishops of Rome wrote and preached in Greek. As empire and church aged, Latin began to win out, especially in the West. It was natural that priests and bishops began informally to translate the Greek New Testament and Septuagint into Latin. The initial Latin version is called the Old Latin Bible. No complete manuscript of it survives. Much of the Old Testament and most of the New, however, can be reconstructed from quotations in the early church fathers. Scholars believe that an Old Latin Bible was in circulation in Carthage in North Africa as early as A.D. 250. From the surviving fragments and quotations there seem to have been two types of Old Latin text, the African and the European. The European existed in an Italian revision also. In textual study the major importance of the Old Latin is in comparative study of the Septuagint because the Old Latin was translated from the Septuagint before Origen made his *Hexapla*.

From every quarter, church leaders voiced the need for an authoritative and uniform Latin translation of the whole Bible. Pope Damascus I (366–384) had an exceptionally able and scholarly secretary named Jerome (c. 340–420), whom he commissioned to make a new Latin translation of the Gospels in 382. Jerome completed the Gospels in 383; Acts and the rest of the New Testament evidently followed. The Gospels were a thorough and painstaking retranslation based on the European Old Latin and an Alexandrian Greek text. The rest of the New Testament, however, was a much more limited effort with the Old Latin remaining dominant unless the Greek text demanded change. In all probability it was not the work of Jerome himself.

Jerome left Rome in 385, and in 389 he and a follower, Paula, founded two religious houses near Bethlehem. At one of these Jerome presided. There he turned his attention to the Old Testament. He realized that what was needed was a retranslation from the Hebrew, not a revision of the Greek Septuagint. He used Jewish rabbis as consultants and completed work through the books of Kings by 390. Jerome reworked an earlier translation he had made of the Psalms and completed the prophets, Job, Ezra, and Chronicles in 390–396. After a two-year illness, he picked up the task again and translated Proverbs, Ecclesiastes, and Song of Solomon.

In 404 he worked through Joshua, Judges, Ruth, and Esther. Soon afterward he did the apocryphal parts of Daniel and Esther and translated the apocryphal Tobit and Judith from Aramaic. He did not touch the Wisdom of Solomon, Ecclesiasticus, Baruch, or the Maccabean literature, so those apocryphal books passed into the official Latin Bible in their Old Latin form. Jerome's work was not uniform in quality, nor did he gather it all together into a unified Bible.

Jerome's work was fiercely criticized, and though he defended it with facile pen and ready temper, he did not live long enough to see it win universal respect. Yet his life's work passed into what is now known as the Vulgate Bible (*vulga* meaning the "vulgar" or everyday speech of the people). Evidence seems to indicate that the compiling of all of Jerome's work into one book may have been done by Cassiodorus (died c. 580) in his monastery at Scylacium in Italy. The earliest extant manuscript containing Jerome's Bible in its entirety is the Codex Amiatinus written in the monastery at Jarrow, Northumbria, England, around 715. The old texts of the Vulgate are second only to the Septuagint in importance for Hebrew textual study, for Jerome was working from Hebrew texts that antedated the work of the Jewish Masoretes.

Only very gradually did the Vulgate supplant the Old Latin Bible. It took a thousand years before the Vulgate was made the official Roman Catholic Bible (by the Council of Trent in 1546). That council also authorized an official, corrected edition, which was first issued by Pope Sixtus V (1585–1590) in 1590 in three volumes. It proved unpopular, however, and Pope Clement VIII (1592–1605) recalled it and issued a new official Vulgate in 1592 which has been the standard edition to recent times.

COPTIC VERSIONS

Coptic was the last stage of the Egyptian language and thus the language of the native populations who lived along the length of the

Nile River. It was never supplanted by the Greek of Alexander and his generals or even threatened by the Latin of the Caesars. Its script was composed of twenty five Greek uncials and seven cursives taken over from Egyptian writing to express sounds not in the Greek. Through the centuries it developed at least five main dialects: Akhmimic, sub-Akhmimic (Memphitic), Sahidic, Fayumic, and Bohairic. Fragments of biblical material have been found in the Akhmimic, sub-Akhmimic, and Fayumic. No one knows whether or not the whole Bible ever existed in these dialects. They gradually faded out of use until—by the eleventh century—only Bohairic, the language of the Delta, and Sahidic, the language of Upper Egypt, remained. They too, however, had become largely forgotten or strictly religious languages used only in Coptic churches by the seventeenth century because of the long dominance of Arabic that began with the Islamic conquest of Egypt in 641.

The earliest translation was in Sahidic in Upper Egypt, where Greek was less universally understood. The Sahidic Old and New Testaments were probably completed by around A.D. 200. Greek was so much more dominant in the Delta that the translation of the Scriptures into Bohairic probably was not completed until somewhat later. Since Bohairic was the language of the Delta, however, it was also the language of the Coptic Patriarch in Alexandria. When the Patriarchate moved from Alexandria to Cairo in the eleventh century, the Bohairic texts went along. Bohairic gradually became the major religious language of the Coptic church. The Copts had separated from the Roman Empire, or the so-called Great Catholic church, over doctrinal issues after the Council of Chalcedon in 451 and had then been isolated from Western Christendom by centuries of Islamic rule.

GOTHIC VERSION

The Gothic language was an East Germanic language. The earliest literary remains known in any Germanic tongue are the fragments of the Bible done by Ulfilas (or Wulfila), who made the translation to bring the gospel to his own people. Ulfilas (c. 311–383), one of the early church's most famous missionaries, was born in Dacia of Roman Christian parents who had been captured by the raiding Goths. He traveled to Constantinople from his tribal area, and he may have been converted there. While in the East, he was ordained as bishop around 340 by the Arian bishop, Eusebius of Nicomedia. Ulfilas himself was of the Arian persuasion (believing that Christ was Savior and Lord by divine appointment and by his obedience, but that he was less than God or was subservient to God).

Ulfilas returned to preach to his people, evidently invented an alphabet for them in order to reduce their language to writing, and then translated the Scriptures into that written language. Records from that time say Ulfilas translated all of the Bible except the books of the Kings, which he excluded because he felt they would have an adverse influence on the Goths who were already too warlike. Scattered fragments of his Old Testament translation survive and only about half of the gospels are preserved in the Codex Argenteus, a manuscript of Bohemian origin of the fifth or sixth century now at Uppsala in Sweden.

SYRIAC VERSIONS

One of the family of Semitic languages, Syriac, was the predominant tongue of the region of Edessa and western Mesopotamia. The version known today as the Peshitta Bible (still the official Bible of Christians of the old Assyrian area churches and often lacking 2 Peter, 2 and 3 John, Jude, and Revelation) developed through several stages. One of the most famous and widely used translations in the early church was the Syriac *Diatessaron,* done by Tatian, a man who had been a disciple of Justin Martyr at Rome. The *Diatessaron,* Tatian's harmony of the Gospels translated from the Greek about A.D. 170, was very popular among Syriac-speaking Christians. Syrian bishops had an uphill battle getting Christians to use "The Gospel of the Separated Ones" (meaning the manuscript in which the four gospels were separated from one another rather than blended) in their churches.

Other portions of the Bible were also put into Old Syriac. Quotations from the church Fathers indicate that some type of second century Old Syriac text existed along with the *Diatessaron*. In fact, the Old Testament may have been a Jewish translation into Syriac which Syrian Christians made their own, just as Greek Christians had done with the Septuagint. It then underwent a more or less official revision around the end of the fourth century, emerging as the Peshitta (meaning "basic" or "simple") text. Tradition indicates that at least the New Testament portion of that version may have been made at the instigation of Rabbula, bishop of Edessa (411–435).

In the meantime, Syrian-speaking Christians underwent a schism in A.D. 431 when the Monophysite (or Jacobite) groups split off from the Nestorian believers (the battle was over the view of the Person of Christ). For a time both groups used the Peshitta, but the Jacobite groups began to desire a new translation. Working from the Septuagint and Greek New Testament manuscripts, Bishop Philoxemus (or Mar Zenaia) of Mabbug (485–519) on the Euphrates River did a new Syriac translation that was completed in 508. The importance of that version was that it included for the first time 2 Peter, 2 and 3 John, and Jude, which then made their way into the standard Peshitta text.

Though the Peshitta has been in continuous use since the fifth century, and reached as far as India and China in its distribution, it has not been nearly so important a source for textual scholars as the Septuagint. That is because it had undergone constant revision through comparison with various Greek texts at Constantinople, Hebrew texts, Origen's *Hexapla* Septuagint, and the Aramaic Targums; therefore, its witness to an early textual source is very difficult to trace. One of the most valuable Peshitta manuscripts extant is the Codex Ambrosianus of Milan which dates from the sixth century and contains the entire Old Testament.

ARMENIAN VERSION

Syrian Christians carried their faith to their Armenian neighbors in eastern Asia Minor. As early as the third century, with the conversion of Tiridates III (reigned 259–314), Armenia became a Christian kingdom—the first such in history. Sometime during the fifth century an Armenian alphabet was created so that the Bible could be translated into the language of these new believers. The Armenian translation is considered one of the most beautiful and accurate of the ancient versions of the Greek, even though textual evidence indicates it may have been done from the Syriac first and then modified to the Greek. (The Armenian language is allied closely with the Greek in grammar, syntax, and idiom.) An old tradition says that the New Testament was the work of Mesrop (a bishop in Armenia, 390–439) who is credited with inventing both the Armenian and Georgian alphabets. The book of Revelation was not accepted as part of the canon in Armenian churches until as late as the twelfth century.

GEORGIAN VERSION

The same tradition that credits Mesrop with translating the Bible into Armenian also credits an Armenian slave woman with being the missionary through whom Georgian-speaking people became Christian. The earliest manuscripts for the Georgian Scriptures go back only to the eighth century, but behind them is a Georgian translation with Syriac and Armenian traces. Evidently the Gospels first came in the form of the *Diatessaron;* therefore, Georgian fragments are important in the study of that text. There is a whole manuscript copy of the Georgian Bible in two volumes in the Iberian Monastery on Mount Athos.

Along with the Armenians and Georgians, a third Caucasian people, the Albanians, apparently received an alphabet from Mesrop for the purpose of Scriptural translation. Their church, however, was wiped out by the Islamic wars and no remains of that version have ever been found.

ETHIOPIC VERSION

By the middle of the fifth century a Christian king ruled in Ethiopia (Abyssinia), and until the Islamic conquests close ties were maintained with Egyptian Christianity. The Old Testament was probably translated into Old Ethiopic (called Ge'ez) by the fourth century. That version is of special interest for two reasons. It is the Bible of the Falashas, that remarkable community of African Jews who claim to be descendants of Jews who migrated to Ethiopia in the time of King Solomon and the Queen of Sheba. Further, the Old Ethiopic version of the Old Testament contains several books not in the Hebrew Apocrypha. Most interesting of these is the book of Enoch, which is quoted in Jude 14 and was unknown to Bible scholars until James Bruce brought a copy to Europe in 1773. The apocryphal 3 Baruch is known only from the Ethiopic also.

The New Testament was translated into Old Ethiopic somewhat later than the Old Testament and contains a collection of writings mentioned by Clement of Alexandria, including the Apocalypse of Peter. Both Testaments are extant in Ethiopic manuscripts. None, however, is earlier than the thirteenth century, and these manuscripts seem to rest rather heavily on the Coptic and the Arabic. Nothing survived the total chaos that reigned in Ethiopia from the seventh to the thirteenth centuries. Because they are so late, the Ethiopic manuscripts have had little value for textual study.

ARABIC VERSIONS

Around A.D. 570 Mohammed was born in Mecca. At the age of twenty-five he married a wealthy widow, Khadijah. His "call" came at the age of forty. In 622 the "Hegira" to Medina took place. In 632 he died, the undisputed master prophet of Arabia. Within a hundred years Islamic domains stretched from the Pyrennes through Spain, jumped the Gibraltar Strait, embraced all of North Africa, and captured Egypt and the Bible lands. Thus began a relentless pressure on Byzantium that culminated in the fall of Constantinople in 1453. Eventually, the Islamic conquest extended to lands as far east as India. Arabic became the most universal language the world had seen since Alexander had spread Greek over nine centuries earlier.

There were a number of strong Jewish communities in Arabia in the time of Mohammed, and the vast conquests engulfed hundreds of Christian communities, a few of which stubbornly survived. Yet the Bible in Arabic evidently did not come into existence until the work of Saadya Gaon. Saadya was born in the Fayum in Upper Egypt in 892 and died in Babylon in 942. He translated the Pentateuch from the Hebrew. Other parts of the Old Testament followed—Joshua from the Hebrew; Judges, Samuel, Kings, Chronicles, and Job from the Peshitta; and the Prophets, Psalms, and Proverbs from the Septuagint—not necessarily the work of Saadya. The resulting version has been used by Arabic-speaking Jews down to this century. The Qara'ites, disapproving of Saadya's rather free work, made rival translations, the most notable that of Japheth ben-Eli-ha-Levi in the tenth century. New Testament translations into Arabic sprang up from Syriac, Greek, and Coptic sources in the seventh to the ninth centuries. Arab writers say that John I, a Jacobite Patriarch of Antioch (631–648), translated the Gospels from Syriac into Arabic. Another John, Bishop of Seville in Spain, is said to have produced Arabic Gospels from the Vulgate around 724. The final form of the Arabic New Testament rested most heavily on the Coptic Bohairic. Because of their late date and mixed background, Arabic texts have had little importance in textual studies.

SLAVONIC VERSION

Though the Slavs were one of the great ethnic groups contiguous to the centers of early Christianity, Bible translations into Slavonic cannot be traced earlier than the ninth century. Two brothers, Constantine and Methodius, sons of a Greek nobleman, began by putting church liturgy into Slavonic. With the approval of popes Adrian II and John VIII (as noted above), they translated the Bible. Constantine (who later changed his name to Cyril, 827–869) and Methodius (826–885) worked among the Slavs and Moravians. Constantine invented the alphabet that bears his saint name— Cyrillic—to facilitate the translation. Manuscript portions from the tenth or eleventh centuries survive, but the oldest manuscript of the whole Bible is the Codex Gennadius in Moscow, which is dated 1499 and is too late to be of much value for textual study.

BIBLIOGRAPHY

Ackroyd, P. R. and C. F. Evans, eds. *The Cambridge History of the Bible,* Volume I, *From the Beginnings to Jerome,* 1975.

Greenslade, S. L., ed. *The Cambridge History of the Bible,* Volume III, *The West from the Reformation to the Present Day,* 1975.

Lampe, G. W., ed. *The Cambridge History of the Bible,* Volume II, *The West from the Fathers to the Reformation,* 1975.

Metzger, Bruce. *The Text of the New Testament—Its Transmission, Corruption, and Restoration,* 1968.

———. *The Early Versions of the New Testament—Their Origin, Transmission, and Limitations,* 1977.

Price, Ira Maurice. *The Ancestry of Our English Bible,* 1956.

Weiser, Arthur. *The Old Testament: Its Formation and Development,* 1968.